WOMEN AND THE POPULAR IMAGINATION IN THE TWENTIES

Women and the Popular Imagination in the Twenties

Flappers and Nymphs

Billie Melman
Lecturer in Modern History
Tel-Aviv University

MACMILLAN
PRESS

First published 1988

Published by
THE MACMILLAN PRESS LTD
Houndmills, Basingstoke, Hampshire RG21 2XS
and London
Companies and representatives
throughout the world

Filmsetting by Vantage Photosetting Co. Ltd
Eastleigh and Southampton
Printed in Hong Kong

British Library Cataloguing in Publication Data
Melman, Billie
Women and the popular imagination in the twenties:
flappers and nymphs.
1. English fiction – 20th century – History and
criticism   2. Popular literature – History and
criticism   3. Women in literature
I. Title
823′.912′09352042   PR888.W6
ISBN 0–333–39195–0

For Yossi and for Yotam, who was conceived and born with this book

Contents

Acknowledgements

I am particularly indebted to Professor John A. Sutherland, of the California Institute of Technology, formerly of University College, London, a rare combination of patient instructor and scrupulous critic, whose advice and guidance have, I hope, benefited my work. Dr David Trotter of University College, most careful of readers, has shown interest in this book from its inception and went over the final draft.

There are others, individuals and institutions, to whom I am indebted in many different ways. Professor Walter Laqueur of the Institute of Contemporary History and Georgetown University; Professor Saul Friedländer of the Graduate Institute of International Studies, Geneva and Tel-Aviv University; Professor James Joll and Professor Elie Kedourie of the London School of Economics; Ms Victoria Glendinning; Mr Terence De Vere White; Ms Julia Birley, daughter of the late Margaret Kennedy, who allowed me to look at unpublished material and quote from it; Professor Zvi Yavetz of the Department of History, Tel-Aviv University; the Fred Lessing Foundation; the Aranne School of History, Tel-Aviv University; the Staff of the London Library; Mr David Doughan and Miss Katherine Ireland of the Fawcett Library; Miss Kathleen Hays of the Newspaper Library at Colindale; Miss Mary Hurworth of the Reading Room at the British Library; the staff of the British Library at Woolwich; Ms Christa Wichtmann; Mrs Jacky Carby; Mrs Perlina Varon, for her dedication; and last, but first, my parents, Glila and Samuel Rosencweig.

London and Tel-Aviv   B.M.

ix

List of Abbreviations

AP	Amalgamated Press
GF	*Girls' Friend*
GFL	*Girls' Friend Library*
HMSO	Her Majesty's Stationery Office
JBA	Julia Birley Archive
MN	*Mizpah Novels*
NYTBR	*New York Times Book Review*
TLS	*The Times Literary Supplement*
VS	*Victorian Studies*
WWL	*Woman's World Library*

Early issues of the *GFL*, *MN* and the *WWL* carry no dates. Only a probable year of publication can therefore be cited, allowing for a lapse between the issue of a number and its stamping in the British Library.

Introduction
1918–28, Contexts and Texts

A decade, to repeat a truism, is not a fact. It is an arbitrary measurement of time, retrospectively imposed upon events in the past by the tidy-minded student of history. It is at the peril of being accused of tidy-mindedness, as well as of a distorting reading of the past, that I use the terms 'decade' and the 'twenties'. They are interchangeably applied in this book to the continuum between two spots in time, 6 February 1918 and 29 March 1928.[1] On the first date the last of the four Reform Bills became law and 13,671,480 electors, the biggest increase ever in Britain's electorate, were added to the Parliamentary Register.[2] The new Representation of the People Act extended the franchise to males over 21 years and to females over 30 years who (except when they qualified in their own right) were the wives of local-government electors. The 'matrons' vote' – as it was appropriately labelled – was, essentially, a household suffrage. A residue of some 5.5 million females remained voteless until, about ten years later, an almost undivided House of Commons passed the Representation of the People Equal Franchise Bill. During the interim the disfranchised female haunted the popular imagination. She was distinguished from the rest of her sex, marked out and labelled 'flapper', a curious epithet that, after three centuries of near obscurity, suddenly acquired life and meaning. And universal female suffrage, which met no serious *political* opposition, popularly became known as the 'flapper vote'. The epithet had a significance beyond its literal meaning and specific political connection. It conjured up an ambiguous and historically peculiar image of the young woman. And, in the image itself and various others associated with it, there co-existed diverse and contradictory notions on the female as androgyne, a figure characterised as sexless but libidinous; infantile but precocious; self-sufficient but demographically, economically and socially superfluous; an emblem of modern times yet, at the same time, an incarnation of the eternal Eve. The equivocal figure became the centre of a polyphonic debate of many voices, simultaneously carried on on various platforms. Orchestrated by the mass-circulation newspapers of the Harmsworth brothers, the debate was to reverberate, through the decade, in popular novels and in the mammoth body of pulp magazines. In its scope and intensity it surpassed earlier discussions on women and sexuality. At certain points and on certain platforms, obsession with the flapper developed into a madness of sorts.

In its historical coverage, then, the book overlaps the period 1918–31, normally defined as the 'twenties'. And the contiguity of the shorter period I concentrate on and the longer interlude between universal war and world-wide depression is not merely one of time. The Great War redefined the role of women in British society and remoulded popular attitudes towards them. The central images of the female and dominant notions about feminine sexuality can be comprehended only in their relation to the universal cataclysm and the demographic and social eruptions it caused. A connection between the rise of the female androgyne and the Great Depression less easily evinces itself. From historical perspective it seems improbable, ludicrous even, that universal female suffrage brought about, or even precipitated, the economic crisis. But, as I later show, contemporaries often related the electoral reform to those elements of crisis immanent in Britain's post-war economy and its society: chronic unemployment, the decline of the old industries, and class conflict. The 'flapper vote' came to symbolise instability. It was regarded as a reflection of the disaster of the war and a catalyst to imminent catastrophes.

Of course, to isolate the decade from the stream of history is, to say the least, misleading. For was obsession with the young female new? And was the myth of the flapper an entirely novel one? Did it break with historical or even universal notions about femininity? The post-war debate seems to echo earlier ones. The reticent Victorians, it is now clear, had engaged in two, autonomous discourses on sexuality, the one secret and hardly audible, the other public and loud. The 1860s, 1870s and 1880s, those *decennia mirabiles* in the annals of vice, had witnessed a growing tumult about venereal diseases, birth-control propaganda and child prostitution.[3] And underneath the surface of propriety the 'other' discourse – as Steven Marcus and Peter Cominos would phrase it – had been carried on: in the underworld, in the private language of diaries and epistles, in the recesses of pornography and, disguised and coded, but decipherable, in the Victorian novel and in (as Peter Gay terms it) bourgeois experience and consciousness.[4] The Edwardian era was to see the 'rights-of-women' question erupt through the façade of middle-class liberal complacency with an unknown violence.

Yet the interest of the Victorians and Edwardians had focused on issues and had touched territories *outside* the orbit of respectability. For over half a century the debate gravitated towards the deviant, both morally and *politically*, with concern about disease, juvenile delinquency, the 'amorality' of working-class women, and the subversiveness of militant suffragism. And, significantly, the public debate had a distinct reformist streak. The furores in the Victorian press had been intertwined with the great morality campaigns of that age: the 'Repeal' crusade in the 1870s, for instance, or the outcry, in the mid 1880s, for the abolition of child prostitution.

Conversely in the 1920s the topic of feminine sexuality became central, public and, most important, legitimate. It was promoted from the domain of the esoteric, the outlawed and the subversive to the area of respectability. At the centre of attention after the war was the ordinary, disfranchised young woman, not the criminal, the poor or the agitator. Moreover, the hitherto largely unacceptable idea of birth control was, for the first time, being welded into the mainstream ideology of monogamous marriage and conjugal love. Suffice it to mention the enormous popularity of Marie Stopes's manuals on sex. To give just one example, *Married Love* (1918) sold over 400,000 copies in hardback between 1918 and 1923, more than the total for all the best-sellers discussed in this book.[5]

But to describe the way in which a society at a certain point in time perceives the female I should prefer to use not the notion of a linear progress, but the image of a vertical structure with several levels – a house, for instance. Ideally there would be in the imaginary house four storeys – a cellar, a ground floor and two upper storeys – each hoarding images and patterns of thought that represent particular lengths of time.

In the cellar would be stored those patterns of imagination which are *ahistorical* and *cross-cultural* and occur at different places in different times. At the centre of these universal, unalterable models is the image of the female as 'other', famously characterised by Simone de Beauvoir: a mirror image of a masculine humanity to which the female gives a negative sense of identification. Where humanity is masculine, absolute, the subject, its 'other' is feminine, relative, the object.[6] It is a tempting interpretation but, to the historians, not very helpful. It fails to explain (and, perhaps even to ask) why a particular image of the female appears, dominates the imagination of an age and, then, vanishes. Why, for instance, did the flapper (supposing that this were merely one version of the archetypal 'other') emerge after the First World War and not survive the decade?

On the ground floor are found those notions about the woman which are peculiar to a culture or a religion. The basic Western concept of womanhood and sexuality had been dominated for over 1500 years by the Pauline – Augustinian doctrine, emphasising that, while mortals *qua* mortals are evil, women are more evil than men. For it had been Eve who had brought upon humanity the *damnosa hereditas* of the Fall.

On the next floor are located modifications to the cultural–religious model which take place over shorter periods – a century would be an appropriate unit of measurement – and are geographically and nationally idiosyncratic. It is a commonplace that English notions about the female had diverged from the continental Augustinian model and that this took place at least twice: first, about the time of the puritan revolution[7] (with the emergence of the ideal of marriage as a spiritual bond), and, more relevantly to this book, in the Victorian age, especially between the 1850s and the 1870s.

In mainstream Victorian thought and literature the relations between the sexes were perceived and described in *terms of space*, or 'spheres'. And that perception was particularly manifest in the notion of the male and the female as 'separate spheres', complementary opposites, biologically, mentally and intellectually poles apart. The differences between the sexes, according to that notion, are nature- or God-ordained and are, therefore, unalterable and determine the moral and cultural 'spheres' that the man and the woman inhabit. The association between space and gender is a well-known characteristic of the Victorian novel and Victorian poetry of domesticity. In both, the 'home' or 'hearth' is the aesthetic and socialised locus of the female and of the feminine experience of reality. And the famous 'Angel in the House', a reversal of Eve, the sinner, incarnates the virtues inscribed in this place. The outside world – economic, destructively competitive and political – is masculine. The domestic space is a buffer against the corrupting influences of life in urban industrial society. The notion of 'separate spheres' had far-reaching political implications, examined by Brian Harrison. Carried to its logical conclusion it meant that reform, indeed any *change* in the position of women, was useless and impracticable, and that conclusion was to become the basis of organised opposition to female suffrage.[8]

The reference to the Victorian ethos returns us to our imaginary house. Its top storey is the domain of the limited and short-term, those modifications and mutations in earlier patterns of imagination and thought which occur in a generation, or a decade. This period may, rather than merely adding to the layers of common inheritance, be marked by a disruption of received attitudes. This was, I think, the case with the twenties. My main purpose is, therefore, to explore the top storey of the symbolic house; to isolate the images of the female and the elements in the discourse on sexuality which are peculiar to the decade from those images and notions which are long-term.

The disruption of established attitudes might be traced to a peculiar and fruitful convergence of two separate trends which, after the First World War, cross-fertilised. The war brought about structural changes in the material conditions of life which particularly affected women. At precisely this time there took place important changes in the texture of popular culture, transforming its character and trajectory. This particular combination, which I proceed to look into in detail, accounts for the rise of 'flapper' and the unprecedentedly wide discussion of the woman and of feminine sexuality. The material changes are the easiest to specify. First and most significant was the shift in the balance between the sexes, a surplus of 1,920,000 females whom the popular press labelled 'super-fluous women'.[9] Second, there was a steep decline in the birth-rate, consequent on the spread of artificial contraceptives. Third, related to this, both the pattern and the ideal model of the family changed: this can be summed up as the consolidation of the *nuclear* unit. Fourth, there was a change in conventions and in social behaviour, a change commonly associated with marginal groups or élites, but noticeable in society at large. Fifth, there was a marked change in the physical appearance of women and the clothes they wore. The emergence of the boyish figure as the ideal of feminine beauty may seem to belong to the history of fashion, but contemporaries regarded this figure as the symbol of the new morality, a sign of the transition from a sexually and socially heterogen-eous society to one that was unisex, uniform and classless. Sixth, the state became increasingly involved in the lives of individual women and the family, a trend which was reflected in extensive legislation. Seventh, and last, despite the trend, after the Armistice, from paid occupations 'back to the home', the standard of living of most women rose.

None of these phenomena was entirely new. Females had outnum-bered males since 1802. The birth-rate had been declining since the 1870s, and as a result the British family had become progressively smaller. And the appearance of the 'modern' female had been deplored since the 1890s. What singles out the twenties is not the changes in themselves but their extraordinary pace and scope, of which contemporaries were fully aware. The statistical surveys are eloquent. Between 1801 and 1914 the proportion of females to males in England and Wales never rose above 1068 to 1000. In 1921 the average was 1096 females to 1000 males and the disparity was higher in three age groups. Between the ages 20 and 24 the proportion was 1176 to 1000, between the ages 25 and 29 1209 to 1000, and between the ages 30 and 34 there were 1186 females to every 1000 males.[10] The age groups where the surplus of women was most conspicuous were, significantly, those of the 'lost generation', an expression with distinct masculine connotations that in the context of the demographic imbalance was to acquire a new meaning.

The war affected the birth-rate as well as the rate of death. The number of births in 1870 had been 1,072,295, in 1913 1,102,500 and from that year onwards (with the exception of two prolific years, 1921 and 1922) the decline was alarming: 900,130 births in 1923, 777,520 in 1926 and 761,963 in 1931.[11] The curve was reflected in the shrinking size of the British family from an average of 5.5 members in the mid-Victorian era to

2.2 between 1924 and 1929.[12] Systematic practice of birth control had started among the middle classes in the 1870s and had spread downwards *before* the First World War. But the war effectively legitimised the use of contraceptives. And the surge of popular interest in the topic of birth control is reflected in the wealth of literature, aimed at large, uninitiated readerships, on that topic (Dr Stopes's spectacular successes may again be cited in illustration).

The twenties also present an eventful chapter in the legal history of women. No fewer than 18 major bills concerning the status and welfare of single and married women were enacted between 1918 and 1925. Only a few of these acts, however, had to do with the position of women outside the home: the Sex Disqualification Removal Act (1919), State-registration of nursing (1919), and the act regulating the practice of midwifery. The bulk of legislation reinforced the status of women *within* or *in relation to*, the family. The Matrimonial Causes Act of 1923 made it possible for women to sue for a divorce on the grounds of adultery alone (where, before, cruelty or desertion, as well as adultery, had had to be proved). Significantly, the legislatory effort of the early and mid twenties was an appendix to Victorian legislation. The largest category of acts consists of amendments of the most conspicuous anomalies in nineteenth-century bastardy laws and the laws of illegitimacy and guardianship: the Bastardy and Legitimacy Acts (1923 and 1925), the Guardianship Act (1925), and so on. At the root of the post-war legislation, which itself manifests the general trend towards collectivism and state intervention, are two contradictory assumptions. On the one hand, parenthood and particularly motherhood are considered the responsibility of the state rather than the individual. On the other hand, the number of laws concerning irregularities in the family was, in itself, an admission, albeit belatedly, that the conjugal unit was in danger. Characteristically, the law did not prevent change but merely regulated it.

There was one important area where the war brought a dislocation rather than acted simply as a catalyst of change: namely, occupation outside the home. The years 1914–18 saw an explosion of the labour market, accompanied by changes in the traditional patterns of female and male occupation. The number of employed women rose from 5,966,000 in August 1914 to 7,311,000 just before the Armistice.[13] More importantly, the workforce gravitated from the classical female occupations (the textile and cloth industries and domestic service) towards male ones, notably the munitions and ordnance industries. Within less than two years, however, the trend was completely reversed. In 1921 the number of employed women fell to 5,062,332, and the pattern of occupation was reverting to that before 1914. However, the trend away from paid work had no dramatic effect on the material condition of the majority of women in Britain – mainly because they benefited from the general rise, despite periodic spells of slump, in the standard of living and a subseqent growth of spending-power. The average wage of a female industrial worker increased from 11s 7d on the eve of the war to 28s. Wages in the cotton industry averaged 27s 3d, in engineering 27s 7d, and in the better-paid new industries 30s[14] (still about a third of the average male income, but a significant improvement on pre-war standards). The potential working-class consumers, together with the swelling contingent of lower-middle-class suburbanites, formed a definable consumer group which, in turn, was the basis of a new female reading public.

The shocks and transitions in material life noted here combined with, rather than determined, important structural changes in popular culture. Again the war was the catalyst rather than the prime cause of change. The Northcliffe press, the cheap edition and the film – those three *signa* of cultural *Gleichschaltung* – and a unified mass civilisation had established themselves well before 1914. The twenties witnessed the rise of their fully developed mutations: the mass-circulation daily (as opposed to the *class* paper), the best-selling novel (significantly, the term came into common usage only around 1920), and the massively capitalised film. The change was not merely one of volume. It was intertwined with a significant structural change in the reading public. Novel-reading remained a predominantly female and middle-class occupation. There were, however, clear signs that the readership was coming to include more and more from the lower middle class and even further down the social scale. Serial fiction and the periodical in general underwent an even more radical transformation, as what had been a middle-class commodity changed into one that was distinctly working-class. 70 all-story papers, three times the figure in 1914, catered for the new female audience in Britain's industrial areas.

Clearly the economic changes alone do not account for such an expansion, or for the explosion of mass-production romantic fiction. The causes of both these phenomena are to be located in the transformation of the mental world of women, related to the changes in the material conditions of life and the physical environment. Society as a whole had to come to terms with the loss of a generation of men and a surplus of women in the reproductive age groups. Moreover, what for the majority had been established patterns of sexual behaviour were now superseded by new ones. Marriage and the conjugal family seemed particularly precarious. Equally important was the influence of the changes in the pace of life in the larger urban centres. The twenties were the decade of the suburban explosion, of the growth of a mass-market for cheaply produced consumer goods and the flowering of forms of mass-entertainment such as the film and wireless. The experience of reality of the mass of British women became wider and more complex than ever before. And, understandably, this sudden broadening of the 'feminine sphere' exposed women, at all social levels, to diverse influences against which the relative and protective narrowness of their experience had hitherto guarded them. The increasing complexity of *real life* after the First World War is, I think, the main explanation for the mass escape into the uncomplicated world of romantic fiction, with the vicarious satisfaction it provided. Hence the rise and flowering of new escapist genres that displaced actual social problems into the world of fantasy. These genres were, to give them the names by which they were known at the time, and are therefore referred to here, the 'sex novel', meaning a novel on women, or on feminine sexuality (a newly discovered topic so far as the mass-production novel was concerned); the 'oriental novel', or 'desert-love novel', set in the Middle East, a genre with allegiances to the pornographic novel; and the 'Empire romance', a development of late nineteenth-century imperialist adventure fiction (see Chapters 2, 6 and 9).

To invoke again our image of a house, in the top storey, it will be recalled, are located the multiple currents, undercurrents and counter-currents of popular thought about women and society. Though characteristic of a particular period, they do not form a narrative. Nor can they be arranged in linear fashion. They should, therefore, be compared with a *discourse*, or rather, with several autonomous but confluent discourses which are carried on simultaneously. My usage of the word 'discourse' here is indebted to the opening volume of Michel Foucault's monumental project of a *History of Sexuality*, a project cut short by his death.[15] Foucault explains sexuality in historical terms and distinguishes modern sexuality (which he dates from the Counter-Reformation) from what preceded it by the need felt, in the last three centuries, to *discuss* sex. That is to say, the history of sexuality over this period has been the history of the *discourse* on sexuality. In Foucault's well-known usage, a 'discourse' is inseparable from the pursuit of power, which he conceives as an omnipresent, omnipotence *will to know*. In this book 'discourse' is dissociated from that particular association of power and knowledge. Nor is this book directly concerned with sexual dominance, or with the regulation or control of sexuality. I apply the term 'discourse' to that dynamic and continuous exhange of shared perceptions, prejudices and ideas that take place in a diachronic, pluralistic society at a certain period in time. And, since the main currency of such an exchange is written language, my chief concern is with texts and their idiom. Verbal utterances are excluded not because I think them unimportant, but because they require a different book with different disciplines, and for the same reason non-verbal discourses such as the film are referred to only in passing.

The danger of reading one's own prejudices *into* the twenties, rather than 'reading the twenties' (Bernard Bergonzi's term) is apparent enough. Work on women has understandably shown a tendency towards a selective and somewhat obfuscating vision of the past. And this particularly applies to studies on women in literature, or women and literature, after the First World War. Most such studies focus on certain 'canonical' texts, consumed by minorities and deriving their authority from (contemporary or later) literary or ideological movements.[16] More worrying is the lacuna in the history of attitudes (of which the canonisation of certain texts is, from the historian's point of view, a department) and everyday life. Whereas the Victorian and the Edwardian experiences have been continuously explored and mapped, the experience of the majority of women after the First World War is, to the historian of *mentalités*, still *terra incognita*. Martha Vicinus's recent *Independent Women* is one notable exception, but it deals with middle-class minorities and ends in 1920. In the field of politics as in the cultural field the twenties are reduced to an appendix to the eventful and glorious decades of the struggle for political rights.[17]

Outside the pale of authority stretches the largely unexplored territory of writings aimed at, and consumed by, the bulk of the reading public, writings which are either not, or are not directly, political but had an immense influence on their readers. I seek to bring into the spotlight the mass-circulation paper, the pulp magazine and some long-forgotten and despised popular novels; to describe the diverse ways in which such publications dramatised preoccupation with the 'modern' woman and 'modern' feminine sexuality. It is precisely the generic non-durability of the popular artefact ('dispensability' is Hannah Ahrendt's appropriate term), the fact that it did not survive its historical moment, the very reason why it has been despised by critics, that makes it invaluable to the historian. The best-seller with a brief claim to fame, the instantly consumed magazine or paper, are sensitive seismographs of the shifts in the attitudes and moods of majorities.

At first the range and variety of material seem to present insurmountable problems of selection and discipline. After the First World War there were in Britain 16 national newspapers, 21 Sundays and about 130 provincial papers (41 morning and 89 evening papers).[18] In 1924 the number of popular magazines was, according to the *Newspaper Press Directory and Advertiser's Guide*, about 14 times this figure. The number of novels is a mystery. In 1924, to take a representative year, the general output of books was 12,690, the bulk of them novels.[19] A rigorous selection is obviously inevitable, the main problem being, of course, according to which criteria? Sales figures, an evident pointer, are scarce and very unreliable. There are the self-advertised (and fairly accurate) estimates of newspaper circulation publicised by such dailies as the *Daily Mail*, the *Daily Express* and the *Evening Standard*. The figures for the sales of novels are an enigma. There were no best-seller lists in Britain at the period and publishers are extremely furtive about sales. The standard answer to queries about sales figures is that the files containing that information were destroyed during the Blitz – an off-putting answer in those cases where the material in question did survive the Luftwaffe raids. Information about the circulation of magazines is next to nothing. The first Audit Bureau Circulation publications appeared in 1931, and the massively read penny-halfpenny and tuppenny weeklies disappeared before the Second World War. Clearly the picture of changes in the reading public is largely impressionistic.

But the lack of such vital information is less serious a handicap than it at first seems. One of the underlying assumptions of this book is that popularity is not quantifiable and that the significance of *an* artefact for *a* particular audience is not – indeed, cannot be – registered by the rise and fall of sales. Accordingly the book focuses on key texts selected because of their impact upon the popular idiom. This impact can be gleaned from the wealth of material in 'minority' publications – whether the literary supplements, or organs of the publishing trade, in both Britain and the United States – as well as in publications for the masses – notably the daily press. More weighty than the problem of selection is that of discipline. Popular fiction and journalism are a no-man's land, claimed by sociologists of literature and 'culturalists', still despised by students of literature, and woefully ignored by historians. There is a plethora of studies on 'literature in the market place' – the various aspects of the production and consumption of books and papers – but they do not deal with the texts themselves. And individual texts, the cultural historian's chief material, are conspicuously absent from the impressive attempts to construct models of the mass-production novel and the mass media.[20] The result of all this is a lack of common critical vocabulary and agreed tools of research, so that the requisite vocabulary and tools have to be arrived at while dealing with the texts.

A historical reading seemed to me the most appropriate approach, because, in the first place, I was concerned with the specific and time-bound. Secondly, the generic limitations of the texts themselves, their short life, dictates such an approach. By a historical reading I seek to place select texts within wider social contexts, as well as within the peculiar circumstances of the impact of the individual artefact and its producer upon a particular audience. But, more importantly, by a historical reading I attempt to reconstruct the vocabulary of the twenties, or, rather, the two vocabularies: the common idiom of feminine sexuality, and the critical terminology used by minority audiences in discussing popular culture. Two distinct but intertwined sets of words loom large, creating a grid of cultural reference. The first set includes the terms 'flapper', 'surplus woman' or 'superfluous woman', 'modern man', 'he man', 'sheik' and 'It' (the contemporary term for sex appeal), which constitute the culturally charged currency of the discourse on sexuality. The second vocabulary reflects the sense of a cultural transformation, and its key words are 'best-seller', 'sex novel', 'high-', 'middle-' and 'low-brow', and 'the Great British Public' ('GBP' in its abbreviated, journalistic form) — addressing mass as opposed to minority audiences. The two vocabularies cross-fertilised — indeed, the first truly popular discourse on sexuality could not evolve separately from the debate on an emerging mass culture. An accurate reading must, therefore, take into account this important connection.

The first impression is of a chorus of discordant voices. There are, first, the three languages of sexuality corresponding to the three main discourses: the rhetoric of the press, the language of 'sex novels', and the idiom of fiction magazines. Within these rather large divisions may be discerned the voices of different authors, editors and publishers, with their individual nuances. Viscount Rothermere's voice differs from Lord Beaverbrook's, which, in turn, differs from Arthur Pearson's; the woman's press is a prism of notions and ideologies which reflect a diversity of tones, and nowhere is the voice of the individual writer as distinctly audible as in the best-seller. This diversity has imposed itself on this book and dictated the use of three different critical languages and a rigid organisation on the lines of the tripartite division of popular writing. As I have already stressed, the diversity of the discourse does not yield a single narrative. But clearly the very notion of the female androgyne was historical and political. It is therefore necessary to keep to a chronological organisation of the material, as well as to an organisation of it according to the form of discourse, to weld, as it were, the vertical structure of popular imagination into a continuum. This particularly applies to the first part of the book, which deals with the political meanings of the 'flapper'.

Part One, then, is a glossary and a calendar, examining the key words of the discourse on women in their specific context. The *Daily Mail* and *Daily Express* have been selected for discussion not only because they were mass-circulation papers but because they started off the debate and set its terms. In the rest of the book the chronological framework is loose. Part Two examines the connection between the language of sexuality and that of the emerging mass culture in what was, perhaps, their most significant junction, the 'best-seller'. The novels selected for discussion not only sold more than others but also had a special impact on the reading public, influenced attitudes and became cult objects. The images of the woman they conjured up do not form a sequence. Thus the 'masculine' social novel dealt with in Chapter 3 is typical of the earlier part of the decade, but it co-existed with, rather than preceded the erotic oriental fantasy discussed in Chapter 6, and the novels distinguished as 'feminine' and looked at in Chapters 4 and 5. The works selected are regarded as complex wholes in which a variety of elements merge: the 'market-place'; the rapport between the best-selling writer and his audience, or, rather, various audiences; and, last, but by no means least, the peculiarities of the individual work and its producer. Part Three describes the connections between structural changes in the magazine industry and changes in the reading public of women's magazines. It then proceeds to examine the combined influences of those changes on working-class serial fiction, isolating two typical genres: the industrial 'Lancashire' romance and the 'Empire story'.

From this complexity emerge six images: the disfranchised woman; the superfluous female; the oversexed, libidinous heroine; the precocious adolescent as victim of her gender and sexuality; the expatriate – the emigrant who finds new life abroad, the outcast adventurer, the exile from 'civilised' society; and, last, the manual worker as emblem of working-class virtues. Behind this profusion of images, vocabularies and tones there are several unities or unifying elements, which are summarily analysed in the concluding chapter. First there is the unity of discourse, those idiosyncrasies characteristic of *a* form of writing or performance (the 'sex novel', the newspaper, the magazine serial, the film). The second unifying element is the relation between image and idiom on the one hand and between image (or language) and class on the other. Third, there is a unity of theme: those motifs which recur in each and every one of the images of femininity, regardless of the discourse in which they developed.

While this book was in print three books appeared which deal with some aspects of women's experience during and after the First World War. Trevor Wilson's panoramic view of the war, *The Myriad Faces of War* (Polity Press, 1986) has a chapter on women and the suffrage campaign. Sally Lewis's collection *Labour and Love* (Blackwell, 1986) is concerned mainly with the family and women's work between 1850 and 1940. See also J. M. Winter, *The Great War and the British People* (Macmillan, 1986), especially Part III: 'The Legacy of the Great War'.

Part One
'The Idiom that the General Public Possesses'

1

The Superfluous Woman, the Flapper, the Disfranchised Female and the Rothermere Press

'The idiom that the general public of the twentieth century possesses is not merely crude and puerile; it is made up of phrases and clichés that imply fixed, or rather stereotyped, habits of thinking and feeling, at second-hand taken from the journalist'.[1] The voice is, unmistakably, that of Mrs Leavis. The words are not characteristically hers. The story of the British reading public after Lord Northcliffe's revolution is told as one of unarrested decline. The narrative, which conventionally begins in 1896, the year the *Daily Mail* was launched, chronicles a process of cultural *Gleichschaltung*. The audience was semi-literate; its life became impoverished, its idiom vulgar and its ideas about life second-hand — received, manna-like, from the sinisterly powerful new press.[2] There is no doubt that the new press had a levelling-down effect on the audience, in that by putting in circulation catchwords and images it dangerously standardised habits of thought. The rhetoric of the debate on the flapper clearly illustrates all this. Yet this rhetoric was not, or not merely, the fabrication of Fleet Street hacks. It reflected certain anxieties and uncertainties, largely connected with the demographic imbalance after the First World War. Certainly the mass media dramatised common prejudices and inflated the fears aroused by the discovery of the new feminine sexuality. But by no means were the fears inauthentic ('second-hand' would be the Leavises' term). And any description of the press and the public as two separate mechanisms, the one manipulating, the other passive and receptive, obfuscates the topic of communications.[3] In what follows I treat the dailies of the twenties and the dailies' audience as — what Raymond Williams calls — two reciprocating, communicating systems, the one feeding on the other, mutually shaping common attitudes.

Let there be no misunderstanding. I do not deny that organs such as the *Daily Mail* and *Daily Express* were complex financial and politically motivated structures, cynically pursuing power. Alfred Harmsworth,

Viscount Northcliffe (1865–1922), who owned the *Mail* until his death, his brother Harold, Viscount Rothermere (1868–1940), who stepped into his place, and Lord Beaverbrook (1879–1964) certainly ran their papers for profit. This particularly applies to Rothermere, who conducted the financial side of the Harmsworth empire with unrivalled business acumen. When in the early thirties the *literati* bewailed the effects of the Northcliffe press it had already passed its zenith. The *Mail*, whose circulation slumped from 1.8 million to 1.5 million, was losing the fierce circulation war with the *Express*, and Rothermere had sold his monster magazine empire. But the twenties can be justifiably described as his era. By the middle of the decade he had a complex network of publishing interests worth some £24 million. He possessed half the £1 ordinary shares in Daily Mirror Newspapers, 51 per cent of the shares of the *Daily Mail*, the *Evening News*, the *Weekly Dispatch* and the *Overseas Daily Mail*, and in 1923 he purchased 49 per cent of the shares of the *Express* from Lord Beaverbrook. Until 1926 Rothermere also owned the mammoth Amalgamated Press, which at that time could boast over 100 magazines, over half of them catering for female audiences.[4] Beaverbrook owned, in addition to shares in the *Express*, the *Sunday Express* and the *Evening Standard*. The three magnates shared an appetite for politics that had a significant influence on the crusade against the disfranchised female. There is no doubt that the *Mail*'s support of the reform of 1917 was consequent on Northcliffe's allegiance to Lloyd George. Conversely, the paper's vehement opposition to universal female suffrage was, partly, the result of the well-known breach between Rothermere and Stanley Baldwin.

Both the *Mail* and the *Express* manifested an obsession with any topic related to women and both were aggressively verbose when dealing with the flapper. There were, however, some significant differences. In the first place, the *Express*, slightly more progressive in outlook than the *Mail*, was also more tolerant towards the 'modern woman'. Secondly, the *Mail*'s interest in female suffrage was topical, but largely political, and during Baldwin's term as Prime Minister this interest had distinct personal as well as anti-Conservative overtones. Thirdly, and most important, the proprietor of the *Mail* assumed the double role of editor and censor. In utterances on the topic of female suffrage, especially in leading articles, his own voice (and not that of Thomas Marlowe, his editor) is distinctly audible. Beaverbrook's voice was hardly audible and his editorial presence less obtrusive.[5]

At the very beginning of the decade, however, the discordant tones were subdued. The general attitude towards women was clement. Indeed, the later opposition of both Harmsworths to universal female suffrage is glaringly inconsistent with their support for it (in limited form) during the war. Their papers hailed the fourth Franchise bill as a just reward for women's patriotism. Northcliffe himself, a fierce opponent to the 'vote' before 1916, was converted to the cause towards the end of that year and orchestrated a noisy campaign in his halfpenny papers and in *The Times* for the Representation of the People Bill, which proposed a limited female suffrage.[6] It seemed, at first, that this conciliatory mood would survive the Armistice. On 26 November the *Mail* emphasised,

> The need for association of women in the deliberation and government of the national affairs was never greater than now. . . . The protective instinct of women is equally at enmity with all those disruptive and destructive tendencies which may seek to introduce a new social order, . . . now that we have admitted and realised the rights of women it seems almost incredible that we should have attempted to touch the fringe of such problems while more than half of the population were excluded from any share in the management of their nation's affairs.

But, as the demobilisation of some 4 million men progressed, the image of the patriotic female, epitomised in the figure of the woman munitions worker, was being superseded by that of the parasite who 'takes men's jobs'. From the beginning of 1919 the contemporary young woman was criticised on every conceivable ground. Her appearance was derided, her manners were deplored, and her newly gained freedom was regarded with suspicion. The pages of the *Mail* and *Express* overflow with features on the modern female's dancing and smoking; her frequenting of night clubs, her hair styles and the length of her skirts. There is also comment on more weighty matters: the new morality, the decline of marriage, birth control and – most portentous of all – the degeneracy of the race.

In this welter of misogyny four themes loom large: the excess of young females; the competition between women and men in the economic and social spheres; the physical appearance of the young female; and, finally, the perils for society of the enfranchisement of women under 30. Each of these disparate themes develops from, and revolves around, one or more of the stock of key words and phrases that together form the basic currency of journalistic discourse. Comment on the imbalance between the sexes revolves around the phrase 'surplus woman' and, later in the decade, 'superfluous woman'. Discussion on the increasing involvement of women in the economic world and in civic life makes use of a vulgarised Darwinist vocabulary, with the phrase 'sex war' as its keynote.

Of course, the themes intermingle, and phrases that are typical of one of them may recur in discourse on another. The Darwinist jargon characteristic of commentary on women's work also appears in debates on the disproportion between the sexes and in parodies on the modern woman's physique. Moreover, certain patterns of discourse are more frequent than others: a preference for ambiguous, equivocal clichés; a systematic resort to innuendoes, often verging on the salacious; use of repetition, to hammer the idea home; and, last but not least, an extraordinarily aggressive tone of utterance. Notwithstanding these interconnections, the themes are separated in what follows and looked at individually.

The major cause, the *primum mobile*, of the obsession with the modern woman was the fear aroused by the disparity between the sexes. In the eyes of many contemporaries, a society in which fertile females were plentiful and males were scarce was politically, socially and morally imperilled. The surplus of young women was the main argument against universal suffrage. For women to be in the majority in the electorate would impair political equilibrium. Similarly, equal opportunities in the labour market would threaten the outnumbered male sex. The problem of surplus women was also associated with the decline in morals, the erosion of the British family and the degeneracy of the Anglo-Saxon race. Finally the socio-demographic imbalance was interpreted as a sign of universal disequilibrium − a fall as it were, from a 'natural' state of harmony between males and females.

The Harmsworth papers first took up the topic in the summer of 1919. On 30 June, in an article titled 'Our Surplus Girls', the *Mail* claimed that there was now 'a large excess of females' in Britain and actually proposed massive emigration of young, unmarried women to the dominions to remedy the situation at home. On 5 February 1920 the tone was even more pugnacious − not 'Our Surplus Girls', but 'A Million Women Too Many, 1920 Husband Hunt'. Over a million females of child-bearing age, revealed the *Mail*, cannot marry. The hordes of celibate women go out into the world to earn a living, thereby driving men to emigrate. In the same issue the degeneration of *mores*, the generation gap and the decline of the family are all causally related to the surplus of women:

> The social effects of sex disproportion are seen in the crumbling of the old ethical standards. The freedom of the modern independent girl from the supervision of her parents, the tendency to rebel against discipline . . . the cry of pleasure for pleasure's sake − all these tend to encourage a lower standard of morality . . . the social butterfly type

has probably never been so prevalent as at present. It comprises the frivolous, scantily clad 'jazzing flapper', irresponsible and undisciplined. . . . There is a large proportion of physically attractive girls with strong reproductive instincts and they are ever vying and competing with each other for the scarce and elusive male.

In the summer of 1921 the demographic issue acquired a new significance. The adjective 'surplus' was superseded by 'superfluous', and the combination 'superfluous woman' (in use before the war)[7] was to bcome a household phrase after Northcliffe, on a visit to America, publicly referred to 'Britain's problem of two million superfluous women' (a somewhat confusing figure: a year before there had been only 'one million women too many'). 'Superfluous' is a conveniently equivocal epithet indicating something excessive or superabundant, but also that which is needless and, therefore, dispensable. And 'superfluous women' implies that the superabundant females endanger the male population, society and the state, while reducing these same females to the category of the residual and, subsequently, the insignificant and harmless. In its second meaning the phrase irresistibly evokes an image of socially and economically dependent spinsterhood that can be dated from the 1830s and 1840s.

What lends journalistic writing on Britain's population problem a certain spurious veracity is the repetitive use of a popularised Darwinist vocabulary that can be described as scientific jargon. Characteristically the catastrophic implications of the imbalance between the sexes are described in 'high-falutin' sub-evolutionist terminology. On 8 August 1921 the *Mail* prognosticated a glum future for Britons and for mankind in general:

Women are an indication of what the human race is coming to. Most women hope that nature will adjust the balance between the sexes. But the hope is vain. The disproportion, already great, is steadily growing greater. . . . The human race is going through an evolutionary process which some hundred thousands of years ago or more was taken by that highly organised society of hive-bees. Mankind is going to move towards a state in which there will be a small proportion of mother-women to maintain the race, and a host of male drones. They will be supported by the labour of an immense number of sterile female workers. Men will be utterly ousted. . . .

In 1921 the metaphor of hive bees was immensely emotive, because, if the role of the modern human male was solely to fertilise his mate, then his fate could be compared with that of the drone: annihilation by the race of females he was destined to perpetuate. Implied in the passage is also the notion that sexual intercourse itself is deadly. Similar metaphors of destruction of the male by the new species of women were evoked through the decade. And, in a society living in the shadow of the greatest-ever carnage of males, such metaphors never failed to have an effect. Moreover, from the beginning superfluous women became synonymous with 'spinsters', an equally derogatory epithet. It was invariably the unmarried young females, not the wives and mothers, that the popular press described as a menace to the country's economy and its social and political order. Examples are legion and may be picked at random. On 8 September 1922 the *Mail* observed that 'In these days of emancipated femininity the superfluous women are . . . supposed to be those without husbands.' The equation 'superfluous women–spinsters' is elaborated, again, on 26 June 1923: 'Modern economic civilisation has been deteriorating men for 270 years, and now it begins to destroy womankind. . . . The superfluous women are a disaster to the human race. . . . Spinsters compete with men and aggravate the economic war.' And on 17 June 1924: 'as she [the spinster] preponderates in numbers she will gradually dominate the electorate'.

Aside from its 745,000 dead, the First World War left some 160,000 men wounded or gassed. It is hardly surprising that alongside the metaphors of gender annihilation there emerged the image of the mutilated and deformed male, an image rich in literal as well as figurative associations. The popular dailies never tired of emphasising that the war which had destroyed one generation of men and had invalided and (it was merely implied) castrated another had simultaneously invigorated the younger generations of women. Typically the notion of a deformed, debilitated masculinity was juxtaposed with that of a muscular, healthy 'new' womanhood. 'Women are the Strongest Sex'; 'Healthy Young Girls are More Boyish than Boys'; 'The Female Species is more dangerous . . . the modern girl is fitter . . . taller, lithe and athletic.'[8]

Such was the obsession with the ubiquitous, physically superior spinsters that the idea of state-controlled emigration of 'redundant females', propagated in the 1860s and occasionally floated in the second half of the nineteenth century, surfaced again. It was advocated in the Harmsworth press and in Westminster, especially at the time of the debate preceding the second reading, in the Commons, of the Representation of the People Equal Franchise Bill of 1928.[9] But advocacy of female emigration never reached the level of serious policy. True, emigrants were officially assisted, but the emigration figures dropped from a post-war peak of 256,000 in 1923 (as compared with 389,000 in 1913) to 92,000 in 1930.[10] And there is very little evidence that female, rather than male, emigration was officially encouraged. Still, when the comments on the topic in the press are examined in the broader context of the superfluous-women hysteria, they cannot be altogether dismissed. It is significant that the quasi-racial element evident in the discussion on the disparity between the sexes can also be detected in discussion of female emigration. The dominions seemed to be the ideal outlet for Anglo-Saxon spinsters. Other parts of the Empire, such as India (a traditional outlet for male enterprise and resources), were not mentioned, nor was multi-racial America, the typical immigrant society. As early as 8 September 1922 the *Mail* argued that 'There is no room even for the two millions of superfluous women in the free lands of the new world; perhaps a home and a husband in Australia or Canada are worth more than a job in London.' On 26 June 1923 it was earnestly proposed to restore the balance between the sexes by establishing a 'consulary imperial system' that would encourage female emigration to the dominions and the colonies and would prevent by legislation the migration of single women to Britain: 'Legislative measures should be taken for the prevention of too heavy a flow of foreign virgins into the country. . . .' On 5 February both regulated emigration of females and state-controlled traffic in baby boys (for the purpose of adoption by well-to-do families) were suggested.

The idea of state-controlled female emigration was, perhaps, the most extreme expression of the sense of a demographic crisis. And, preposterous as it may seem today, the idea appealed to the readers of contemporary magazines. The extremely popular Empire or Commonwealth romance (discussed in Chapter 9) related the life and adventures of the unmarried British immigrant in one of the dominions or a Crown colony. And it seems more than a coincidence that this particular genre, whose vogue overlaps the period between the enfranchisement of women over 30 and universal female suffrage, predominates in the magazines of the Amalgamated Press, owned until 1926 by the chief opponent to women's political emancipation. Characteristically, romance solved the problem of surplus women by reversing the balance between the sexes. In the magazine stories it is the males who are plentiful and superfluous. The young female colonisers and adventurers are scarce and much coveted.

Dramatisation of the surplus-women problem was one way to come to terms with the anxieties and fears the demographic imbalance undoubtedly aroused. Ridicule of the female sex was another. Derision had always been one of the most efficient weapons of the opponents to women's rights. (The celebrated *Punch* cartoons lampooning the Edwardian 'New Woman' and the suffragette inevitably come to mind.) And, in a broader, ontological rather than historical, context, mirth has always had a special role in human life: to help the individual and societies comprehend the novel and unfamiliar; to protest against that which cannot be changed; and to control, symbolically, that which otherwise cannot be controlled. Naturally, physical deformities and peculiarities have always been an object of satire. And after the First World War there was a change in the physical appearance of women that made them – both in the literal and in the metaphorical sense – figures of fun. No other topic, it seems, inspired contemporaries with greater ribaldry and witticism. The caricature of the contemporary woman is familiar. The tube-like silhouette is that of a juvenile androgyne, exaggeratedly emaciated and curveless. With it goes the heavily painted face, the 'bob' and, from the mid twenties, the 'shingle' and the inevitable cigarette. Writings on the subject of this emblematic figure tend to be ambivalent. To the contemporary mind there was something alluring in the blurring of the distinctions between the sexes, in the very unwomanliness of the modern young woman. On the other hand, the effacement of gender seemed to be, and was interpreted as, a symptom of decay, an outward sign of an internal racial degeneracy and moral decline. Characteristically the new look of women and men was described as both unnatural and immoral – a lapse, as it were, from the ideal feminine and masculine shapes (this is a curious reversal of the initial Platonic notion of androgyny, with which the majority of readers were probably unfamiliar). It is significant, for instance, that the changes in the female physique and the post-war decline in the birth-rate were assumed to have a cause-and-effect relation. Sterility and infertility seemed well-deserved punishments for 'unnatural' appearance and conduct.

As with the population issue, so with the androgynous female, popular journalese massively resorted to 'scientific' authority. Articles on the topic in the *Mail* and the *Express* are an amazing blend of ambiguous, nonsensical rhetoric and the self-assured tone of the expert. The descriptions are richly pictorial. 'The modern woman', lamented the *Mail* on 26 April 1927, 'is as slim as a lamp-post, her look is worried and her smile quick and nervous.' It continued,

> The smiling dimple, for years a subject for poets and essayists and an inevitable accompaniment of the Victorian heroine has disappeared from the face of the modern woman and is as rare now as the long skirt. . . . her face is harder . . . the craze for slimness of body is also reflected in her face.

The satirical column of 26 July 1927 bearing the title 'The Eternal Flapper who at 60 Looks 25' was even more graphic:

> Is that sylph with an abbreviated Greek tunic just a little less vivid than her lips, swaying well above her slim, flesh-coloured knees, a girl or a grand-mother? . . . Her hair is bronze, her complexion vivid, her skin unwrinkled, her lithe body as fit as a school boy is.

The physical appearance of the contemporary woman was often adduced as an argument against any extension of the franchise. On 26 April 1926 this argument was taken on by the popular novelist and veteran suffragist Mrs Desmond Humphreys ('Rita', as she was commonly known), founder of the Writers Club for Women, whose reprimand of the flapper is typical of the pre-war feminists: 'She had paid the man the poor compliment of imitating all his worst and few of his best qualifications.'

The *Mail* was surpassed by the *Express*, which regularly came up with articles by medical experts on the pernicious physical and mental effects of the new feminine look. Some were probably concocted in Fleet Street. But there are quite a few unmistakably genuine pieces which certainly made the desired impression of respected authority. The medical profession was more outspoken and less inhibited on the topic of the new look than journalists were. On 29 December 1924, Sir William A. Lane, consultant at Guy's Hospital, warned that 'In trying to look like boys women of the present day destroy the character of their sex . . . they are poor creatures sheathed from throat to hips in rubber.' Naturally the *Express* made the most of the unsavoury metaphor. The title reads, 'Modern Women Dancers in Rubber Sheaths'. On 12 November 1924 the modern woman's physique was given ample front-page space. The craze for slimness, smoking and dancing, it was revealed, was the cause of cancer, venereal diseases, 'deterioration of the brain, bones and muscles'. Moreover,

> With short hair, skirts little longer than kilts, narrow hips, insignificant breasts, there has arrived a confident, active, game-loving capable human-being, who shuns the servitude of household occupations. With her smaller, lither, more ornamental figure and greater capabilities, she has ousted the less capable or less fortunate men out of their occupations. . . . this change to a more neutral type . . . can be accomplished only at the expense of the integrity of her sexual organs.

The catalogue of illnesses and physical deformities is in curious juxtaposition to the references, cited earlier, to a new race of Amazons. But, then, juxtaposition is inherent in a popular myth as equivocal as that of the surplus woman.

The contemporary woman had a counterpart in the 'modern young man'; unnaturally effeminate, dolled-up, dispossessed of gender characteristics and (in contrast to the young female) divested of sexuality. The phrase 'modern man' came to signify impotence in both the literal and metaphoric sense of the term. The post-war man was conventionally juxtaposed with the archetypal *homme moyen sensuel*, dominated and driven by sexual impulses, and had distinct class characteristics. Effeminacy was associated with minorities, cliques such as the Bright Young People or literary sets, notably Bloomsbury. Intellectualism (or, in the idiom of the period, 'high-browism') and an upper-class breeding were commonly coupled with physical degeneracy and sexual malfunction, or with homosexuality – never openly discussed, but often implied in the editorial columns. On 6 July 1925 the *Express* described the 'modern girl's brother' as a 'slim, overdressed youth about town . . . who is concerned with what other men wear'. Two days later there was a frontpage feature on the disappearance of manliness. The 'affected nincompoop', opined the *Mail*, thrived especially in the universities, but his languid pose and affected gestures could now be noted in other public places. The key phrase, however, is 'He is not a worker.' *Punch* was even more terse about the 'modern girl's brother'. In a dialogue titled 'Beauty and the Ballot' between Mr Punch and the cynic, the latter remarks that

> Women have long ceased from any desire to attract the male, and naturally enough, for the male is growing less and less worth attracting. That is Nature's way: when our women become men she rectifies the balance by seeing to it that our men become women. I confess the gloomiest forebodings about the physical features of the race.[11]

Unlike the young woman, who came to embody the spirit of 'modernity', the effeminate male made no impact on popular writing and the collective imagination. At best he provoked criticism and at worse he was a figure of fun, to be exaggerated and sneered at. Either way he never inspired the fears that the supernumerary, omnipresent female inspired. Yet fear was not enough. For the debate on the demographic imbalance to reach its peak a concrete issue was needed – an economic, or political issue so acute as to make real both the image of the superfluous woman and the vulgarised Darwinist vocabulary evolving round it. That issue was, before 1926, women's work and, afterwards, reform of the franchise.

The debate on 'women in men's jobs' lasted over five years and had four peaks: from summer 1919 until autumn 1920 – a period roughly overlapping the final stage of demobilisation; spring 1923; November – December 1924; and winter 1925. During the spell of relative stability that preceded the Great Depression, interest in women's work petered out and the popular press sought new crusades to fight. This chronology is essential. For it indicates that, despite some connection between the economic situation in Britain and popular views on women's employment, the areas of material conditions and mental attitudes were not causally related. During the months of demobilisation, when nearly three-quarters of a million women were forced to leave industry, the national dailies were reticent. A similar silence characterises the recession of 1921 and 1922, when unemployment reached the unprecedented figure of 2.5 million. Conversely, the fiercest campaign against working women was waged in 1923 and 1924, a period of economic recovery and relative peace in labour relations. The real causes of the crusade were, it seems, not economic. They should be looked for in the sphere of mental attitudes and prejudices.

The pattern of evolution of the discourse is, by now, familiar: introduction of a phrase, emotionally appealing and easy to absorb; repetition and excessive, albeit effective, resort to popular 'scientific' vocabulary. In the whole English language there were, in the twenties, few words as emotive as 'war'. And the combination of 'war' and 'sex' was, to the contemporary ear, especially evocative. 'Sex' in particular was intriguing, adequately ambiguous (for it signified not only gender but also intercourse) and still sufficiently novel to the dailies' reading public. The phrase 'sex war' and the images associated with it smacked of the vulgarised socio-Darwinist idiom with which this public was by now familiar. And both the phrase and the concept it stood for offered a simple and simplifying explanation of the pace and scope of the changes which had recently occurred in relations between women and men. And, if those changes were – as it was popularly argued – part of a universal struggle between the sexes, if the new woman was a new species, then there was little humans could do to reverse them. In other words, the popularised Darwinist idiom helped contemporaries to comprehend, after a fashion, and come to terms with the phenomena of modern femininity and feminine sexuality, precisely because it presented those phenomena as biologically inevitable and nature-ordained rather than as cultural or social and, consequently, alterable.

Furthermore, economic problems such as the slump, unemployment or inflation could now be related to the demographic imbalance and explained in the Darwinist jargon. Significantly, the labour market became a popular metaphor for competition. And the metaphor, ideally, combined evolutionist notions of the struggle between the species and the survival of the fittest with a vulgarised interpretation of the liberal notion of *laissez-faire*. The least important development concerning women's employment was described in terms of a struggle between warring species. A petty dispute between women bank employees and the Bank Clerks' Guild was elevated to a 'sex war'. The decision of the Cambridge authorities not to admit female students to full membership was typically reported: 'women defeated in sex war'. On 12 October 1921 it became clear to the *Mail* that 'a series of sex skirmishes may easily develop into a pitched battle between man and woman as such'.[12]

The debate on employment graphically illustrates the customary hyperbole on verbal violence. Discourse in, say, 1924 or 1925 was distinctly more aggressive than in 1919 or 1921. Especially bellicose was the campaign against the payment of unemployment insurance to women, an issue that Rothermere's dailies cleverly related to the problem of the shortage of domestic servants. Initially the campaign was launched against 'government waste' – a favourite target with both the *Mail* and the *Express*. The tirade started in March 1923. The object was unemployment benefit; the slogan, 'scandals of the dole'. But the publication of two articles on 'women and the dole' brought such a response that the *Mail* soon diverted from its original course to the topic of unemployment and women. The debate, in which the public took an active part,[13] did not die down until 1925. Naturally, the payment of the dole to women was less to be approved than unemployment benefit for men, and unemployed women were encouraged to enter domestic service. Service was seen as women's natural vocation, an ideal preparation for a life of motherhood and domesticity, the appropriate sphere of the female. On 19 November 1924 the *Mail* pilloried the '$\frac{1}{4}$ million women living by doing nothing when at the same time tens of thousands of homes are disorganised'. On 18 March 1925 it revealed that 'Young women would rather idle away their time at home to join the already swollen ranks of the unemployed . . .', and continued, 'Rents are kept high, discontent is caused, unemployment is increased and home-life disorganised, all because the young woman of today . . . will not undertake the proper and natural employment that is awaiting her.' In 1925 the phrase 'sex war' was less explosive than it had been in 1919 or 1920 and it was seldom used; but the vocabulary revolving around it and the images it conjured up were still there. The relations between women and men outside the domestic sphere were still described in terms of a struggle over territory and territorial rights, between two species biologically and culturally apart. But the keynote of the debate on the disfranchised women was sounded by the epithet 'flapper'. And its day was yet to come.

Of all the words and phrases that formed the currency of discourse on womanhood and feminine sexuality, 'flapper' was the oldest (it had had a history of more than 300 years), the most semantically complex and, to the contemporary mind, the most emotive. The evolution of this epithet, which has not previously received the attention it deserves, conveniently presents three significant phases. The first and longest phase had lasted from the end of the sixteenth century until the second half of the nineteenth. 'Flapper' over this period had been an obscure word, largely neutral, that had existed in dialect and literature and in both had designated first inanimated beings and subsequently animals. The second phase, lasting from about 1870 until the end of the First World War, had seen the progress of the word from dialect to general speech, together with a two-sided change in meaning. 'Flapper' now became applied to humans – invariably females – and at the same time became distinctly derogatory. The third and final phase, covering the years 1918–28, was also the most crucial. Three disparate changes coincided to elevate the flapper into one of the most popular myths of the twenties. The word was transformed from a largely passive and somewhat obsolete term into a living one; it became a term of opprobrium; and finally, while still maintaining some of its older connotations, it acquired new social and political meanings. After this brief flowering the word gradually returned to its former, obscure status. And it is now largely unfamiliar, a curiosity mainly identified with the spirit of the twenties. But to separate the final phase from its antecedents would be historically wrong – especially since the meanings of the word after the war can be fully grasped only in relation to their precursors. And, since the history of the word has not been the subject of a full published account, I outline it in brief.

Literally 'flapper' means something that slaps or strikes. Figuratively the word has been applied to both animals and humans – the earliest example of the latter application being the flappers kept by the absent-minded philosophers of Laputa, whose business was 'to strike . . . the mouth of him who is to speak, and the right ear of him . . . to whom the speaker addresseth himself'.[14]

It seems that in the early nineteenth century 'flapper' had disappeared from standard English, but had remained alive in various dialects, signifying 'young fowl' – typically, a waterfowl just able to fly. 'Flappers

. . . puir beasts that couldna yet flee – and therefore are ca'd flappers' (1865); 'Auld drake and an auld dyuck wi' about a dizzen flappers' (1869); 'A couple of flappers start out from a clump of rushes and take a short flight across the Broad . . .'[15]

Around 1870 'flapper' acquired two novel meanings. It came to signify a female adolescent on the eve of her *début* in society, recognisable by the mane flapping down her back. The image this particular usage conveys is one of indecorous and sexually innocent youth. 'A flapper is a girl of the bread and butter age'; 'A red-faced flapper with lots of freckles and a pigtail' (1903); 'The first appearance of a "flapper" at a ladies' golf championship was in 1895. . . . Two long-haired, long-legged colleens were the most famous lady-golfers the world has yet produced' (1909); 'She was the jolliest flapper I had seen, with her long plait of hair down her back' (1915). There had also evolved a variety of derivatives describing the state of being a flapper: 'flapperhood', 'flapperdom' (both implying flippancy and clumsiness) and 'flapdoodle' – the last indicating silliness, a characteristic regarded as generically 'flapperish'.[16] At about the same time 'flapper' had come to signify a child prostitute – 'A very young girl trained to vice' (1899), 'a very young prostitute' (1893) – and, occasionally, the male sexual organ.[17] The two usages, the one celebrating sexual innocence, the other vice and deviance, are closer than they first appear to be. For they both describe real or ideal pubescence, that stage between childhood and womanhood when the female body is capable of procreation, but gender may be difficult to discern and the sexual identity is blurred. Typically in the first usage the flapper is boyish, often tomboyish. In the second usage there is an emphasis on physical immaturity, combined with a precocious sexuality.

The simultaneous emergence of the two meanings reflects the ambivalent attitude of the Victorians towards feminine youth and sexuality. Until the last quarter of the nineteenth century feminine childhood has been seen as an undifferentiated whole – a vestibule, as it were, preceding entrance into adulthood. But in the 1870s and 1880s a particular phase in the female's life was specified, recorded and named. And the peculiarly equivocal meanings of the term 'flapper' mirrored the ambiguous sexual role the Victorians assigned to the adolescent. On the one hand, the image of the socially segregated girl was one of perfect purity and chastity, the ideal of desexualised womanhood. On the other hand, this very image epitomised illicit sexuality in one of its most sinister forms: a thriving trade in child prostitution.

After the First World War the term 'flapper' was to acquire an even broader and more versatile range of significance. While still designating a young female, it came to mean not so much an immoral young girl as, more characteristically, a disfranchised adult (i.e. a young woman past her twenty-first birthday).[18] On 28 May 1928 Stanley Baldwin, addressing the Conservative Women's Association at the Albert Hall, commented on the confusion caused by the nonsensical 'inclusion of all working women . . . under the generic term of flappers'. Several months earlier *Punch* had stated that 'Flapper is the catchwood for an adult woman aged twenty one to thirty, when it is a question of giving her the vote under the same qualification as men of the same age.'[19]

There is one major difference between the late Victorian and the post-war usages. The former had placed the young female outside the pale of polite adult society, whether on its fringe (the child prostitute) or upon the threshold of social life (the middle-class adolescent). The latter usage brought feminine youth and sexuality into the orbit of adult life and the social and civic worlds. Of course, the new usage still retained many of the old connotations of the word. 'Flapper' still implied childishness, precocious sexuality and, more often than not, inanity, fickleness and inconsistency. Popular journalese occasionally resorted to the antiquated, eighteenth- and even seventeenth-century usages, evoking the old associations with fowl and fish in a denigrating analogy with young women. On 1 September 1919 the *Mail* reported on the 'dismissal [from government offices] of flappers and pig-tailed messengers while the barnacles remain firmly attached to their posts'. The same Dickensian metaphor reappeared in another article: 'Flappers go first and big limpets stick.'[20] The *Express* outshone the *Mail*. On 18 July 1926 it carried a recipe for 'roast flappers' with gluttonous undertones.

> I love a daintily dressed flapper. There's no better company at dinner. I love her more if she is tender and wild. . . . If you really roast them, then roast your flapper or duck. If you can and do roast them, there's a sauce: flappers love to be discreetly sauced. . . . Slowly half bake your dicky bird in pan with plenty of butter, to prevent the poor dear from becoming dry. . . . Then pop the whole into a big marmite, adding enough stock to cover up birdie. Put it into a not too fast – nice flappers do not like anything too fast – oven for about three quarters of an hour.

The jocose salaciousness could hardly escape the contemporary reader. It was spelled out in the barely disguised innuendoes and in a plethora of equivocal Swiftian phrases: 'daintily dressed flappers'; 'tender and wild flappers'; 'flappers love to be discreetly sauced'; 'fast flappers'; and so on. It hardly needs adding that eating as a metaphor of intercourse is as hackneyed as the comparison between women and birds.

Yet the peculiarity of the post-war usage of the word 'flapper' was not in its ties to a remote past, but in its relation to contemporary political issues. And that relation elevated the word, with its various shadings into a forceful symbol. The peculiar course of semantic evolution after the war can be chronicled year by year and, from the spring of 1927, almost day by day. Early in 1920 flappers apparently disappeared from the popular dailies, a significant event. There was, of course, mention of the word in the early and mid twenties, but on a relatively small and insignificant scale. 'Superfluous women' and 'sex war', it will be recalled, were the dominating phrases in debate on the contemporary woman. Then, on 31 March 1927, 'flapper' reappeared. It was not a sudden reappearance, nor a temporary one. Henceforth the epithet was to be aired daily on the news pages, in the editorial columns and in readers' letters. Few other events in the twenties were covered as thoroughly as the uncontroversial and unsensational 'Flapper Bill' of 1928. And few other campaigns – and the Rothermere and Beaverbrook press had launched many – were more ferociously fought.

The storm broke when Joynson-Hicks, the Home Secretary, proposed a bill granting women the vote on the same qualifications as men. The bill was based on a pledge made by Baldwin during the election campaign of 1924 to reform the franchise before the end of his term as Prime Minister. The *Mail* dismissed the pledge, calling it 'a case of the unimportant and unknown "Votes for Flappers" promise', but at the same time described this promise as 'a leap in the dark. . . . a proposal that will add some 4,500,000 new voters – many of them quite irresponsible persons – to the electorate – is thoroughly unpopular in the country and worthy of Bedlam.'[21] Two tonalities may be detected here: the one, dramatic, is pronounced in the phrases 'leap in the dark' (originally describing the Second Reform Bill) 'worthy of Bedlam', 'thoroughly unpopular'; the other, casual and belittling the issue of the reform, is apparent in the adjectives 'unknown' and 'unimportant'. This juxtaposition of tonalities was to become a set pattern. On 14 April the *Mail* warned that

> If the absurd project of Votes for Flappers is seriously pressed the only conclusion can be made that the government is using it as a kind of smoke-screen to enable it to escape from carrying out its reiterated and solemn pledges in the matters of economy, and the protection of England against Zinoviev and his Moscow bandits. M.P.s are wasting their time on such questions as Votes for Flappers, while urgent and important questions are left untouched.

The reading public had been acquainted with the President of the Third International and his 'Moscow bandits' three years before, when the *Mail* published the famous letter, allegedly signed by Zinoviev, to the Communist Party of Great Britain, so stirring up a Red-spy hysteria in the national press. Henceforth the mere mention of Zinoviev was sufficient to excite the audience. It is typical that, while the article describes the bill as a mere 'smoke-screen', it elsewhere refers to it as 'the most momentous step taken by a government for many years'. The nonsensically contradictory implications conjure up an ambiguous image: the bill is 'silly' but 'momentous', 'unknown' but 'thoroughly unpopular', 'unimportant' but strangely portentous. And there is yet another paradox. The allegedly insignificant reform was copiously and obsessively discussed, an obsession that belies the apparent insignificance of the issue. Ambiguity is increased by the calculated use of equivocal phrases, especially in the headlines. The passages quoted above are all from a series of articles entitled 'Stop the Flapper Folly'. And 'folly' may mean, in this context, stupidity or feeble-mindedness (both generic characteristics of the flapper), and also madness, or unreason. What makes the title particularly intriguing is the fact that 'flapper folly' suggests both the folly of flappers and the folly of giving them the vote. True, the Rothermere press had never had a monopoly on ambiguous expression and tonality. As William Empson puts it, the popular press substituted a compact and vague discourse for clarity of expression, and a certain flatness for simplicity. In the journalese of the Northcliffe era, single words and phrases came to stand for a mass of ideas which the journalist had no time to explain.[22] What singles out the discourse on the 'flapper vote' is not the ambiguous writing, not the vague, equivocal terminology, but the degree to which they were both elaborated. In 1927 'flapper' had become so equivocal a word, and could cover so many meanings, that it appealed to a mass audience of diverse tastes.

The argument behind the *Mail's* harangue was somewhat stale. The proposed bill, it ran, would create an overwhelming majority of young female voters in the electorate. Such a change would undoubtedly have serious consequences. It could bring down the Conservative government, or it could end in the creation of an Amazonian state ruled by a 'petticoat government', or an even greater calamity might be visited upon British democracy – namely, a Bolshevik revolution. At the heart of the *Mail's* oratory was the idea that an imbalance between the sexes could threaten the political, economic and social systems. But the rhetoric was new. The superabundance of flappers was still described by carefully chosen equivocal catchwords. But from the spring of 1927 these were gradually superseded by statistics. Estimates of the number of female voters that a reform would add to the electorate were now endlessly repeated. Calculations of the relative proportions of male and female voters were published daily. And it is evident that the function of this profusion of data was not to inform but to validate the argument against franchise reform and invest it with scientific authority.

On 19 April 1927 it was confidently revealed that according to the census of 1919 there were in Great Britain as many as 3,320,000 women aged 21 to 30 years. A day later their number alarmingly multiplied: there were now between 4.5 and 6 million flappers in the country. On 23 April the *Mail* announced that if the bill passed there would be a majority of 4 – 6 million 'young and ignorant women, most of whom will vote Labour'. Careful use was made of titles and cross-heads. On 16 June 1928 the compressed language of the newspaper headline produced a dramatic effect:

Flapper Issue Resumed
Election Swamped by Women
Conservative Alarm at Flapper Vote Results
Men Outnumbered Everywhere

The text that follows overflows with figures. The relative proportion of male and female voters in the event of reform are carefully examined for some 40 constituencies. In Kensington there would be 47,000 women voters to only 19,000 men; in Blackpool, 54,000 women to 31,000 men; and so on. 'In almost all the constituencies women will outnumber men and will dictate the politics of the country.'

Unlike the *Mail* the *Express* was not politically opposed to the idea of universal female suffrage. But the topic of 'votes for flappers' made news and could easily be capitalised on. Sophisticated layout techniques counteracted the paper's relatively moderate tone. On 13 April 1927 one front-page headline spoke more eloquently than columns of diatribe in the *Mail*: 'Women to Vote at Twenty-One, Great Franchise Expansion'. The cross-head that follows is divided into two blocks by an inserted photograph of a shingled, heavily made-up woman smoking a cigarette, the proverbial image of flapperdom. On the left of the photograph the words 'Cabinet Takes the Plunge' appear in heavy type, and on the right (also in heavy type) is printed 'Girls on Age Equality with Men'. The choice of the word 'Girls' and not 'Women' is significant. Furthermore, the same print is used in the feature as in the cross-head, so that the division between heading and text virtually disappears. This American poster technique successfully changes the emphasis of even the most straightforward and balanced report.

The obsession with the arithmetic of the flapper vote was infectious. Even *The Times* gave extensive editorial space to the topic of the imbalance between men and women in the new electorate.[23] And pamphlets, probably originating from the Independent Labour Party and distributed in the spring and summer of 1927, sought to beat the mass-circulation press with its own weapon.[24] Like the assault of the Rothermere press on the 'Flapper Vote Bill' the ILP backlash was designed to overwhelm the audience with apparently well-founded information, presented in an aggressive manner.

The introduction of the rhetoric of figures into the discourse on the disparity between the sexes was timely. For 'superfluous women' and 'sex war' were both loaded phrases, and in the twenties both were unmistakably opprobrious. After being endlessly repeated they could lose their power even with the least discriminating audience. Figures appear factual and unbiased. When massively quoted they are a powerful weapon. True, the figures offered for the size of an enlarged female electorate were grossly inaccurate and calculatedly misleading. But they had the appearance of 'scientific' authority – neutral, precise and seemingly irrefutable, and they could provide the most fatuous argument against universal suffrage with some illusory veracity.

At its peak, from April 1927 until the autumn of 1928, the campaign against the flapper was intertwined with other sacred crusades of the popular press. The flapper and the flapper vote were continuously coupled with the *Mail*'s favoured scapegoats: Baldwin and the 'Socialist Party' (the word 'Labour' was anathema in Rothermere's days); the International and 'Bolshevik menace'; the trade unions and the 'radicals' – an extraordinarily resilient term that could be usefully applied to any enemy. Here indeed was a novelty. Before 1927 female voters were described as more proof against change than the male ones. During the election campaigns of 1919, 1922 and 1924 women were addressed as potential supporters of the Coalition or the Conservative Party,[25] the preservers and stabilisers of the social order. Of course, this was barely disguised propaganda, but, more important, the female electorate at the time was composed of 'matron' voters, those women over 30 with the property qualification. Flappers, on the other hand, were presented as generically unstable, uprooted, socially subversive and politically radical.

At first glance the blending of anti-socialist propaganda with propaganda against the 'Flapper Vote Bill' may seem odd. For the social unrest of the early and mid twenties ended with the fiasco of the General

Strike and organised labour embarked on a path of co-operation with the parliamentary system rather than action outside it. It may seem that in 1927 and 1928 the threat of revolution was even less real than it had been in 1919, or 1926. Yet seldom before had the tirade against the 'Moscow band' been as vehement and as persistent as during the campaign against the 'Flapper Vote Bill'. And close examination of the material suggests that the anti-socialist propaganda was actually a weapon against the Conservative government and, more important, that this propaganda fed on popular, deep-rooted fears of universal revolution. Flapperdom was first associated with subversion on 14 April 1927, when the *Mail* proposed to make tax-paying a qualification for the franchise. Flappers and paupers (the latter also disfranchised), it was argued, were 'parasitical minorities'. (The reference to the much feared hordes of flappers as a 'minority' is ludicrous.) 'It is tax-payers, not flappers who need effective enfranchisement.' Many a reader felt that abolition of the property qualifications for the franchise was hazardous. On 15 April the proposed new recruits to the female electorate were described as 'irresponsible, unpropertied and ill-informed on public-affairs'. The crucial adjective is 'unpropertied', for hitherto the word 'flappers' had been applied to all female adults without the vote and had never included a class element. Henceforth, however, it would be applied mainly to disfranchised working-class women and would be associated with politics of the Left. On 23 April a leading article predicted that the votes of the ignorant young female workers of the industrial North and the Midlands would sweep Labour to power. Two days later the leader bore the metaphoric title 'The Coming Massacre' – 'massacre' being the fate of the Conservative Party in the coming general election. On 27 April the *Mail* returned to the same metaphor:

> The socialists are convinced such a massacre will place them in office for many years, and will mean for them the capture of a host of Conservative seats at the next general election. In their secret conclaves they revel in the fact that in the great industrial areas the young working women and girls are already organised and regimented in trade-unions which are under socialist control and that they can be trusted to vote almost in a mass and without exception for socialist candidates.

'Secret conclaves' echoes one of the most powerful myths of the twenties: that of a world-wide conspiracy, designed in Moscow and executed by the communist and socialist parties of Western Europe, to destroy capitalist civilisation and democracy. True, the notion of a universal, destructive power is much older, but in the inter-war years the myth of a Bolshevik conspiracy reflected middle-class fears of a revolution. In the late twenties the British newspaper-reading public had long been acquainted with the jargon of the conspiracy theme. Both the 'Red Letter' scare of 1924 and the General Strike were vivid memories in the collective imagination of the age. The insinuations that the franchise reform was part of an international Bolshevik conspiracy were brilliant propaganda. The incorporation of the conspiracy myth into the ambiguous image of the superfluous, socially subversive flapper made this image especially powerful. Naturally the 'Red menace' was omnipresent. It was said to have infiltrated the highest seats of authority: the Conservative Party, Parliament and even the Cabinet. Stanley Baldwin, whose brain-child the reform was believed to be, was alternately described as the victim of a Bolshevik plot and its instigator. On 11 October the *Mail* proposed to postpone the enfranchisement of flappers until after the coming elections, so as not to 'revolutionise the electoral system'. On 12 November the paper demanded the leadership to purge the Conservative Party of a 'socialist clique', insisting that 'It is to the effort of this clique that the pernicious proposal to give votes to "flappers" is due. They are known to be responsible for the disastrous intention to saddle British industry with a new Factory Bill.'

By the end of 1927 the political purpose of the crusade against flappers had become clear. Baldwin personally was continuously attacked and it seems that Rothermere sought to bolster opposition to the bill within the Cabinet and the Conservative Party.[26] At this stage of the campaign a change in tone can also be detected. Discourse is less compressed and economic. Everything is spelled out. And the direct, unequivocal attacks on the reform are less effective than the language of *double entendre*. On 18 November, Rothermere himself stepped into the limelight and openly addressed Baldwin. The rhetoric of the address is that of populist propaganda, cunningly playing on the emotive powers of such words as 'patriotism' and 'democracy'. Characteristically, the *Mail*'s proprietor assumed the task not only of critic and guide, but also of authorised interpreter of the public's will. And it was largely from this persistent identification of the addresser with the addressed audience that organs such as the *Mail* and the *Express* derived their power.

The votes which put the Conservatives in power were given for a specific purpose. They were cast by patriotic men and women in the cause of anti-Socialism and for drastic action against Bolshevist interference from abroad. Yet you now continue your policy of promoting legislation of a Socialist character by using your majority to give Votes to 'flappers'. How, I ask you will all respect, can it be reconciled with the principles of democracy, to force into law a measure like 'Votes For Flappers'. . . . Its most important effect will be to transfer political power in Britain from the male to the female sex. *This is a Revolution. You are setting a precedent of entirely altering the basis of government of this country without any reference to the electorate.* . . .

Politically, the campaign against the flapper failed. On 30 March 1928 the Representation of the People Equal Franchise Bill passed with an overwhelming majority of 387 to 10 in the House of Commons, and it was later endorsed in the Lords by a majority of 114 to 35. In July 1928 the bill became law.[27] It was outside the sphere of politics that the campaign had a fateful significance. For neither 'flapper', nor 'superfluous woman', nor the other opprobrious epithets used to designate the modern female were merely press catchwords. They became 'umbrella' pejoratives, so resilient and all-embracing that they covered multiple and diverse images and meanings: the image of adolescent purity and juvenile deviance; asexuality and hypersexuality; feminine independence and superfluity; social order and subversion. And it was precisely the versatility of these words and their emotive power that made them portentous slogans. They all, but especially 'flapper', came to be associated with, and to reflect, a cluster of social and economic problems that had no apparent connection with the sexual issue: social tension; the fears of revolution, unemployment and socialism.

The campaign had two other effects. First, the mass-circulation dailies put the controversial topic of feminine sexuality into the spotlight and impressed on it the stamp of respectability. The disappearance of the associations of 'flapper' with child prostitution is noteworthy. The sexuality of adult women, not that of the female adolescent or the delinquent child, was now at the centre of public concern. And the former topic was legitimised by those organs that identified themselves, and were popularly identified with, the attitudes and moods of the Great British Public. There was another effect. Inadvertently, the popular dailies liberated the discourse on womanhood and feminine sexuality. Never before had it been brought to so large and heterogeneous a public with such intensity. And never before had the public debate (as opposed to the private, clandestine discourse in 'forbidden' literature, or the learned debate in publications for élite audiences) been more open and its language more aggressive. Of course, the Rothermere press vulgarised common feelings and modes of thinking about women. But it also made feminine sexuality popularly discussable and put a repository of words and images at the disposal of both the writing and the reading publics. Without acknowledging this role of the press as mediator it is impossible to comprehend the emergence of the 'sex novels' of the twenties.

Part Two
'Furtive Excitement' The
Discourse in Post Colonies

2

'Sex Novels': A New Kind of Best-seller

One might easily say that half the love novels and half the love-films today depend entirely for their success on the secret rubbing of the dirty little secret. You can call this sex-excitement if you like, but it is sex-excitement of a secretive, furtive sort, quite special. The plain and simple excitement, quite open and wholesome, which you find in some Boccaccio stories is not for a moment to be confused with the furtive excitement aroused by rubbing the dirty little secret in all secrecy in modern best-sellers.
(D. H. Lawrence, *Pornography and Obscenity*, 1929)

The brief fame of the word 'flapper' coincided with the emergence of the term 'best-seller', or, in the currency of the period, 'big seller' or 'super-seller'. These three synonymous epithets were at the centre of a discourse on the nature and trajectory of mass-market fiction, a discourse which overlapped and often intermingled with that on the contemporary woman. For the new motions on womanhood and sexuality to reach a large, disintegrated reading public the apparatus of best-sellerdom was needed. On the other hand, this apparatus, which in Britain began to develop after the First World War, would not have emerged at this particular moment had there not been a public aware of, even obsessed with, the phenomenon of modern feminine sexuality.

But, unlike 'flapper', 'best-seller' is a wholly modern term. It was only in the twenties, nearly three decades after its first appearance in America, that it came into common usage in Britain.[1] Examples of its use can be found dating from the 1900s and early 1910s, but they are isolated and insignificant.[2] It was only after the war that the best-selling book became the subject of public discussion and the term 'best-seller' itself spread to the popular idiom. The pattern of evolution curiously parallels that of the key words in the vocabulary of sexuality. An obscure word is given a new significance and is circulated by the national press. The word retains some of its primary meanings but acquires new ones, which can be understood only in their specific context (the context of the socio-demographic crisis,

41

as is the case with the derogatory sense of 'superfluous woman', or the changes in the texture of popular culture, as is the case with 'best-seller').

As in America, 'best-seller' in Britain normally signified either a book that, over a limited span, sold more than other books, or its creator. But for the British 'best-seller' was a new phenomenon, an innovation of the age, one that needed to be specified and recorded. It is significant that in the early and mid twenties the terms 'big seller' and 'super-seller' were used interchangeably with 'best-seller'. Only later in the decade did the last become the favoured description of the mass-market book and its creator.

But, more important, the best-selling novel was regarded as an evil wrought by the First World War, epitomising the maladies and malfunctions of post-war society. Philistinism, levelling-down and moral degeneracy were emblazoned in this 'new kind of book'. And, last but not least, the unprecedented demand for this commodity was seen as a reflection of the need for escape from the reality of modern life to a vicarious existence. The familiar criticism offered by the Leavises in fact echoes in critical rhetoric the diagnosis of publishers and book-sellers. 'The demand for fiction on such a wholesale scale', wrote Michael Joseph, 'must be due to the artificial complexities of a civilised state. Men and women, especially women, seek in the vicarious realm of fiction the wider range of human experiences which a complex and narrow life denies them'.[3] Joseph's emphasis on the hunger of feminine audiences for escapist fiction, a hunger that is by implication largely generic, is characteristic. It was on this particular point, to do with the relation between fiction and gender, that the attention of his contemporaries was focused. One type of novel was isolated, given a label and catalogued – the 'sex novel'. And, if the best-seller as such reflected the cultural and moral maladies of the age, the sex novel epitomised them. Furthermore, the latter, it was observed, had its own distinctive features. First and foremost, the heroine was a contemporary young woman. Second, the genre displayed an obsession with modern sexual morality. Third, it provided a realistic presentation of woman's sexual experience and openly discussed the topic of feminine sexuality. Lawrence's indignant remark on the coded, furtive 'rubbing [of] the dirty little secret' in the modern best-seller is an isolated one. The majority of critics regarded the discourse on sexuality as unprecedentedly liberated, or even licentious and dangerously salacious in its frankness. Fourth and last, the growing demand for escapist novels about sex was related to the expansion of the female reading public and its greater social diversity. Opinion on the sex novel was divided. On the one hand, the new freedom to discuss topics that had previously been hushed up was welcomed. On the other hand, the preoccupation with feminine sexuality was diagnosed as symptomatic of a deep social and cultural malaise, an indication of decadence. Elizabeth Drew's reaction to the 'new licence' in mass-market fiction is typical:

> The collective mind of contemporary society is now impregnated with a new consciousness of sex. It has indeed become such an obsession with some sections of it, that there are many, as Mr Edwin Muir humorously remarks, who see the curves of a woman's body in every subject not actually flat. . . . The new licence in the presentation and depiction of sexual phenomena has created a new type of best-seller that is characteristically modern.[4]

The press occasionally coupled the new freedom of expression with high-browism and described it as a marginal phenomenon, unhealthy and un-British. In the chorus of middle-brow disapproval the voice of Gilbert Frankau was specially audible. The prolific Frankau was a steady rather than a best-seller, a self-appointed interpreter of national tastes and preferences and relentless campaigner against the *outré* and subversive in literature. His platform was the *Express* and, later in the decade, the BBC. (It was one vicious attack on the wireless that prompted Leonard Woolf to vindicate the high-brow in the now almost forgotten *Hunting the Highbrow*, published in 1927.) A typical diatribe appeared on 2 March 1924:

> The modern highbrow novel represents a tendency towards the *outré*, the bizarre, and the a-moral. . . . [it] presents life from the angel of 'Cracked Chelsea' or 'Reckless Russell Square'. . . . That this contemptible minority, however, has the slightest influence on the behaviour of actual Englishwomen and English girls, I refuse to believe.

But more characteristically the sex novels were classified as middle- or low-brow, a classification that, *ipso facto*, associated them with the masses of the Great British Public, rather than with esoteric minorities. The new licence seemed so pernicious because it was most likely to affect those readerships who had always been regarded as uncritical, 'actual English-women and English girls'. And the female reader of all ages, with the adolescent male, seemed to be more exposed than adult males to the corrupting influences of vicariously experienced sex. Behind the forebodings of critics can be detected the familiar axiom that feminine nature is fickle and infantile, and masculine nature mature, stable and discriminating. Yet it was universally granted that the demand for what Lawrence called 'sex-excitement' came largely from the public that needed the greatest protection. A review of Edgar C. Middleton's controversial play *Potiphar's Wife* (1927) attributed the vogue of sex novels and sex plays to the preferences of a predominantly female audience: 'A first-class play may fail because it has no love-affair. There was not one theatre success since the war which did not enjoy what is predominantly described today as *It* [sex appeal].' The modern play, the reviewer summed up, 'deals with sex and sex alone'.[5] On 29 November 1927 the *Express* devoted about half its editorial page to an address of James Douglas, editor of the *Sunday Express*, to 'the vilest of all war profiteers', the 'best-sellers of sex-novels'. The letter, duly publicised in the Beaverbrook press, is an orgy of scurrility, offensive even by the standards of the *Mail* and the *Express*. But the difference between Douglas's tirade and other attacks on sex novels and the sex novelists is merely one of degree:

> Mimes, Cads, Bounders, Sniggerers, Innenduists, Pornocrats, Garbage Mongers, Purveyors of Pruriency, Vendors of Vice, Sewer Rats, Carrion Crows, Maggots of Decadence, Hookworms of Salacity, Literary Lepers and Yahoos; You are one of the ten plagues let loose upon us by the war, and I am afraid that no pestologist will exterminate you before you have completed your corruption of defenceless youth and your mercenary demobilisation of the English novel . . . you have turned marriage into mockery. You have glorified lust and lechery. You have made the world safe for pornocracy. It is your crowning shame that you have transformed sex into a synonym for sensuality, so that this once honest word is now a lewd leer reeking of lubricity. Sex novels, sex plays and sex films are a marketable commodity. . . . Not long ago I retched over a novel by a female procuress which explored abysmal horrors that hitherto have been the monopoly of psycho-analysis. Sweet girl graduates read it and discuss its esoteric abnormalities and fetid mysteries. . . .

Today Douglas's oratory seems pathetic, but in 1927 it certainly had weight. For here was the voice of authority, an expert opinion on the taste and morals of the British public. A sophisticated layout (two columns instead of the standard four) and print (both the cross-heads and part of the text are in heavy type) probably had additional effect. The verbal violence of the 'respectable' mass-circulation press set the terms and tone of an unleashed journalistic and critical attack on sex literature. Paradoxically, the language of the uncensored dailies is far more offensive than that of the technically pure sex novels. Literary critical comment also is intemperately aggressive. Inadvertently, the ceaseless barrage against sex literature and modern sexuality contributed a great deal to the 'new licence' it continuously deplored.

Thus the modern best-seller was popularly regarded as a feminine artefact, produced by women for women – a form of communication, as it were, between distinctive female writing and reading publics. It is significant that even sex novels by male writers were commonly referred to as effeminate. There recurs a significant distinction between straight-forward masculine fiction and unhealthy, emasculating and emasculated literature by 'affected' authors – females and males. A. S. M. Hutchinson, Sir Philip Gibbs, Robert Keable, Warwick Deeping and C. P. Wren, all of whom specialised in social melodramas with male heroes, were in the first, 'masculine' category. Gilbert Frankau was an interesting border-line case. A 'manly' author by conviction, he nevertheless capitalised on the vogue for the modern emancipated heroine and the topic of the new morality. In the second, 'effeminate' category can be found, lumped together, reputed pornographers such as E. M. Hull; romantic novelists such as Elinor Glyn and Ethel M. Dell; H. De Vere Stackpoole, author of the famous *Blue Lagoon*; and Michael Arlen, whose romantic fantasies were invariably labelled 'affected'. It is largely to writers in this second category that the derogatory description 'sex novels' was applied, and the novels themselves were characterised as perverted, unnatural and 'foreign'.

The classification of literature according to gender was hardly an innovation. Since the late eighteenth century the novel had been thought of as a specifically feminine form, the appropriate vessel to reflect the domestic world of women and their experience of reality and to transmit this experience to a primarily female audience. And from about the middle of the nineteenth century (as it has since been observed) the English novel had materially influenced the ideology of domesticity and desexualised femininity.[6] What was so peculiar to the twenties was, therefore, not the distinction, as such, between a masculine and a feminine literature, but the idea that the female public sought escapism in the form of vicarious sex as independent of, even opposed to, romantic love and matrimony. This concept involved a notion of the modern woman as a sensual and sexually motivated being, far more sensual than her male counterpart. Indeed, many contemporaries maintained that women rather than men sought 'sex-excitement'; that women were the consumers of erotic literature; and, finally, that they were far more expressive than men on topics related to sex. What Douglas blatantly spelled out others insinuated. A *Bookman* feature on the sado-masochistic novels of Ethel M. Dell argued that 'the less intelligent and less sensitive girl dreams of an ardent lover and gets a humdrum fellow who makes love without spirit and without inventiveness. To such a girl the Dell hero is a whiff of romance. She responds to him with a sort of masochistic delight.'[7] Michael Joseph, commenting on the rapid change in conventions, observed that 'Women novelists, in particular, are far more outspoken on sex matters than most men writers. Very often they can deal with sex themes with far less self-consciousness than men appear to do.'[8]

The much-commented-upon change in conventions accounts for the rise of the new genre. It does not explain the unprecedented levels of production and consumption of feminine literature on sex. Several material changes made it possible for the new artefact to become a mass-market commodity. In what follows I offer a sketch of some possible connections between, on the one hand, the pattern of life and leisure of urban populations and, on the other, the book market.

It is usually the first decade of the twentieth century, not the third, that is regarded as an era of expansion in the book industry. The twenties are described as a period of consolidation rather than change and there certainly is substantial evidence to support this claim. Between 1913 and 1923 the annual output of books rose from 12,379 to 12,690 titles, an insignificant rise in comparison with what occurred in the previous decade.[9] But these figures do not reflect the two inverse trends in the market after the war: a decline in the volume of new titles (about a quarter of the figure for 1923 consists of reprints) as against a dramatic rise in the number and size of editions.[10] Or, as Per Gedin put it, in the Americanised British market the decisive factor was the peaks of sales rather than the total range of books.[11] Examples are legion. 51 editions of *If Winter Comes* were issued between June 1921 and 1923. 17 editions of *The Green Hat* appeared between June 1924 and August 1926. C. P. Wren's *Beau Geste* ran into 27 editions between October 1924 and January 1927; three editions appeared in March 1927, one in April, two in May and two in September. But the most conspicuous example is E. M. Hull's *The Sheik*, which, between 1919 and 1923, ran into 108 editions in Britain alone.

The demand for cheap editions could not be met. The standard price for a novel in cloth covers remained 7s 6d (there was, however, a wide range of novels at 3s 6d). The price for a cheap edition in soft covers was considerably lower. When Nash and Grayson first published *The Sheik* it cost 3s 6d, but the spectacular sales of the novel in Britain and America enabled the publishers to cut the price of a copy to 2s 6d, and a cheap edition eventually cost only 1s. Firms such as Werner Laurie, Cassell, Hutchinson and Nash, and companies such as the Readers' Library diversified into magazine-publishing and mass-market pulp editions. Conversely, newspaper and magazine magnates such as the Harmsworths and George Newnes increased their hold on the market for cheap editions. Newnes's shilling publications for 1924 included reprints of Richmal Crompton's popular William novels and a crop of Edgar Wallace's latest thrillers. Among the lucrative 'Newnes Classics', priced at 2s 6d, were *The Blue Lagoon*, one or two of Gene Stratton Potter's favourites, and several of Rider Haggard's works.

The cheap editions catered for a reading public that was larger and less unified than its Victorian and Edwardian predecessors. The pattern of change evident in newspaper audiences can also be detected in the novel-reading public. As it expanded, it included more and more readers from the lower-middle class and then the working class, until these came to comprise the bulk of the readership. In other words, audiences that before the war had access only to magazines and the Sundays could now afford to purchase or hire reading-matter in book form. A cheap edition was hardly distinguishable from a cheap magazine. Printed on pulp paper or newsprint, in an economic two-column layout (typical of Newnes and Readers' Library reprints), the cheap editions competed successfully with the middle-price story papers. The average price of a typical household miscellany such as the *Corner Magazine*, *Complete Story Magazine* or *Happy Magazine* was 7d. Fortnightly story magazines for women, such as the *Violet Magazine*, *Red Magazine* and *Yellow Magazine*, cost between 6d and 7d. By the late twenties all the contemporary best-sellers and the 'popular classics' could be bought for 7d or less, or they could be cheaply hired from the lending libraries of the high-street chain stores Boots and W. H. Smith, or from the back-street 'tuppenny dram shops' that prospered in the poorest areas. The magazine look of the best-seller was likely to appeal to that audience which by tradition and social allegiance was a magazine- and not a novel-reading public, the *petite bourgeoisie* and the better-off working class. Indeed, the boom of the novel can be related to three changes in the texture of life in urban areas: first, a dramatic expansion, over a short span, of Britain's larger cities; second, a rise in the standard of living of the majority in the poorer classes; and, third, the spread of new popular entertainments such as the film. Of these factors, the first was, probably, the most decisive.

The urban landscape changed after the war. Two movements took place: one from the populous industrial fringes to the residential centre; the other (traceable from the 1830s, but dramatic in the twenties) from already built-up areas to new and expanding suburbs. The population of London's outer ring (i.e. suburbs outside the county of London) swelled by 27 per cent between 1921 and 1930, and corresponding growth on a smaller scale took place in Britain's other conurbations.[12] But the suburban area stretching between the old centres and the open country was a 'waste-land', with neither focus nor sense of community. The main reason was that, in contrast with earlier urban development, which had tended to be compact, radiating from an economic or civic centre, the new neighbourhoods sprawled linearly, along the routes of an expanding transport system. The inhabitants of 'commuterland', daily pouring into the cities and out of them, were an ideal audience for fiction and journalism that could be cheaply purchased and easily digested and dispensed of.

Since the 1860s critics of culture had associated the emergence of mass-market literature with urbanisation and the spread of railway networks. The latter phenomenon in particular had symbolised 'machinery' and the 'machine age'. 'Railway' fiction, in its derogatory Arnoldian and Jamesian meanings, had become a metaphor for the debasement of culture. It is possible, even probable, that the simultaneous growth of the suburbs and the expansion of commuter transport influenced the history of popular fiction as significantly as the rise of the railways. Observers in the twenties were aware of this connection. In the idiom of the period the epithet 'suburban' came to be what 'philistine' had been in the 1860s. Both epithets denoted mediocrity and a propensity to cheap emotionalism. But in the twenties the word 'suburban' became synonymous with a markedly feminine way of life. And the suburban female (whether the inhabitant of a huge working-class estate or the occupant of a villa) personified the hollowness of existence in the modern big city. Her image was somewhat ambivalent. She still possessed some of the stock characteristics of the Victorian prig: prudishness, hypocrisy and middle-class respectability. But she was also endowed with a libido. She was the typical consumer and projected heroine of erotic fantasies. Elizabeth Drew attributed the success of *The Green Hat* to the delight of the British housewife in vicarious experience of a 'reasonable amount of adultery'.[13] The *Bookman*, in the article on Ethel M. Dell quoted earlier, revealingly described the contemporary male as a 'humdrum fellow who catches the same train every morning'. Not surprisingly, his spouse was inclined to indulge an appetite for sado-masochistic fantasies about uncivilised but masculine 'cave men'.[14]

Those who sought such escapism could now afford it more easily than ever before. Books became readily available to the mass of the population, not only because they were relatively cheap but because of a significant rise in the standard of living of the poorer classes. Despite periodic spells of recession and chronic unemployment, the period between the First World War and the Great Depression witnessed a sharp improvement in the conditions of life of most members of the British working class. The number of wage-earners, forming its core, fell to 15 million and the proportion of salaries swelled by about 10 per cent. Average wages rose by 95 per cent while the cost of living increased by only 75 per cent, and shorter hours in the industry (the average working week had been reduced to 48 hours) meant more leisure.[15] These changes contributed to the phenomenal growth in domestic consumption, which in turn acted on patterns of leisure. Mass manufacture of consumer goods such as readymade clothes, canned food and labour-saving appliances made housekeeping less demanding. Two groups in the swelling class of consumers are of particular importance here: young working women and lower-middle-class housewives. Both these groups, particularly the former, benefited from the war, and their growing spending-powers attracted the expanding book and magazine industries. True, the reading-matter of most British working-class females still consisted predominantly of periodicals. But this traditional form of entertainment now faced competition from two quarters, the mass-produced novel and the film.

The 'pictures' had been a popular entertainment since their inception, aimed at large audiences with low incomes. But it was in the twenties that the making and showing of films was transformed from small-scale private enterprise into a commercialised, massively capitalised industry. Cinema-going became a regular feature in the life of the working class, bringing a decline in two traditional pastimes: drinking and attending music-hall performances. The rise of the 'picture palace' coincided with the steep decline of vaudeville and a relative decline of the pub. Drinking had begun to decline during the war, when the consumption of spirits and beer fell dramatically. And vaudeville as the 'expressive art of the working-classes' was in decline. When in 1923 T. S. Eliot predicted the disappearance of music halls and their replacement by cinemas he was, in fact, recording a process already well advanced.[16] Like the suburban estate and the local branch of Woolworth's, the lucrative 'picture palace' was a prominent feature of the changing urban landscape. Cinemas adorned even the poorest neighbourhoods. And there is evidence that cinema-going was particularly high in the most depressed areas. According to one estimate, there were by 1928 some 3768 commercial cinema halls in the United Kingdom. 33.5 per cent of the cinema-going public went to the 'pictures' once a week and 47 per cent twice a week, while a year later only 23.5 per cent went once a week and as many as 60 per cent twice a week.[17] The cinema-going public was larger and substantially more heterogeneous than the novel- and newspaper-reading publics. The burgeoning industry catered particularly for the low-income urban audiences, a fact that is evident from the low admission prices and frequent changes of programme, especially in the poorest districts.

There was a dynamic interchange between the sex novel and the new industry. The film popularised not only works of fiction which the mass of the British working classes could not, or would not, purchase or hire, but also stylised fictional images of the woman and particular notions about sexuality. It is an aesthetic commonplace to observe that visual images may have a greater impact than verbal ones. And in the silent film the expressive human face, or a gesture 'frozen' by the camera, was as conventionalised as the *tableau vivant* and as articulate. The camera imprinted on the collective imagination of the age stereotypes that would otherwise have been forgotten. What made the celluloid idols of the twenties so easy to identify with was the fact that they were inseparable from the persons of the stars. And it was the illusory disappearance of 'aura', or the distance between the authentic, *unreproducible* artefact and the spectator – what Walter Benjamin describes as the 'phony aura' of the screen – that made the stars figures of cult.[18] Greta Garbo in *A Woman of Affairs*, the first, bowdlerised version of *The Green Hat*, was Arlen's promiscuous heroine; Clara Bow, oozing sex appeal, *was* the essential flapper; Agnes Ayers, only implicitly violated in the filmed version of *The Sheik*, *was* the well-bred virgin turned into a woman, and millions of female spectators identified with her. Like the mass-circulation paper, the film served as mediator between a minority of writers and an audience far more diverse than the novel-reading public.

The popular paper and the film disseminated the sexual idiom and the stereotypes which dominated contemporary sex literature. But the film went beyond the paper by literally changing words into images. The word 'It', as a euphemism for sex appeal, was coined in 1927, in Elinor Glyn's famous novelette. A few months later came Metro-Goldwyn-Mayer's version, with Clara Bow as the 'It' girl. The persona of the actress was sex incarnate. Another example is provided by the term 'Sheik', which in the idiom of the period denoted a masculine lover. The first appearance of that particular meaning was in Hull's notorious best-seller. Despite its success there is no doubt that the implausible oriental hero became a sex symbol because of the extrinsic appeal of the inimitable Valentino to female audiences.

It is difficult, even impossible, to isolate one single factor and measure its impact upon the production and distribution of sex novels, or upon their readers. The influence of the growth of the London Underground on the consumption of reading-matter in the metropolitan area cannot be measured. Nor is it possible to calculate the effect that the rise in the real wages of factory girls had on their reading-habits. Taken together, however, the three factors identified above had a decisive influence. For they brought about the emergence of a new type of reader, the lower-middle-class or working-class female, economically better off than her Edwardian predecessor, socially freer and, most important, exposed to various cultural influences. There was the influence of the expanding market for mass-production goods, a development that transformed urban populations, and the working classes in particular, into a consumer society. There was also the impact of the new forms of communication and popular entertainment – the sex film or the mass-circulation newspaper – which made feminine sexuality so marketable. But, more than any *one* influence, it was the overall effects of life in the post-war 'megalopolis' which contemporaries regarded as most pernicious. And that peculiarly urban experience was diagnosed as the prime cause of escapism on such a massive scale.

3

1921: *If Winter Comes* – a 'Masculine' Novel

1921 was an inauspicious year. The boom that followed peace came to an abrupt end. Trade slumped. Wage rates fell and a succession of stoppages and strikes swept the country. On 1 April the long-threatened miners' strike broke out. A strike order to the railway and transport workers for midnight on 12 April was then postponed, and three days later the Triple Alliance called off the strike. 15 April, 'Black Friday', became a symbolic landmark in the social history of the decade. There was talk of an averted revolution. In June, unemployment reached 2,171,888, an ominous figure, not to be passed until the Great Depression.

In August, Hodder and Stoughton brought out a novel by Arthur Stuart Menteth Hutchinson, a successful journalist who had been editor of the *Daily Graphic* and written three other novels, all mildly received by the critics and scarcely remembered by the public at large. The arrival of his fourth novel was timely. There could not have been a more opportune moment for a book photographically reflecting the atmosphere of disillusionment and despondency than that summer of discontent.

Hutchinson dwelt upon the issues of unemployment and class conflict; national strife and international crises; the crumbling of the institution of middle-class marriage and the erosion of the family. Yet, despite its gloom, the picture he drew was sentimentally optimistic – so much so that many a reader felt that *If Winter Comes* was 'something we needed without knowing it',[1] a book to be recommended even to a dying man, 'so spontaneous, so fresh, so humorous . . . as full of life as a May morning'.[2] Publishers described it as a 'phenomenal success', 'one of the most notable events . . . in years' in the history of the trade.[3] Hodder and Stoughton reported that the original edition, published at 7s 6d, sold over 100,000 copies in Britain in 12 months. The American sales soared to 400,000 by April 1922.[4] After 51 editions the cascade of sales tapered off and the fifty-second edition appeared in June 1927. But these impressive figures cannot measure the extraordinary resonance the book had. *If Winter Comes* was the focus of what was possibly the earliest articulate public debate on the phenomenon of the best-seller. In April 1922 *The Times* launched its weekly literary column with the query 'Why is *If Winter Comes* a Best-Seller?' The response was overwhelming. The correspondence columns for April, May and June overflow with letters that, apart from their topical interest, cast light on the obscure mechanism of relations between popular novel, professional criticism and the reading public.

The first impression is that contemporaries saw *If Winter Comes* as 'untypical' of its genre, lacking intense action and sex interest and not at all 'gripping'. On 21 April one reader commented that, 'Although novels which achieve such volume of sales are ordinarily either luscious or thrilling, either sentimental or sensational, Hutchinson's novel is neither.' Two days later another reader wrote,

> When entire families read the book and each member speaks of it with affectionate enthusiasm, we ask why? Ordinary best-sellers explain themselves. Their authors can tell a story, and they deal with popular types and popular sentiment. But *If Winter Comes* . . . is written by a man of letters and it lacks the form and purpose of popularity.

Hutchinson's style was 'jerky and oblique . . . not what the public wants'.

Yet the book did have one of the allures of a popular novel: an anti-hero with whom contemporaries found it easy to identify. Mark Sabre was the book's greatest appeal. Today the evangelistic streak in him seems absurdly mawkish. But the contemporary reading public thought this 'Christian spirit' both elevating and edifying. Sales in America were boosted after the book was commended by thousands of clergymen (who actually made Sabre the subject of their Sunday sermons), and it became required reading in several schools in New York, along with George Eliot and Shakespeare.[5] In *The Times* the ineffable Margot Asquith opined that 'what gives the book true power is that in Mark Sabre the author has brought out the highest qualities of man and those generally associated with Christ — Tenderness, Patience and Compassion'.[6] More restrained and far more judicious was a letter of 21 April: 'The book does not flout religion, patriotism, convention in their present state: it upholds them stoutly and then points out that, good as they are, they needed overhauling in this new world.'

If Winter Comes was not a 'feminine' novel. Among the letters and features published over a period of three months, one alone refers to the women in it. This reticence is significant. Of the weaknesses of the novel — and it undoubtedly has a few — the portrayal of the female character is the most glaring. Contemporaries found them at best anaemic, at worse implausibly odious. This weakness in characterisation was partly owing to Hutchinson's inability to draw women, but mainly attributable to the literary convention within which he worked and which he to a great extent formulated.

For, despite descriptions of it as an 'untypical best-seller' – an individual, idiosyncratic text – *If Winter Comes* represents a genre which flourished between the wars, the story of the return of the warrior to civilian life. Nor was this type of story peculiarly English. It was widely popular in both France and Germany. But with a few exceptions – such as Jean Giraudoux's *Siegfried et le Limousin* (1922) – the first French novels on the demobilised soldier appeared in the thirties. In fact, the most influential of them, Pierre Drieu La Rochelle's *Gilles*, covering the era between the Armistice and the Spanish Civil War, saw publication in 1938. Erich Maria Remarque's *Im Westen Nichts Neues* (1929) and Arnold Zweig's *Der Streit um den Sergeanten Grischa* (1928) are set on the front and do not actually deal with the conflict between the demobilised soldier and civilian society. The term *Heimkehrerliteratur*, applied to novels on the soldier's return home, dates from after the Second World War. Only a handful of plays and novels on the topic appeared in Germany in the twenties: Jacob Wassermann's *Faber oder die rerlorenen Jahre* (1924), Ernst Toller's *Der deutcher Hinkemann* (1923), Leonard Frank's *Kare und Anna* (1927), Gerhard Menzel's *Tobboggan* (1928) and Ernst Von Salomon's autobiographical *Die Geächteten* (1930) and *Die Stadt* (1923), and of these works only Frank's can be classified as an early example of the genre.

Things were altogether different in Britain. Four of the seven blockbusters of the first half of the decade revolve around the theme of the problematic return of the soldier to civilian life; one deals with it directly; and many books of lesser fame but a wide following capitalise on its vogue. Robert Keable's *Simon Called Peter*, relating the crises of a military chaplain in wartime France and in contemporary civilian London, appeared in the same year as *If Winter Comes*. 1923 saw the publication of Philip Gibb's *The Middle of the Road*. Warwick Deeping's *Sorrell and Son*, dramatising the predicaments and social purgatory of the demobilised officer as no other popular novel did, appeared in 1925. The early rise of the genre in Britain may be attributed to material conditions in the early twenties: the recession of 1921 and 1922; chronic unemployment; industrial strife; the Irish problem; and so on. But, more important, the genre adequately reflected the disillusionment that followed the war, the sense that 'it was not worth it'. True, the economies of both France and the Weimar republic suffered even graver crises and the sense of disillusionment prevailed in both countries, but in neither did those crises coincide with a political-reform episode as controversial as the Representation of the People Equal Franchise Bill.[7]

In terms of the customary classification of twenties best-sellers, the novels on the demobilised soldier are distinctly masculine creations, told from a man's point of view.[8] And they invariably contain some autobiographical material. The four British writers in this genre who have already been mentioned all had first-hand experience of conditions at the front during the war. A. S. M. Hutchinson served in France with the Royal Engineers: Philip Gibbs was one of the five accredited correspondents with the Allied forces; Warwick Deeping served with the Royal Army Medical Corps in Gallipoli, Egypt and Flanders; and Robert Keable was military chaplain with the South African Corps in France.

The predicaments unfolded in the works of these veterans (and those of their French and German contemporaries) are men's, not women's. Typically, in the British version of the genre, the hero is an ex-officer and a gentleman, physically and mentally invalided, financially hard-up, rejected and misunderstood by an ungrateful civilian society. He possesses a certain degree of practical intelligence, but is not an intellectual. It is significant that, while the French ex-serviceman novels condoned intellectualism (Gilles, for instance, is the archetypal intellectual longing for 'real' action), their British counterparts typically condemned it. But, most important, the British ex-serviceman hero possesses an extraordinary fortitude and an unbending tenacity. Like his blueprint, Mark Sabre, he stands for sanity and moderation, 'the middle road' between violent extremes. In overall literary–historical terms, this hero is a distant relation of the Waverley type, inaugurated by Sir Walter Scott in 1814. In the narrower context of the twenties, Hutchinson's hero and the novel inaugurated a popular type of story which falls into the broader category of social melodrama and whose primary purpose is to reconstruct a concrete reality and record concrete popular moods.

And the reality of the ex-serviceman is distinctly masculine. The ideals emphasised are the camaraderie of men-at-arms, a Christian compassion and self-sacrifice for higher causes. This world is typically juxtaposed with civilian life during and after the war – crassly materialistic, morally degenerate and dangerously emasculating. Invariably this life is identified with, or personified by, a female figure, intolerant and selfish (Mabel Sabre; Hilda, Peter's fiancée in *Simon Called Peter*; and Joyce Bertram Pollard's flapper wife in *The Middle of the Road*) and grossly sensual (Julie in *Simon Called Peter*, and Dora Sorrell in *Sorrell and Son*). The manner in which the female antagonists are presented by the narrators varies from the perfunctory and indifferent to the openly hostile. At first glance it may appear that they are merely a foil to the male characters. But women do have important thematic and structural roles in this masculine genre, and to assess those roles the model to all the ex-serviceman novels has to be carefully examined.

Hutchinson's claim to originality lies in the displacement of the political and social problems of 1920 and 1921 onto the seemingly idyllic days before 1914. When the story begins it is 1912, and Mark Sabre, junior partner in a respectable firm of furnishers and designers, lives at Crawshaws, a spacious house in picturesque Penny Green, a place with 'the Kate Greenaway Touch'. His fortune and position depend entirely upon two of the pillars of the old order, the Established Church and the public school. His firm specialises in ecclesiastical and school furnishings and he himself writes history textbooks. Sabre's besetting weakness is an admirable ability to see both sides of every issue. He sympathises with both the striking miners and their employers, the Unionists and the Republicans in Ireland, the suffragettes and the public. In his middle-class, provincial surroundings he alone can foresee the coming catastrophe. But Penny Green cannot tolerate his prescience. Sabre ruffles his partners and antagonises his narrow-minded wife Mabel, whose lack of understanding drives him to an infatuation with the enticing Lady Tybar, wife of the local grandee. But Sabre overcomes temptation and clings to the ideal of the sanctity of marriage and to a miserable bond. When the war breaks out, his personal predicament becomes entangled with the universal cataclysm. He enlists as a private, refusing a commission, is invalided in Flanders and is honourably discharged. It is now that the real crisis begins. Sabre's place in the firm has been taken by another and he finds himself doomed to a retired life with a wife who understands him less than ever. But the inadvertent instrument of his fall is Effie Bright, Mabel's paid companion, who gives birth to an illegitimate child. Sabre offers asylum to both the mother and the infant, and Mabel – with the unanimous approval of Penny Green – divorces him. When Effie, driven to insanity, kills the infant and commits suicide, he is suspected of murder. A self-righteous jury acquits him of the charge of murder but finds him responsible for Effie's act. He collapses and is taken to a sanatorium. At this point, when his fortunes are at their nadir, there appears, like *dea ex machina*, Lady Tybar, now a widow (her husband having been conveniently disposed of on the battlefields of Flanders). She nurses the invalid, restores him to health and to faith in the human race and, naturally, marries him – an oddly conventional end for a novel whose writer once declared that 'all love stories are wrong'.[9]

Sabre's tribulations and his personal tragedy are illuminated by the greater, common crisis collectively experienced by the contemporary reading public. The chain of international events, leading to the outbreak of the First World War, is painstakingly reconstructed. And the national scene is carefully set: the social unrest of the early 1910s, the situation in Ireland, the suffragette campaign – all are narrated from the point of view of the 'simple man': that is from the reader's point of view. Contemporaries could easily identify those past crises with the current ones. Furthermore, the plausibility of the fatuous story depends upon the historical facts. Indeed, there is evidence that the ex-serviceman yarn was seen as a well-documented sketch of life in Britain and Europe after the war, a social history of the age, as it were. Hutchinson, Gibbs and Keable were expected, first of all, to dramatise the familiar social context. The portrayal of full-blooded men and women and the plot were of lesser importance. Clearly, for a social melodrama a discourse other than the literary was needed, and it was to be found in the national press. Both Hutchinson and the other prominent 'masculine' author of the early twenties, Philip Gibbs, were accomplished journalists, and both made extensive use of newspaper material and contemporary journalistic jargon. Gibbs, in a detailed answer to Mrs Leavis's famous questionnaire to best-selling writers, emphasised that

> *The Middle of the Road* . . . deals with the problem of the ex-officer and the conditions of life after the war in England, France, Germany and Russia. I suppose people read it . . . because I dramatised the post-war world and tried to show the way out from hatred and conflict. Most of my novels have been a kind of social history.[10]

Significantly Gibbs compared his own coarse writing with 'the kind of coarseness' of another war novel, Remarque's *All Quiet on the Western Front*. This was written six years after the publication of *The Middle of the Road*, but already in 1923 a critic writing in the TLS could observe that the flatness of Gibb's characters was not a serious setback:

> it is enough for his purpose that they should be flat. His aim has been to bring before us all the various currents of opinions and the economic or social causes which have kept and still keep Europe in ferment. He has produced a kind of film of Europe after the war and a very lively one it is.[11]

As the analogy with film implies, the best-selling author, like the photographer, or journalist, is a recorder of external, visible events, not the interpreter of an inner reality. Interestingly, the analogy also evokes the fragmentary, episodic nature of all three forms.

In Hutchinson's own particularly fragmentary narrative, the female characters have a structural as well as a thematic role. They bind together various incidents in the hero's life and provide a framework for what contemporaries regarded as 'piecemeal' writing. The novel is divided into four parts, covering four years in Sabre's history, each part bearing as title the name of one or all of the three main female characters: 'Mabel', 'Nona', 'Effie' and 'Mabel, Nona, Effie'. Each part is subdivided into chapters, which are further segmented into compact, self-contained episodes. Into this personal history are introduced documentary paragraphs, briefly relating the national and international history of the years 1912–16. Part III, which spans the period between 1913 and Sabre's discharge from service early in 1916, characteristically opens, 'And in October of the following year, October 1913, life was going along at a most delirious and thrilling and entirely fascinating speed. There never was such a delicious and exciting and progressive year as between October, 1912, and October 1913.'[12] For Sabre, 1913 is the year when his situation at home and his position at the firm reach a dead end. It is also the time when his passion for Lady Nona Tybar awakens. But the significance of 1913 for the hero is brought to the reader not by a description of his personal, uneventful life, but by an impersonal newsreel report on national events and their effects on the public:

> It was a year of deliciously varied and intense excitements. Thoroughly stimulating shocks were delivered to the public by the newspapers at least once a week. You never knew what the militant suffragists were going to do next; you never knew what next terrific sensation would burst out of the conflict between the determined Government and the stubborn, imperturbable Lords; you never knew what airman, and what prodigious attempt was next going to break his neck; you never knew what infamous strike was next going to fill you with deliciously virtuous hatred of those damned trade-unions; you never knew what superbly loyal armed threat in Ulster was next going to discomfort the determined Government. You never knew what splendid sensation was next in store for you in 1913; but there always was a splendid sensation, lashed into the most deliciously agonising thrills by the Press. . . .[13]

In 1921, the wry catalogue of newsworthiness read like a newspaper report. The contemporary reader could not miss the mock journalese of words and phrases such as 'shocks', 'terrific sensation', 'thrills', 'infamous strike' and 'determined Government'. The use of newspaper material is characteristic of all the social novelists. Hutchinson's technique is, however, specially elaborate. For he distinguished between the fictional, intimate parts of the narrative, which are also the novel's 'feminine' parts, and those parts which are historical and 'masculine' by using two different discourses: effusive prose for the former and facetious journalese for the latter. The interesting result of this device is the tension between two idioms which reflect the conventional classification of prose literature according to gender. Moreover, the fictional 'feminine' parts are ludicrously magniloquent and unconvincing. As one New York critic, exasperated with Hutchinson's style put it, 'What in the name of sense and lucidity is one to do with his sentences . . . some times [his] tortured syntax does not come off at all.'[14]

Those episodes related to the women in Sabre's life are a curious stylistic blend of polemic and bathos. On the one hand, *If Winter Comes* has all the ingredients of a sob story: a miserable marriage; a heroically suffering saint for hero; a sub-plot evolving from the theme of 'pure', unconsummated love and a vulgarly sentimental end. On the other hand, it is evident that what really appealed to the writer was not the history of a broken marriage, but the problem of marriage as a social and economic institution, a problem which he approached and treated in a characteristic polemical manner. The novel and its imitations are scathing commentaries on the state of modern marriage and the relations between the sexes. Typically, the theme of the marriage of opposites manifests the collision between the 'ideal' masculine world of the ex-officer and the 'real' feminine, civilian world. The *Middle of the Road* describes the gulf between an unemployed officer sympathetic to the Labour Party and his selfish wife. In *Sorrel and Son* matrimony is the epitome of a Darwinistic struggle between the male and the female species. The Sabres' union is not an individual relationship, but a repudiation of Victorian notions of marriage. Significantly, those notions are personified in Mabel, a parody (and a very crude one) of the 'Angel in the House', with more than a trace of Mrs Grundy in her make-up. The reader is given several pages of analysis in which her innumerable flaws are mercilessly catalogued. Mabel is stupid, mean, insensitive, unimaginative, incurably prejudiced and incorrigibly snobbish. The following passage supplies typical examples of Hutchinson's polemic:

Her life was living among people of her own class. Her measure of a man or of a woman was Were they of her class? If they were she gladly accepted them and appeared to find considerable pleasure in their society. . . . The only quality that mattered was the quality of being well-bred. She called the classes beneath her own standard of breeding 'the lower classes', and so long as they left her alone she was perfectly content to leave them alone. She liked a 'civil tradesman' immensely; she liked a civil charwoman immensely, she liked a civil workman immensely. . . . She read the caption under one of the pictures of the wives and families of the 429 colliers killed in the Senghenydd mine. . . . The point she noted was that all the women 'of that class' wore 'those awful cloth caps'. . . . She thought charity meant giving jelly and red flannel to the poor; she thought generosity meant giving money to someone; she thought selfishness meant not giving money to someone. She had no idea that the only real charity is charity of mind, and the only real selfishness, selfishness of mind.[15]

The emphasis on 'class' and social prejudices is characteristic. Like all else in the novel, the three women in Sabre's life are classified and labelled. Nona is a Lady with a capital 'L', redeemed from a perverse bond with a man of her own class by the worthy, middle-class Sabre. Mabel is the proverbial *bourgeois* bigot, and Effie, the archetypal seduced servant, is the daughter of a respectable working family who, forgetting her place in the social hierarchy, becomes the victim of her new surroundings. In the ex-serviceman novel, marriage is no solution to class conflict. Indeed, a romantic relation between unequal parties does not reconcile social differences but sharpens tensions. This attitude in a genre popularly classified as documentary probably reflects the middle-class response to the social unrest of the early twenties. Sorrell is openly hostile to the 'masses'. Pollard's marriage to an upper-class woman in *The Middle of the Road* is a failure, and the Nona episode in *If Winter Comes* is a gratuitous exception. Sabre's happy union with a woman above his station is an imposed, banal end to what might otherwise have been a story of a certain originality.

Mabel is in her element in an exaggeratedly domestic setting. A model woman but pre-eminently a model housewife, she presides over Crawshaws and keeps it to perfection. The Hall and the places the Sabres occupy in it both elaborate the notion of separate masculine and feminine spheres. Mark and Mabel are worlds apart. And, significantly, the incompatibility between them is perceived and presented in terms of their relation to a socialised space. Two important episodes are connected with the rearrangement of the rooms at Crawshaws. The first relates Mark's placement in a 'den' of his own, the idea of the 'den' reflecting Mabel's commonplace notions about 'manliness' and sex-roles in general:

> she called it his 'den', and Sabre loathed and detested the word 'den' as applied to a room a man specially inhabits. It implied to him a masculine untidiness, and he was intensely orderly and hated untidiness. It implied customs and manners of what he called 'boarding house ideas' — the idea that a man must have an untidily comfortable apartment into which he can retire and envelop himself in tobacco smoke, and where he 'can have his own things about him', and 'have his pictures and his pipes about him', and where he can wear 'an old shooting jacket and slippers' — and he loathed the ideas they connoted. . . . Above all he loathed and detested the vision which the word 'den' always conjured up to him. This was the vision of the door of the typical den being opened by a wife, and of the wife saying in a mincing voice, 'This is George in his den', and of boardy-house females peering over the wife's shoulder. . . .[16]

The second episode concerns Mark's banishment from the nuptial bed to a separate chamber, a symbolic event that marks the effective, if not the legal, end of the marriage. Significantly, the Sabres are childless, and their childlessness is often associated with Mabel's mental and physical sterility and, implicitly, her frigidity. The distinction between a feminine and a masculine space and the identification of the latter with the domestic sphere, centred around the 'Angel in the House', are both recognisable clichés in the nineteenth-century novel. In the mass-market novel of the twenties the domestic *genius* is virtually nonexistent. Had Mabel been more humane, she would have been seen by the contemporary reader as an anachronism. As it is, the stereotype of the homely wife provides the best foil to the socially conscious hero. Mabel is superfluous in both the Victorian and the post-war sense of the word. Economically useless, she is also dispossessed of sexuality and the functions of gender. The sterile spouse fails in her vocation and role as woman and makes Sabre's own life a misery. She is not an angelic châtelaine, but a monstrous gaoler. Many a contemporary found her too monstrous to be credible. The reviewer in the *TLS* complains,

> We never in our lives . . . met anyone quite like her . . . of course she was the daughter of a dean, but even so she is a perfectly monstrous compound of density, meanness and complacency. Why should Sabre

have married her? Quixotism? Rebound? Mr Hutchinson does not tell us.

And he adds, 'It is not a woman but a mechanical assemblage of all the vices and all the virtues that one instinctively dislikes.'[17]

Hutchinson returned to the metaphor of the divided house in his fifth novel, *This Freedom* (1922), a work which throws more light on his attitude towards women and marriage. *This Freedom* is not a 'masculine' novel, but the history of an emancipated woman, from oppressed child in a Victorian household to independent adult. Like its predecessor, *This Freedom* articulates social and political issues in a typically polemical manner and retrojects problems of the post-war years onto the pre-war era. There is also the familiar divison of the novel into four parts with symbolic titles. 'House of Men' describes Rosalie's childhood in a rectory dominated by a tyrannical father and run by a host of superfluous, incapable females. 'House of Women' is set in a London educational establishment for girls and in the City. The close sorority of students and teachers, in an abode charged with sexual tensions, is juxtaposed to the austere and exclusively masculine surroundings of Lombard Street, where Rosalie begins her apprenticeship. Her new environment is both the real and symbolic embodiment of her independence. In the last two parts, appropriately entitled 'House of Children' and 'House of Cards', Rosalie is a brilliant banker – a rare career for a woman in 1922, let alone in the 1900s and early 1910s, when most of the story takes place – but she fails as mother and wife. The final episodes outdo even the lugubrious parts of *If Winter comes*. A series of catastrophes is visited on the luckless heroine: her older son is gaoled, her flapper daughter dies of blood-poisoning after an abortion, and her youngest, the apple of his parents' eye, is killed by a train. The penitent Rosalie, realising that she is to be blamed for the massacre of her family, returns to the 'home' and to a sedentary life.

In their strictness Hutchinson's critics did not spare his rhetoric, nor his style, nor his views on marriage and the family. They particularly resented his vindictiveness and the disproportion between Rosalie's 'sin' and her punishment. The author went out of his way to prove that a married woman cannot have a career outside the home and 'Not the sturdiest supporter of the old ideas and methods . . . could mistake Mr Hutchinson's story for good sense. It is a piece of violent *ad captandum* pleading. . . .'[18] Evidently the polemical tone that was acceptable in the misogynist ex-serviceman genre seemed ludicrous and inappropriate in a 'feminine' *roman de problème*. Such was the outcry that Hodder and Stoughton included in the 1924 cheap edition a Preface by the author, which was publicised in the press under the heading 'Mr Hutchinson Apologises for Himself and his Reader'. But Hutchinson was *not* apologetic. At the end of one particularly convoluted paragraph, he, for once, made himself clear:

> It is the mother who makes her home; and the mother only and not the father, who in the true meaning of home life can work it. I believe that home life in the dimension that has helped to make us is passing; and this book, in Rosalie's attitudes towards her children, notes its passing. . . .[19]

The conclusion of *If Winter Comes* implies that, where the domestic female failed, an independent and active woman may succeed. However, *This Freedom* (and the Preface to the 1924 edition in particular) clearly shows that Hutchinson's refutation of Victorian notions of domesticity was spurious. In the latter novel the role assigned to women is that of mothers and wives. It is significant that, despite superficial similarities with the hero of *If Winter Comes*, Rosalie is not a female Sabre but a version of Mabel: selfish, unfeeling and, to her masculine surroundings, dangerous.

In summary, the story of the ex-serviceman is, *sui generis*, anti-feminist and even misogynist. It presents woman and man as symmetrical opposites, symbolising the emasculating and the masculine; 'home' and the 'front'; the perturbed peace and the idealised war; selfishness and self-sacrifice. In the severely masculine world that Hutchinson and his imitators depicted, there is little or no place for women, except as satellites or in the familiar role of the 'other'. In the novels of Hutchinson, Gibbs, Deeping and Keable, the feminine figures are superfluous. Their superfluity has three distinct aspects. First, despite their thematic and structural roles, these figures are subsidiary and, in some cases, dispensable. It is significant that the popular debate on the genre focused on the heroes and that even today we involuntarily identify with them and not with the narratively remote heroines. Second, in the world of the demobilised officer, the female is needless and unnecessary. She has no hold in the fraternity of men-at-arms, nor in their ideas. In all of the novels, relationships between man and woman, whether in the form of marriage or in the form of extra-marital liaison, are inferior substitutes for a sublime human relation which is not sexual: comradeship between men; religion; a political affiliation. Sabre's main allegiance is to 'the middle road', a basic humanity. Simon, in *Simon Called Peter*, is committed to God. And *Sorrell and Son* is about a father's morbidly destructive self-sacrifice for his son. Third and last, the female figures are superfluous in the two post-Victorian senses of the word. On the one hand, they are dependent and unreproductive. On the other, they threaten the hero's world. Not only do they compete with him in the social and economic spheres: they degrade and emasculate him. The scene in *Sorrell and Son* in which Sorrell carries his wife Dora's bags as hotel porter and is tipped by her epitomises the humiliation of the returning hero by the feminine and effeminate civilian world.

The vogue of ex-servicemen novels overlapped the turbulent years between the Armistice and the Great Strike. Read together they seem to illustrate clearly enough certain attitudes of mind consequent upon the economic instability and social unrest of the early twenties. In a literal, narrow sense the novels record the plight of the demobilised soldier. In a broader sense they articulate the anxieties of a larger middle-class public: the fears of revolution and great uncertainty in the face of a rapidly changing world. On both these levels, the sense of instability is communicated in, and personified by, a female figure, the embodiment of life in the aftermath of the war. It is highly significant that, despite their sentimentality, the view the novels present of the relations between the sexes is depressingly pessimistic. The society they depict is polarised: there is no sympathy or understanding between man and woman.

4

1924: *The Green Hat*

The Green Hat vexed the critics. Ralph Wright, reviewing it for the *New Statesman*, found Michael Arlen 'an irritating writer'. Wright was particularly irritated by the 'smart and thin style' of Arlen's prose, the boastful parade of knowledge about modern literature, and, last but not least, by the self-assurance of the man-about-town on matters related to women and sex:

> There is a sort of epigrammatic cocksureness on all the details of love-making that I find particularly unpleasant: an assumption that love has something to do with silk underclothing at one moment and at the next a rhetoric outburst on almost Wellsian lines of optimism. I do wish he [Arlen] would be a little more modest and show a little better taste when dealing with the subject.[1]

The epithet 'irritating' and the personal, curiously puritanical tone are characteristic. They recur in numerous comments on Arlen. There were several reasons why contemporaries were put out yet, at the same time, intrigued by *The Green Hat*. A first reason was its euphemistic but suggestive language. A second was the sophisticated lifestyle of a promiscuous élite, which Arlen, more than any other best-selling writer in the twenties, celebrated. Observers regarded his novel as a history of modern Mayfair and Belgravia, a faithful chronicle of contemporary morals. A third reason was, undoubtedly, Arlen's 'smart' and easily recognisable style. Fourth, and most important, there was the difficulty in placing his work satisfactorily.

Reviewers dismissed the novel as 'sentimental tosh' but nevertheless applauded its style and sophistication. Elizabeth Drew, for instance, dedicated a whole chapter of *The Modern Novel* to *The Green Hat*, which she described as 'sentimental tomfoolery' and 'pure Ethel M. Dell and A. S. M. Hutchinson', but went on to compare it with Fielding: 'In a pitiful milk and barley water backboneless way the writer is trying the same thing as the author of *Tom Jones*.'[2] Claude C. Washburn, who bracketed Arlen's work with the melodramas of Elinor Glyn, Ouida and Richard Le

Gallienne, also juxtaposed it more honourably with Ford Madox Ford's *Some Do Not*. The two novels, according to this critic, typified the widespread tendency towards a sophistication that was a 'sentimental' rather than 'an intellectual condition'. However, Arlen's awareness of this condition and his self-mockery made him an artist superior to Ford. Where *The Green Hat* was intriguing, *Some Do Not* was merely pompous, a 'rewriting in a grand style of *If Winter Comes*'.[3]

This inability to catalogue Arlen's work as high-, middle- or low-brow probably explains why the critics focused on his personality and tended to ignore his craft. He was labelled a 'best-seller' and cited as the exemplar of the successful artist: a mere money-maker, a shrewd manipulator of the machinery of best-sellerdom and of its entrapped audience. To the reading public as well as to the critics, he was personally as fascinating as his characters. Few other contemporary writers enjoyed more headline publicity. The identification between Arlen's lifestyle and the style of his prose is traceable from earlier reviews. When in 1920 Heinemann published *The London Venture*, his first collection of stories, 'Michael Arlen' was generally believed to be a pen-name of the idiosyncratically 'stylish' George Moore.[14] That the real author was not an Englishman but an Armenian born in Bulgaria was known only to few.

Dikran Kouyoumdjian began his literary career in the periodical *Ararat*, the aggressively nationalist organ of the Armenian United Association. Then, after being introduced to A. R. Orage, he started writing for the *New Age*, contributing regularly reviews, essays and stories which were scarely noticed. His breakthrough finally came in August 1918 with the serialisation of his 'London Papers', a sequence of semi-autobiographical vignettes that were to become the basis for *The London Venture*. Arlen's apprenticeship with Orage was, undoubtedly, the formative phase in his career. It was in the *New Age* that he came under the influence of Lawrence, Moore and Orage himself, and between them the three prompted a crucial change in his style – from the uneasy realism of his early writing to the eventual sophisticated and peculiarly artificial mode that was to become his trademark.[5]

The London Venture was followed by a novel, *Piracy* (1922), and two collections of short stories, *The Romantic Lady* (1921) and *These Charming People* (1923) and by 1924 Arlen had already acquired some reputation as short-story writer. Then, in October of the same year, Collins published *The Green Hat, a Romance for a Few People* and it became overnight a *succès de scandale*. Within less than five months Collins had issued 11 editions. Sales were boosted by the sensational American stage production and by Arlen's first visit to America in 1925.[6] On 10 March he arrived at New

York in a blaze of publicity. He was lionised by New York society, and the American press, less restrained than the British, covered his visit in detail.

Arlen became a media hero. And his vogue coincided with the emergence of a new kind of personality cult characteristic of the burgeoning film industry. The successful novelist could now become a star, surrounded by the star's magical aura of glamour. A fabricated image of the best-selling writer, similar to that of the Hollywood personality, could be openly and cynically marketed. The case of *The Green Hat* thus represents an unprecedented commercialisation of the best-selling novel and the persona of the best-seller. In the summer of 1924, green felt hats, of the kind worn by the novel's heroine, became the rage. There is a curious record of this fashion in *Brideshead Revisited*, whose principal heroine 'like most women then wore a green hat pulled down over her eyes with a diamond arrow in it'.[7] More revealing than Waugh's faint echo were the pictures of Arlen that accompanied hat displays in shop windows, and advertisements running, 'The dramatic sensation of the century. The triumph of fiction becomes the triumph of fashion and the Green Hat, symbol of sophisticated chic, is now available to the woman of smart individuality.'[8] The language of advertisers is symptomatic. If fiction is identified with fashion, the novel is, first and foremost, a commodity. And novel-reading ceases to be a pastime or a vicarious existence and becomes living itself. And, in the particular case of *The Green Hat*, to read was to live an elegant, sophisticated life free of constricting social and sexual conventions.

At the beginning of the novel there is a widely quoted passage in which the loquacious narrator, looking from his bedroom window in Shepherd's Market down Sheep Street, observes a yellow Hispano-Suiza and a green hat: 'I saw that it was a green hat, a sort of felt, and bravely worn: being, no doubt, one of those that women who have many hats affect *pour le sport*.'[9] Few other passages written in the twenties inspired more burlesques. A parody bearing the telling title *The Green Mat*, commissioned in 1925 by Arlen's publisher, reads, 'It was a long felt mat, like a want, and gravely worn; being, no doubt, one of those mats that affected novelists find an easy subject *pour rire*.'[10] In another burlesque the mysterious heroine puzzles. 'Do I wear this hat for the style (*pour le style*)?'[11] On the author's peculiar use (and, many critics felt, abuse) of the word 'affect' there are countless puns. And the yellow Hispano-Suiza became the object of endless witticisms, particularly after Arlen, with an unfailing eye for publicity, acquired a yellow Rolls-Royce.

The mysterious stranger who affects the hat is, it transpires, Iris March (or Fenwick, or Storm), the twin sister of the narrator's ill-tempered, solitary neighbour Gerald March. Gerald, however, is so drunk that he does not recognise his sibling and she follows the narrator to his rooms, discusses modern literature with him and ends the night in his bed. In the morning she temporarily disappears from his life. Later the narrator and the reader simultaneously learn Iris's torrid life story from Hilary Townshend and Guy de Travest, a pair of avuncular figures who first appear in *These Charming People*. Significantly, in *The Green Hat* Arlen transformed them from the men-about-town of the early vignettes into staunch upholders of conventions. They describe Iris as 'a woman of affairs', an outcast condemned by polite society. Her history is rich in scandal: one husband killed by his own hand in a Deauville hotel on the nuptial night; another killed by Irish Republicans; and countless lovers during and after her marriages. The real facts of Iris's tragic life are known to few. Her first husband, Boy Fenwick, the idol of Georgian youth, was in fact, a syphilitic bounder who, with atypical gallantry, resolved to take his own life rather than infect his bride. She, in a quixotic gesture, declared that 'Boy died for purity', therefore implying her own impurity and so destroying for ever her good name. The Deauville episode and Iris's sacrifice were regarded by Arlen's contemporaries as extremely fatuous – so much so that 'for purity' became yet another mocked-at catchphrase. Encumbered with a wrecked reputation, Iris plunges into a succession of affairs, frantically changing bed-mates, whom she uses for her pleasure and then discards. But this wanton life is merely a substitute for her enduring passion for Napier Harpenden, whose father, Sir Maurice, has forbidden them to marry. Through the agency of the ubiquitous narrator, Iris meets Napier on the eve of his marriage and it is then that their love is finally consummated.

The story resumes nine months later with Iris dying of blood-poisoning, after a still birth, in a Paris clinic. Again the narrator directs the course of events. He tells Napier that Iris suffers of ptomaine poisoning. When, miraculously recovered, she returns to London, the affair with Napier continues and the couple decide to elope. In the penultimate episode all the protagonists assemble in Sir Maurice's house to talk Iris out of the plan. But, when Napier reveals the real cause for Boy's suicide and Iris's tarnished reputation is redeemed, she makes a final quixotic, and this time fatal, gesture. She crashes the Hispano-Suiza into the symbolic tree on the Harpendens' estate, where she and Napier made love in the idyllic days of their adolescence.

On the whole the novel was well received in Britain and acclaimed in America. The reviewer in the *TLS* observes that 'It has never been possible to question this writer's cleverness, but it has sometimes been impossible not to doubt his artistic sincerity. . . . Mr Arlen has invented a new kind of literary cocktail. . . . The style is pert, mannered, witty. . . . He is full of tricks'; and adds 'The book has a convention of extreme artificiality and once we accept it, the book proves captivating.'[12] The *New York Times Book Review* numbered 'skilled technique', 'sensible story [and] character portra[yal]', 'sonorous prose' and 'grace and charm' among the work's fine points and concluded its panegyric by declaring *The Green Hat* 'a finely wrought sound piece of work'.[13] Even the end, universally regarded as the novel's main flaw, was applauded. Other opinions were more discriminating: 'tosh, but done with craft', 'sophisticated nonsense' and 'witty shining stuff'.[14] Something can be gleaned from the critical vocabulary. Regardless of the judgements they passed on the novel, the language of the reviews is curiously unified. It denotes a certain degree of skill and stylishness, artificial but of a certain originality. After the publication of *The Green Hat* Arlen's style was recognised as his chief trademark. And any typical paragraph of the novel is still easily identified. Arlenese comprises long, twisted sentences, repetitions and suggestive remarks, and, occasionally, phrases in the fashionable jargon that dates Arlen as a writer of the twenties:

> She was fair. As they would say it in the England of long ago – she was fair. And she was grave, so grave. That is a sad lady, I thought. To be fair, to be sad . . . why, was she intelligent, too? And white she was, very white, and her painted mouth was purple in the dim light, and her eyes, which seemed set wide apart, were cool, impersonal, sensible, and they were blazing blue. Even in that light they were blazing blue, like two spoonfuls of the Mediterranean in the early morning of a brilliant day. The sirens had eyes like that, without a doubt, when they sang of better dreams. But no siren she: That was a sad lady, most grave. And always her hair would be dancing a tawny, formal dance about the small white cheeks.[15]

The trick of repetition ('she was grave', 'she was sad'), the insinuating, taunting voice of the narrator and the deliberate use of vague, broken sentences exasperated the critics. But they were impressed by the author's ironic self-awareness of his distorted syntax. And his style, known as 'Arlenesque', came to be regarded as both an asset and a weakness. The emphasis on an artificial, sophisticated phraseology seemed to have been bought at the expense of the plot (notably in *The Green Hat*) and the characterisation. That Arlenesque was regarded as a singularly generic discourse is evident from the oblique tribute of a large number of burlesques and cartoons. Arlen was, I suspect, the most parodied author in the period, and *The Green Hat* the most parodied novel. It inspired countless cartoons and literary spoofs: most famously, *The Green Mat* (1925), *This Charming Green Hat Fair* (1925), *Arabella* (1933) and *Keep It under your Green Hat* (1926). In the last of these, Sherlock Holmes and his assistants, the Rollo Boys, investigate the mystery of Boy Fenwick's death 'for purity'. The ambiguity that surrounds his alleged suicide derives, of course, from Arlen's abuse of English syntax. The passage describing the detectives' attempts to decipher the intricate sentence and insinuating narrative remains amusing:

> As swiftly as possible (which is not only too gosh darned swift) the Rollo Boys and Sherlock Holmes advanced down their intricate maze of twisted phrases, similies, and winding allusions, trying to find their way through the mystery of Mr Arlen's style. Now and then their eyes watered as a loose adjective whipped their faces. . . . On both sides little bypaths lured them from their main course, but they continued resolutely ahead, reading neither to the right nor to the left. . . . 'Pray God we are not too late' prayed good Sherlock Holmes as they followed down the trailing dots. . . .[16]

Alas! the detectives arrive at the scene of crime after Boy and the other protagonists have all killed themselves 'for the purity of grammar'. The reference to 'the trailing dots' is a thinly disguised gibe at Arlen's habit of breaking his sentences in order to insinuate, or to allude to, what he could not in decency write.

But it is doubtful whether the consumer of seven-and-sixpenny novels bought *The Green Hat* (for it was banned from the lending libraries) for its style alone. Suburbia was, probably, indifferent to the proscription of Iris as 'bad grammar'. What mattered most was that she was 'a bad woman'. The reading public – exposed as never before to the newspapers' barrage against the modern woman – was specially susceptible to the stereotype of the libidinous, sexually emancipated female. And Iris typified this stereotype more than any other female figure in the popular fiction of the period. *The Green Hat* stands out in the general trend towards an open discussion on feminine sexuality. Technically the novel is pure'. It contains one offensive word – 'syphilis', which appears in the penultimate episode and which probably was the principal reason for the libraries' ban. Apart from venereal disease, the novel includes references to a miscarriage, a still birth and a major gynaecological operation (these, however, are only implied by the narrator). Yet Arlen's appeal lay not in what he actually said but in his meaningful reticence, in the timely hiatus, in the coded language of innuendoes, in the suggestive tone that taunted contemporary readers.

There was, however, one detail that the evasive Arlen clearly stated: Iris's adultery. Of all the super-sellers of the twenties, *The Green Hat* is the only one with an adulteress for heroine. Iris not only commits adultery, but does so habitually and, it is continually insinuated, indiscriminately, flaunting her sins in the face of polite society. Dominated by strong impulses that she cannot repress, she takes mates to gratify an insatiable libido, devours them and casts them away: 'I am a house of men',[17] she confides to the narrator, and elsewhere adds,

> It is not good to have a pagan body and a Chislehurst mind, as I have. It is hell for the body and terror for the mind. There are dreams, and there are beasts. The dreams walk glittering up and down the soiled loneliness of desire, the beasts prowl about the soiled loneliness of regret.[18]

The confession with the notorious trick of repetition ('dreams', 'beasts', 'soiled loneliness') was, of course, too obvious a butt to be ignored by parodists, cartoonists and other satirical opponents.

Despite such passages as this, even the novel's harshest critics admitted that it was more than a sexual fantasy and its heroine more than a dangerously beautiful vamp. For in Iris Arlen created a quixotic feminine figure: solitary, intrepid and gallant. And these qualities are revealed in the two most flamboyant gestures she makes: her reticence about the real cause of Boy's death, and her suicide. Thematically and structurally, the two gestures are central to the novel. The former is the key to Iris's tragedy and eventually leads to her death. Her code of behaviour is self-denyingly 'masculine'. She regards men as her equals and pursues them openly and aggressively; she is 'chivalrous' (the epithet is Arlen's), impeccably honest and, last but not least, 'clean' of any feminine wiles or tricks. On the morning after their night together, the narrator observes Iris completing her *toilette* by scrutinising her reflection in a mirror:

> It is a commonplace about women, as assiduously remarked by brilliant female psychologists as women's 'caprice' and 'intuition', that every woman must now and then make a 'grimace of distaste' into a looking-glass. But she did not do that, nor need to. She was untouched, unsoiled, impregnable to the grubby, truthful hand of *lex femina*. She was like a tower of beauty in the morning of the world. The outlaw was

above the law of afterwards, impervious and imperious. She was beautiful, grave, proud. How beautiful she was now! It was a sort of blasphemy in her to be beautiful now, to stand in such ordered loveliness, to be neither shameful like a maiden nor shameless like a *mondaine*, nor show any fussy after-trill of womanhood, any dingy ember of desire.[19]

Of course the passage is grossly overwritten. And it smacks of the cocksureness of the man-about-town which the critics found so distasteful. But it seems that the reading public was captivated by the narrator's confidence and his generalisations on sex psychology, and intrigued by the knowledgeable description of private feminine rituals. Such intimate descriptions were Arlen's forte, and in his later novels, especially in *Young Men in Love* (1928), he included several detailed *toilette* and *boudoir* scenes. Equally significant is the reversal of conventional sex roles. Iris feels neither regret nor shame. For her, casual sex is natural exercise and one lover is like another. It is the male narrator who romanticises the one-night affair: 'Romance was more than the licence to be shameless with clouded eyes. Romance . . . did not coil white limbs into the puerile lusts of the mind. . . . To romance, which was the ultimate vision of commonsense, sex, as sex, was the most colossal bore.'[20] Effusive outbursts such as this (and the novel abounds with them) are confined to the male characters. True, Iris is impetuous and irrational, but outwardly she is hard and resilient. Moreover, the sentimentality of the writer–narrator softens Arlen's authorial image as the calculating best-seller. To his critics and audience he was the modern sex novelist, but also an incurable, soft-centred romantic.[21] And it was precisely this odd mixture of cynical suggestiveness and sentimentality that made *The Green Hat* so broadly appealing.

Like all of Arlen's female characters, Iris looms over the men in her life. She is stronger and more honest than her two husbands and Napier. And it is significant that the latter fails to understand her personal code of honour. For it is he who reveals the truth about Boy's death – thus, according to his own notions of honour and chivalry, vindicating Iris's good name. To her 'a name' is of no consequence. Contemporaries found this female figure quixotic and unreal, yet irresistible – so much so that her violent death was often regarded not as a nemesis, but as a tragically gratuitous end to an unhappy life. The *TLS* reviewer wrote that 'it is with a sense of having been cheated that we stand her final whitewashing in the last chapter with its perfunctory inevitable self-sacrifice'.[22] Others thought Arlen's portraiture of her a failure, but a grand one.[23]

This sympathy on the part of the critics can be partly attributed to the narrative technique, especially to the supervisory role of the narrator. The narrator persona first appears in the 'London Papers' and recurs in most of the short stories and novels. Ubiquitous, gullible and annoyingly omniscient, the narrator is, perhaps, the most convincing single character in Arlen's fantasies. With strong autobiographical elements, this character is a fictional–factional version of the author in his first years in London. The major novels of the twenties and several of the vignettes of that period are told from the point of view of an impecunious and ambitious artist, ready to compromise his art for money and fame (Dikran in *The London Venture;* Ivor Pelham Marley in *Piracy;* the narrator in *The Green Hat;* Charles Savile in *Young Men in Love;* the raconteur of the 'Confessions of a Naturalised Englishman'). Typically he falls in love with a society woman who is a connoisseur of literature and who encourages and then betrays him. Invariably the heroine is described through the young artist's adulating eyes. The famous seduction scene in *The Green Hat* takes place after an extraordinary discussion on modern literature. Iris rebukes the narrator for his fanciful, superficial writing, and there follows a *tour de force* designed to impress upon the reader Arlen's knowledge of literature and, indirectly, vindicate his reputation as a serious writer:

Hers was that random, uniformed, but severely discriminating taste which maddens you. . . . She used the word 'common', I think, to denote a thing attempted and achieved scratchily. Mr Ernest Bramah was, for instance, not common. But Miss Clemence Dane in *Legend* was. 'Oh Come!' I said, for to me *Legend* is an achievement in literature. . . . She was loyal to girlish admirations for Mr Locke, Mr Temple Thurston, Oscar Wilde. D.H. Lawrence was 'nice'. 'Nice?' I said, 'Well, wonderful', she said, with wide eyes, so that I was made to seem slow and stupid. Mr Paul Morand was 'common', a 'stunt' writer. . . . She had once enjoyed a book by Mr Compton Mackenzie, a garden catalogue called *Guy and Pauline*. There was Hergesheimer. . . . But perhaps the book she most profoundly liked was *The Passionate Friends*, with perhaps the last part of *Tono Bungay*. 'And of course', she said, '*The Good Soldier*, Mr Ford Madox Hueffer's amazing romance.' From a table she picked up Joyce's *Ulysses*, looked at it vaguely, dropped it absently on the floor amongst the others.[24]

This amazing check list, lumping together writers as different as Joyce and Hergesheimer, has in it something for every taste. And it is evident that the writer addresses two audiences, the *literati* and the large uninitiated public. The clear preference for such writers as Clemence Dane and Hergesheimer and the dismissive references to Lawrence ('nice') and Joyce ('she . . . looked at it vaguely, dropped it') were likely to appeal to the less sophisticated audience. Here is a writer, the passage implies, who knows his art and everything about it, but prefers a good yarn ('the last part of *Tono Bungay*') to a high-brow novel. The episode is an Arlen set piece and recurs in *Young Men in Love* and in 'Confessions of a Naturalised Englishman'. In both these works, the wayward heroine, Iris's reflection, is not merely an object of sexual desire but also a source of inspiration, a critic and an arbiter of art and literature. The libidinous female is assimilated to the male narrator's literary *alter ego*. She has a double role: as true libertine, a rebel against sexual restrictions and taboos, and preacher of the modern and experimental in art and literature.

This ideal *anima* was not the figment of the writer's imagination. For, despite its extravagant fantasy, *The Green Hat*, like all of Arlen's early novels, is a *roman à clef* based on the lives of literary figures and socialites.[25] A. R. Orage makes a short appearance as the publisher and editor Horton. Adolf Stulik, the Austrian proprietor of the Eiffel Tower Restaurant in Percy Street, a haunt of Bohemian *literati*, appears as Stutz (the restaurant is called Mont Agel). Iris is a fictional—factional reflection of one of the arch-rebels of the decade, Nancy Cunard, minor poet, *avant-garde* publisher, committed war correspondent and daughter of the celebrated Lady Emerald Cunard.[26] If for nothing else, she should be remembered for her Paris Hours Press, which printed and sold works by George Moore and Joyce; Beckett's *Whoroscope*; Pound's *Draft of xxx Cantos*; Graves's *Ten Poems More* and Laura Riding's *Twenty Poems Less*; and, in the thirties, the series of leaflets on the Spanish Civil War known as *Les Poètes du monde defendent le peuple espagnol*, with contributions from W. H. Auden, Tristan Tsara, Pablo Neruda and others. Nancy covered the war for the Associated Negro Press and became the soul of the group of Western intellectuals supporting the Republic. Despite this versatile career, she was known to her contemporaries mainly for her unconventional sex life. Already in the early twenties she was a living symbol of rebellious womanhood, sexually emancipated but doomed. The combination of her eccentricity and her wide knowledge of contemporary poetry and painting had a galvanising effect upon many writers and artists, who immortalised her in a number of paintings and novels (among the latter are Louis Aragon's *Blanche ou l'oubli*, Hemingway's *The Sun also Rises*, and probably Huxley's *Point Counter Point* and *Antic Hay*). Arlen knew her intimately, and when, late in 1920, she had a hysterectomy and subsequently contracted peritonitis and gangrene, he visited her during the long convalescence at a Paris clinic; that episode in her life was, most probably, the basis for the latter part of *The Green Hat*. As Anne Chisholm has pointed out, the episode of a gynaecological operation which mortally affects the patient recurs in several of Arlen's early novels. In *The Green Hat* death is associated with confinement and child-bearing.[27] Iris is dangerously ill in a Paris medical institution for 'misbehaved cosmopolitan women' after having been delivered of Napier's still-born child. The whole of the episode is uncharacteristically restrained and realistic — so much so that years later Nancy Cunard was to confirm that 'part of the novel was inspired by the only two real circumstances around me in December 1920 and Jan—Feb 1921. I did nearly die there and he did hear me scream.'[28] And she was even to point to a minor inaccuracy in Arlen's description of her sick-bed.

Arlen himself emphatically denied any relation between his heroine and a living woman. But in a famous interview with the *New York Times Book Review* he admitted that Iris 'is made up of so many people I've really met and known'.[29] The evidence in Nancy Cunard's private notebooks should obviously be taken more seriously than this tongue-in-cheek public disavowal. *The Green Hat* was subject to various forms of censorship and contained enough explosive material to be found libellous. Arlen's caution is more than understandable. And, even if it is assumed that Iris was pure invention, there still remains the fact that contemporaries believed her to have an original and the book to be a faithful chronicle of its times. But *The Green Hat* can claim to be more than a period piece. The novel appealed to different audiences for different reasons. 'Society' could find in its own pleasantly distorted image. To the critics, that select public within the initiated reading public, it offered a scathing self-criticism of a self-conscious middle-brow. To reading suburbia the novel offered a glimpse of the glamorous and delinquent world of Mayfair, the promiscuity which the gossip columns of the large-circulation dailies condemned yet, at the same time, celebrated. And this experience at second hand was specially rewarding; for the novel does not end happily. The rich and fortunate, it implies, are not immune to tragedy and punishment. But, most important, *The Green Hat* was, possibly, the first mass-market novel to describe a female libertine without presenting her as a victim or a fallen woman. Iris *is* made to suffer. Furthermore, her promiscuity is atoned for by a *grande passion* and self-sacrifice. Yet at no point in the novel is her conduct condemned. It is accepted. The libidinous heroine is depicted with frank admiration. She is dominated by uncontrollable impulses but she does not fall to the status of mere sexual object. She is fiercely independent and obeys only her own code of honour. And Arlen would probably have us think of her as a woman who is doomed but is not for that reason a victim.

5

1924, *Annus Mirabilis: The Constant Nymph*

The Green Hat *is the novel of the year. It will be an* annus mirabilis *if it produces a better one.*

Sunday Chronicle

In the annals of modern British publishing 1924 is probably recorded as an *annus mirabilis*. In October, less than four months after the appearance of Arlen's big seller, John Murray published the first of the novels of C. P. Wren, following the adventures of the Geste family. That same month Heinemann brought out a second novel by an unknown Oxford graduate which was to become one of the very greatest successes of the decade. It is difficult to imagine two lives entirely different as those of Arlen and Margaret Kennedy. He was an exotic foreigner; an emblem of 'modernity'; a master in the arts of publicity and best-sellerdom; a wit and a connoisseur of books, on a superficial, social level. She was solidly English; 'the best of Victorian' (the *Express's* description); a real *cognoscente* of the classics and of literature generally.

Margaret Kennedy (*not* Margaret Kennedy Moore, as the name commonly appears) was born in 1896 into the prosperous milieu of the Edwardian professional class. She was the eldest child of Charles Kennedy, a well-to-do barrister of Anglo-Irish descent, and Elinor Marwood, his cousin. Like most females of her background and generation, she had a protected childhood in a household in which the topic of sex was strictly taboo, a proscription which was to affect her writing, particularly in her earlier career. But, unlike most women of her class, Margaret Kennedy enjoyed the benefit of higher education: first at Cheltenham Ladies College (which she was unkindly to lampoon in *The Constant Nymph*) and then at Somerville College, Oxford, where in 1919 she took second-class honours in modern history. Her first published work was a commissioned history textbook about the effect on Europe of the French Revolution, *A Century of Revolution, 1789–1920* (1922). Her first novel, *The Ladies of Lyndon*, followed a year later and was politely received.[1]

When *The Constant Nymph* appeared, it seemed at first that it would follow the undistinguished path of its predecessor. For about five weeks it received little attention. Then, on 6 December, it was taken up in the *New Statesman* by Augustine Birrell, who described it as 'one of the best novels old or new, that had ever absorbed a reader's attention during the still hours', and compared its author with Meredith. Such a panegyric from a critic of Birrell's status was sure to have some weight. The novel was to receive further approval from Hardy, A. E. Housman (who recommended it to Junior Fellows at Trinity high table as 'the best product of this century', but characteristically regretted that it had been written by a woman), Galsworthy, William Archer and William Gerhardie.[2] Bennett was more reserved and in a letter of 5 October doubted whether the bourgeois characters were 'quite as good as the artists'. Parts of the novel he found 'uneconomically organised' and a few of the characters superfluous.[3] In this way Margaret Kennedy became the writers' best-seller. Outside Britain, particularly in France, the novel was regarded as a classic, rather than as a superior best-seller. Jean Giraudoux's translation of Kennedy's own stage version was serialised in 1934 in the prestigious *Revue de Paris* and reprinted in book form. In Italy Antonio Gramsci, who read the *Nymph* twice in his prison cell, paid it the highest tribute of comparing it with *The Idiot*. 'The title *The Constant Nymph*', he remarked, 'is somewhat foolish, but the book is interesting . . . it reminds me of Dostoyevsky's *The Idiot*. . . . It's certainly remarkable, both because it's written by a woman and because of the psychological atmosphere and the world it describes.'[4]

Curiously enough, the average reader was less impressed and far more discriminating than the *cognoscenti*, though granting the novel its due place as an extremely well-written, carefully structured yarn with an engaging adolescent for heroine. On 23 April 1930 the *Sunday Dispatch* announced a literary competition in which readers were asked to choose those six post-war novels that would be admired by later generations. The answers, misrepresented by Mrs Leavis and interpreted by her as further proof of the degeneration of the novel-reading public,[5] are immensely revealing. *The Constant Nymph*, which *The Times* had ranked with *A Passage to India*, was mentioned in only two of over thirty published answers. Neither *If Winter Comes* nor *The Green Hat*, it was thought, would be remembered by posterity.

The popular notion of Margaret Kennedy as a Victorian born out of her time probably derived from the setting of her second novel. To readers in 1924, *The Constant Nymph* could well seem to be an invitation to look back to the years before the war, an evocation of the colourful world of Bohemian men and women, at home and abroad, at the turn of the century. But Margaret Kennedy evoked the past not in a spirit of nostalgic reverence, but in order to criticise her own age. And she staged a drama of tragic adolescent passion against the background of middle-class, Victorian *mores* in order to comment on post-war conventions and morals. Her novel is, therefore, decidedly not a period piece. And, in contrast to the well-documented chronicles of some of her contemporaries (A. S. M. Hutchinson, Warwick Deeping and Philip Gibbs), it is not historically conscious. In fact, apart from a few passing remarks on the period, there is no sense of time in *The Constant Nymph*. And the characters, particularly the female ones, are perceived and presented in terms of their changing surroundings.

The first part of the novel takes place in the Karindehütte, the Sangers' Tyrolean home, and its idyllic Alpine landscape. Albert Sanger, the head of the family, is a Hammersmith-born composer, admired in Europe but ignored in his native country. The expatriate genius moves from one capital to another, always experimenting with modernist, revolutionary music – so revolutionary, in fact, that it can be truly appreciated only by the initiate few. To that élite belongs his family, large even by Victorian standards, but un-Victorian in any other aspect, comprising two children by a long-forgotten first spouse; four offspring by a second, the well-bred, well-connected Evelyn Churchill; the larger-than-life Linda, Sanger's Cockney mistress, and their daughter. This extraordinary ménage is known as the 'Sanger Circus', a collective term particularly attaching to Evelyn's four orphans: Antonia, Teresa (Tessa), Paulina and Sebastian. The four are gifted, precocious and unruly. Neglected by an incapable parent, they grow to command a knowledge of life and sex that is most peculiar in Victorian children their age.

When the story begins Sanger is mortally ill; Linda cuckolds him with a comic Russian impressario, Trigorin, and Antonia has just eloped with Jacob Birnbaum, an opulent young Jew. Onto the already crammed stage another character is introduced. He is Lewis Dodd, Sanger's disciple and himself a promising talent. The master's death leaves the Karindehütte in a state of limbo. The children now homeless and penniless, are grief-stricken; Linda pursues Trigorin and Dodd is helpless. Into this chaos descends Florence Churchill, Evelyn's niece, the glaring opposite of her female relations. Florence is a caricature of the educated female, self-sufficient, self-denyingly disciplined and with an infantile passion for 'games'. Under her capable hands Antonia is married off to Birnbaum and the rest of the 'Circus' dispatched to England. Florence herself marries Dodd, moves him to Chiswick and organises his life. But her attempts to tame the wild musician and her insane jealousy drive him into the arms of fifteen-year-old Tessa, who has always loved him. The selfish Dodd persuades the child to elope with him. And she expires in a grimy boarding-house in Brussels, miraculously intact, a pathetic figure in school uniform, the victim of a lifelong passion.

Margaret Kennedy's initial scheme was to write a *roman-de-problème* on the incompatibility of art and social conventions (or, in her own words, 'art' and 'culture'), the clash between Bohemian and *bourgeois* ways of life. This incompatibility she wished to anatomise by portraying a union between an impecunious, unmanageable genius and a 'great lady', outwardly enlightened but inwardly narrow-minded and coarse. This unhappy relationship was to reach its symbolic *dénouement* in a written-in polemic on art and life: the wife was to represent Ruskin's view on art as a means to educate the masses and the husband to advocate 'art for art's sake'.[6] But already in the process of writing the first of the novel's three versions Kennedy moved the child characters to the foreground. Tessa, not Florence, became the central figure, and Tessa's complex relations with Lewis, rather than the Dodd's marriage and the 'art versus culture' debate, emerged as the story's main strand.[7] The author came to realise the dramatic possibilities in the history of an adolescent uprooted from the protective environment of home and transplanted into the artificial and alien world of society. 'The main subject of the book was to be the tragi-comedy of the heroine transplanted from Bohemia to Kensington.'[8] In the final version Florence became a foil to Tessa and was reduced from an educated, thinking individual to an odious harpy.

Florence is not the only one of the adult characters to conform to an easily identifiable type: Trigorin is the soulful Slav; Jacob Birnbaum is the wealthy Jew; Madame Marxe, the proprietress of the pension in which Tessa dies, is the avaricious Gallic procuress; the Churchills, Florence's father and uncle, offer two economical sketches of the Victorian don and the middle-class philanthropist. Both Florence and Lewis had originals. Lewis's was popularly believed to be Henry Lamb. Florence, as Margaret Kennedy later admitted, was 'reported, the only character in the book who was "drawn from somebody I know"'.[9] As regards characterisation, the novel's forte is the 'Sanger Circus'. The name derived from the celebrated circus of the self-styled 'Lord Sanger' which, between 1848 and the early 1890s, toured South eastern England and the continent (when the *Nymph* appeared, Sanger and Co. threatened to sue Heinemann for libel, but the parties reached an agreement of sorts).[10] The Sanger household was transparently modelled after Augustus John's ménage, with John himself as the prototype for the composer.[11]

But the main appeal of the novel was, and still is, the endearing figure of its adolescent heroine, to whom even Margaret Kennedy's sharpest critics warmed. It is significant that even the lukewarm reviews dating from before Birrell's panegyric referred to Tessa in eulogistic terms. The critic in the *TLS*, for instance, wrote,

> Never is she to change, this constant child, whose flame is quenched before she reaches sixteen. It takes art to make this passion neither flapperish nor pathetic, but actual and tragic, and Miss Kennedy has kept her nymph half pagan, half christian to the end.[12]

The presumption behind the juxtaposition of the word 'flapperish' to 'actual' and 'tragic' is transparent. For in the popular idiom of the period the first of these objectives denoted inconstancy, fickleness and instability, the very reverse of Tessa's enduring passion. The reviewer in the *New York Times Book Review*, on the other hand, was struck by the pathos in her character: 'So subtle a blend of pathos and satire is proof of a literary power of a degree seldom attained . . .', and *Punch* commented that 'the masterpiece of the book is the innocent and tragic figure of Tessa'.[13]

The key to the critical vocabulary is in the words 'constant child' and 'innocent'. What appealed most to the contemporary reviewing establishment and reading public in the character of the 'nymph' was the combination of vulnerable youth with an awakening sexuality. This intriguing combination of juvenile eroticism and actual sexual innocence, so conspicuous in the Victorian novel, was especially appealing to postwar audiences. An ambivalent notion of feminine adolescence was, it shall be recalled, central to the image of the flapper. For that historically peculiar image of the young woman as androgyne combined a blurring of the sexual identity of the modern female with mythical sexual powers. The ambivalence of purity and sensuality is evident in the opposing words comprising the title of the novel. The adjective 'constant' denotes immutability and implies permanence and loyalty, but the noun 'nymph', from its Graeco-Roman origins to the seventeenth century, had been related to nature and had come to symbolise freedom and mutability. And, although they had been associated with the spiritual in nature, the nymphs had often been endowed with sensual powers (in Greek and Roman mythology they are described as akin to the satyrs and the Sileni and even to Pan). Significantly for the author's use of the equivocal term, the oreads, dryads, hamadryads and naiads – female spirits of the mountains, trees and water – were young and mortal and sometimes symbolised death in youth (the nymph in Ovid's *Metamorphoses* immediately comes to mind). It is very likely that Margaret Kennedy perceived the image in its classical rather than Miltonic associations. She was certainly familiar with Greek and Latin mythology, and the novel itself, like several of her other works, abound in classical themes and images (not least among the latter is the recurring reference to Tessa as a Delphic sibyl[14]). However, whether classical or Miltonic in its origins, the image of the free spirit of woman, unspoilt by modern civilisation, is central to the novel. Tessa is in her element in the pastoral landscape of the Tyrolean Alps. And the part of *The Constant Nymph* that describes the awakening of her passion for Lewis bears the allusive title 'Nymphs and Shepherds'. In the corrupting atmosphere of the metropolis this passion becomes tarnished and even deviant and therefore cannot survive.

The female adolescent as the victim of her gender and sexuality is a theme that dominates Kennedy's early works. Its development can be traced chronologically from *The Ladies of Lyndon* (1923), through *The Constant Nymph* and *Red Sky at Morning* (1927), to *The Fool of the Family* (1930). In the first of these novels the precociously mature adolescent is a personification of sinister sensuality. The satyr-like Sir Thomas Bragge is infatuated with the enchanting twenty-year-old Agatha, and his unmasked desires offend the sense of propriety of those who watch him: '[one] felt a faint distaste at seeing them side by side. So fair a nymph and so foul a satyr were too striking an essay in contrast.'[15] Sir Thomas is eventually lured into marriage by an even younger girl, Agatha's flapper sister Cynthia, who calculatingly cashes in her negotiable sexual assets. This is how the old satyr and the maiden become acquainted:

'I'm not out' said Cynthia primly. 'I don't know any young men.' . . . Sir Thomas was thinking how very accomplished she was if this were true. He could have sworn that hers was no prentice hand in the tender game. 'Of course I'm not out. My hair isn't up.' She shook the shining, honey coloured mane upon her white neck. They paused in their walk and Sir Thomas delicately picked up a silky tress between a stubby and red thumb and a forefinger.[16]

The fact that Cynthia is, technically, under age is communicated by the recurring reference to her long, flapping mane. And the priapic, yet ludicrous nature of her union with Sir Thomas is conveyed in the apposition of the girl's shiny hair, the symbol of her alleged purity, with the obese fingers of her elderly suitor. In the early novels obesity, especially in middle-aged or elderly men, is a sure mark of lasciviousness and lustful appetite. In *The Constant Nymph*, for instance, Birnbaum, Trigorin and Sanger himself are all obese and correspondingly promiscuous. And they all prefer young women, who in turn are attracted to the older men's vitality and experience of the world.

In the second novel the cartoon-like cocotte is superseded by a more complex figure, representing a less simple notion of adolescent sexuality. To the image of the nymph is added that of the female child as predestined victim, or even saint. The most important scene in the novel is, perhaps, that in which Tessa, wandering on the mountains, becomes entranced and undergoes a semi-religious experience that leaves her physically and emotionally drained. The scene is at the end of the first part of the novel, between the episode that describes Antonia's return from her escapade and the description of Albert Sanger's death. Both thematically and structurally the mountain scene marks for Tessa the end of her period of childish innocence. Antonia's elopement prefigures her younger sister's future and illuminates – to herself as well as to the reader – the nature of her tragic passion. Tessa escapes from the explosive atmosphere of the Karindehütte (for, in addition to the tension between Antonia and her lover, there is a game of pursuit and seduction played by Linda and Trigorin and her discovery of her own awakening sexuality) and reaches the mountains:

> She climbed a knoll, the highest point near by and stared round her. In every direction she could see for miles, but the view was simple, a succession of serene ranges sticking up into emptiness. The moon had painted them all a uniform black and white, and the sky was of no colour at all. It was a simplification which delighted her; she needed it. There were, usually, too many things. The people and colours and noises crowded her mind. . . . She stared hungrily, trying to stamp this image on her mind and thus secure it for ever and ever. She became entranced with it. As she looked she had an idea, a passionate hope, which took her breath away. If she could ever see but one thing she might easily see God. The thought so moved her that she flung herself down on the short, wind-blown grass . . . waiting, rigid in an effort to reach singleness of mind. Nothing happened. In a few moments she became painfully exhausted and very cold. . . . She pulled herself together for the descent aware that a frightful weariness was aching in all her bones.[17]

And, gazing up the mountain path, she sees not God but Lewis, staring 'in a kind of lost trance'. In this and several other passages the pastoral Alpine landscape is endowed with purifying, redemptive powers. The stillness, cleanliness and simplicity of nature are significantly juxtaposed to the noise, density and colour of that man-made abode the Karindehütte. And this juxtaposition is articulated in the succession of carefully chosen words and phrases that describe the mountains: 'serene ranges', 'no colour at all', 'simplification', 'smooth', 'bare outline', 'emptiness', and so on. The symbolic landscape affects both Lewis and Tessa, but particularly her. Nymph-like she merges into it and undergoes an intense mystical experience. Her 'trance' is a mixture of unfamiliar physical sensations and religious feelings, and it is described in a curious blend of religious vocabulary and erotic symbols. When Tessa reaches the mountain she happens upon a calvary, whose primitive wooden crucifix moves her. She then contemplates a life of solitary prayer and meditation and flings herself upon the ground awaiting some revelation. Her ecstasy and final reaction – a fatigue both emotional and physical – is followed by a vision of Lewis, her *idée fixe*.

Significantly, Tessa, like her siblings Pauline and Sebastian, is named after a saint. And it is possible that her name is meant to recall the sixteenth-century mystic of Ávila, author of *Castel interior*, and not the 'little flower of Lisieux', whose popular autobiography, *L'Histoire d'une âme*, had a vogue in the 1900s and early 1910s. According to Birley the analogue with St Teresa did not draw on *Middlemarch*. Margaret Kennedy was a staunch anti-Catholic and it may appear odd and even unlikely that her 'pagan nymph' could be modelled after a Catholic mystic. But there is enough evidence in the text itself to suggest that the 'saintly', mystical element in the nymph is not pure conjecture. Tessa is unfit for the life of this world. She cannot and will not adjust to the role that society imposes upon her. Lewis himself comes to the conclusion that only the blissful seclusion of a convent could save her from her tragedy-ridden nature and circumstances. He realises that the combination of an unconventional upbringing and ignorance is fatal to a young girl. And in another key passage he foresees her inevitable predicaments, thus confirming what the Antonia–Birnbaum episode merely suggested:

She was barely two years younger than that sister whose history she would inevitably repeat. Pauline, too, was fashioned for the same fate. Unbalanced, untaught, fatally warm-hearted . . . they were both likely to set about the grimy business of life in much the same way. He knew what company they kept; lust, a blind devourer, a brutish, uncomprehending Moloch, haunted their insecure youth, claiming them as predestined victims. . . . She must be shut up. There were too many

Birnbaums about . . . he thought that if she were his little girl he would put her into a convent. He knew little of convents, but he imagined that they were safer for little girls than Sanger's Circus.[18]

Ironically, of course, it is Lewis himself who is to be the Moloch to whom Tessa's innocent youth and life will be sacrificed. And there is further irony in the fact that the danger to Sanger's girls stems not from Birnbaum and his like (for Birnbaum is genuinely in love with Antonia and later marries her), but from their self-appointed guardians, mentors and custodians: the Dodds, the Churchills, the girls' teachers at Cleeve School. The precocious adolescent is threatened and eventually destroyed by the '*bourgeois* characters' (Bennett's term), not Albert Sanger's *demi-monde*. In other words, female youth is most endangered in respectable, segregated society. Significantly, the pillars of social convention and sexual propriety treat the children with indifference and, on occasions, cruelty.

In all four of her novels written in the twenties, Margaret Kennedy conceived female adolescence as a period of intense physical and mental suffering which she implicitly associated with the awakening of sexuality. In *The Constant Nymph* the process of growing-up is not overcome, but destroys Tessa; she dies at the moment when her lifelong passion for Lewis is about to be expressed. The end of the novel, unlike that of *The Green Hat*, is not gratuitous. It is carefully built into the narrative by repeated references to Tessa's illness and to her inability to adapt to a conventional life in a London suburb. Yet by killing her, while preserving her chastity, Margaret Kennedy simply avoided the main issue of the novel, the conflict between nature, or freedom from convention (the 'pagan' element), and society. The death-bed episode is unconvincing. The author was fully aware of this and admitted that 'I could not carry this thing out. . . . I did not know how to manage anything so grim without resorting to crude violence.'[19]

The tragedy of the young woman as expressed in the threefold conflict – between life and art, between the *bourgeois* and the Bohemian, between the genius and the philistine – manifests itself in the familiar theme of the house. In each of Kennedy's novels of the twenties two symbolic abodes are juxtaposed: the one chaotic but full of artistic activity, the other seemingly orderly and harmonious but decaying. In *The Ladies of Lyndon* the Georgian house of Clewer is threatened by Braxhall, the garish mansion of a war profiteer, and the cottage at Bramfield, where Lady Clewer's son, a painter, lives with the servant girl he has married. In *The Constant Nymph* the noisy, colourful Karindehütte contrasts with Dodd's peaceful domesticity at Chiswick. In *Red Sky at Morning* the neighbouring houses of Water Hythe and Monk's Hall symbolise, respectively, the declining pre-war world and the emerging 'new morality'. Finally, in *The Fool of the Family* the decaying *cinquecento* palace on the Grand Canal opposes Caryl Sanger's room in the old Ghetto. Each of these houses is an edifice embued with ideas and values which are identified with one female figure.

Margaret Kennedy's use of the familiar metaphor is wholly within the conventions of the 'feminine' novel. Equally conventional is the perception of the female characters in terms of their relations to places, rather than to time. Her main allegiance, however, was not to the Victorian domestic novel. For her notion of the symbolic house, or household, is opposed to that of the 'home' in the Victorian sense of the term. In the early novels the house is a microcosm of its surrounding world, not an enclosed sphere separated from and resisting the influences of society. True, large families, a typical Victorian theme, held a special fascination for her. And it cannot be denied that her taste for complicated ménages, the relations between siblings and between parents and children, derived from the works of a Victorian writer – Charlotte Yonge.[20] But Margaret Kennedy did not extol the households she so realistically portrayed. She recorded their decline and fall. Furthermore, despite the fact that the heroines are drawn against domestic backgrounds, they are not the angelic spirits of the 'home'.

It is of special significance that the author whose work influenced her most was not a Victorian. From Jane Austen she learnt the use of detail and settings. In addition to writing a biography of the novelist (*Jane Austen*, 1950), she dedicated part of a book on the art of the novel, *The Outlaws on Parnassus* (1958), to the dialogue and setting in *Mansfield Park* and *Pride and Prejudice*, a work with which she dealt briefly in her essay 'The Novelist and his Public' (1963). But it is in the first four novels, particularly in *The Ladies of Lyndon*, that Jane Austen's influence is conspicuous. The model for Lyndon and its spacious park is Mansfield Park. The decay of Lyndon is reflected in the life story of its beautiful but incapable mistress Agatha Clewer. But Agatha is not quite another Fanny Price. She lacks Fanny's moral fortitude and her powers of endurance. And in contrast with Fanny she does not, and cannot, save Lyndon and the way of life it symbolises, but falls with it. The first chapter ends with a meaningful reference to *Mansfield Park*. Agatha, on the eve of her marriage to the heir of Lyndon, finds some consolation in the thought that her future husband, a gentleman with 'good fortune' and 'excellent breeding', would admire and respect her even when her beauty waned. The thought vaguely reminds her of an episode from Jane Austen's novel, which she pulls out from a shelf and, quite by accident, opens at the dialogue between Henry and Mary Crawford after Henry has first proposed to Fanny. The language of sensibility employed in this passage is somewhat anachronistic. And there is a curious disparity between Jane Austen's vocabulary ('liberality', 'good breeding', 'tranquillity') and Kennedy's lapses, particularly in the dialogues, into the jargon of the twenties. But more important is the similarity between the two central episodes in *The Ladies of Lyndon*, which take place in gardens, and the famous Sotherton outing in *Mansfield Park*. In the first of these episodes two couples – Agatha and her cousin Gerald Blair, and the flapper Cynthia and Sir Thomas Bragge – explore the park of Lyndon. Their seemingly aimless wandering is, in fact, a subtle game of seduction that prefigures coming crises. For Gerald is to become Agatha's lover and Cynthia will hook the ageing Sir Thomas. The second episode is set against the background of the newly planted garden of Braxhall, the house built from Sir Thomas's war profits. The estate's grounds plainly recall Sotherton. Both places comprise a formal lawn and a symbolic orchard – nature ordered and 'improved' – and a wild forest. Like the pitiful Mr Rushworth, who wishes to improve his property to impress an unworthy bride, Sir Thomas hires an architect to plan a garden that will make Braxhall 'the embodiment of the new order'.[21]

In *The Constant Nymph* Jane Austen's influence is less transparent, but it is still to be found in the thematic and structural use of places – whether open landscapes or domestic circumscribed spaces. The novel is divided into four parts, of which the first two, 'Sanger's Circus' and 'Nymphs and Shepherds', take place in the Karindehütte and its mountainous surroundings. Sanger's disorderly chalet throbs with unmasked desires. Significantly, Tessa and her sisters are more susceptible to the effects of this pernicious environment than their brothers. Even the refined, inhibited Florence succumbs to the influence of nature. For it is in the Tyrol, so different from her customary surroundings, that she discovers her sexuality and is subsequently transformed from a gentlewoman into a full-blooded female. In the third part of the novel, symbolically entitled 'The Silver Sty', the scene dramatically changes from the pastoral Tyrol to the suburban respectability of Chiswick. The Dodds' house at Strand-on-the-Green reflects Florence's character and her notions of domesticity. There she attempts to regain her usual composure and create a 'civilised', tame version of the Karindehütte and its Bohemian style, 'a sort of civilised Sanger's Circus, don't you know, with all its charm and not quite so much . . . disorder'.[22] Bohemia in a suburb is pitiful, and even Florence, that paragon of self-discipline, cannot order and control nature. Nor can she repress her own desires, or check the passion that grows between her husband and Tessa. The house is shown to the reader not through the eyes of its architect, but through those of the young Sangers – Tessa, Paulina and Sebastian. The three are taken through the labyrinth of rooms by Lewis, who all that time hums a nursery rhyme whose salacious undertones escape the children:

> There was a lady loved a swine,
> (Honey! says she) . . . .
> 'Pig hog', she said, 'wilt thou be mine?'
> (Hunks! said he) . . . .
> 'I'll build for thee a silver sty',
> (Honey! says she) . . . .[23]

The architect of Lewis's new house and life does not achieve the desired effect of orderliness and harmony. The Dodds' household becomes a place of discord. And the condescending tolerance of its enlightened mistress is transformed into an insane jealousy when Tessa and her siblings appear in Strand-on-the-Green. The fifteen-year-old girl takes over the place of the lady of the house. When she enters the cold, impersonal drawing-room it becomes warm and its occupants immediately come into life. But, in the end, the Alpine nymph transplanted to suburbia is destroyed by its hypocritical codes of polite behaviour.

Despite their apparent adherence to established conventions, there are elements in the four novels that are alien to the world of the nineteenth-century novel. Essentially the novels display neither the code of sensibility nor the sentimentality of the domestic melodrama. They are about destructive passion. And the tragic lives of their heroines are dominated by their senses and their sexuality. True, there is in Margaret Kennedy's early work, particularly in *The Constant Nymph*, a disparity, or even a tension, between the subject matter and the general atmosphere of sensuality, on the one hand, and the curiously reserved narrative discourse, on the other. All four novels revolve around one pattern of sexual relations which in the twenties was popularly regarded as sordid or even deviant. An adolescent, technically or symbolically under the age of consent and, therefore, outside 'society', becomes infatuated with, or attached to, an older man and is threatened by her own sexuality and the hostility of the social world. It is an old pattern and a familiar one. Tessa is a descendant of the Victorian child bride, or the beloved ward. But neither a post-war writer nor the post-war reading public could accept the father–daughter relationship (or the relationship of a guardian and a ward).

Margaret Kennedy was a shrewd observer of adolescent and juvenile sexuality. And, unlike many a contemporary writer, she did not attempt to gloss over this and other controversial topics with sentimental prose. Nor did she resort to a suggestive narrative as Arlen did. Indeed, the conversations in *The Constant Nymph*, especially those between the little Sangers, are refreshingly outspoken. But she was reluctant and, perhaps, unable to discuss openly the topic of feminine sexuality. Tessa's death is immensely revealing. Rather kill the heroine than bring the story to its logical conclusion. The contemporary writing and reading publics saw things quite differently. To them the tension between Victorian reticence and 'modern' licence was fascinating and, more importantly, made it possible to have things both ways. The novel could be considered 'clean' and 'healthy'. And any 'uncleanness' in it could be attributed to the promiscuity of the Bohemian or 'artistic' characters. *Punch's* comment is typical: 'the theme . . . is an old one and a tragic one – the mutual incompatibility of artistic and social ideas, presented by a set of moral outlaws'.[24] There is no doubt that Tessa's tragic end as well as the Bohemian and foreign *mise-en-scène* made the sordid topic of juvenile sexuality acceptable. What seemed prurient in *The Green Hat* appeared pure in *The Constant Nymph* precisely because in the latter novel deviant sexuality was apparently relocated outside society.

6

1919–28: 'The Sheik of Araby' – Freedom in Captivity in the Desert Romance

Lovehungry women thought he was a darling . . . he became the gigolo of every woman's dreams.

(John Dos Passos on Rudolph Valentino: 'The Adagio Dancer', 1930)

The mass of our popular literature, the bulk of our popular amusements just exist to provoke masturbation.

(D. H. Lawrence, *Pornography and Obscenity*, 1929)

Until about 1919 English-speaking people had used the Arab term 'sheikh' to describe a venerable Mohammedan, a chief of a Bedouin clan, tribe or village, or a desert potentate. Then, in the early twenties, the word acquired a new significance. 'Sheik' (as it was now spelt in popular writings) still retained its older meanings and associations with the Orient, but in popular Western imagination it came to stand primarily for a new image of masculinity. In the idiom of the period 'sheik' signified a virile, sensual male, a priapic, violent lover who masters females by sexual prowess and physical force. Significantly, the epithet was applied to oriental and occidental men alike. The new idiom became current at exactly the same time as the 'flapper' entered popular myth, and a causal relation between the two developments may therefore be assumed. The image of the desert lover was a reaction against the twin stereotypes of the modern young woman and her male counterpart. Alongside the image of the youth as a sexless androgyne, there emerged that of the male and the female as antipodal yet magnetic poles, drawn together solely by the power of sex. And, alongside the stereotype of the emasculated man, there developed the myth of the male possessed with extraordinary physical powers and a talismanic potency, a myth that was a response to

89

the new type of woman: politically emancipated, economically independent and sexually uninhibited.

The prototype desert lover was the extravagant figment of the imagination of a woman novelist who, before her works became best-sellers, had never visited the exotic places she so vividly dramatised. Edith Maud Winstanley was, as far as can be discovered, the retiring wife of a Derbyshire farmer, and she assumed the pseudonym E. M. Hull for fear of disgracing her family. *The Sheik*, published in 1919 by Evelyn Nash, was her first novel. Its sales were to surpass those of all the contemporary best-sellers lumped together. To her millions-strong reading public, and to a contemptuous posterity, Winstanley was known only by her pseudonym. And even today the basic biographical details about her remain obscure. The popular newspapers which fêted A. S. M. Hutchinson and Margaret Kennedy and chronicled faithfully the social life of Michael Arlen completely ignored E. M. Hull. She was not interviewed, nor did her name appear in the society and gossip columns. To the literary critics her work was beneath contempt. 'A typist's day-dream' was Mrs Leavis's trenchant summary of *The Sheik*.[1] The *Literary Review* described the book as 'a poisonously salacious piece' and added that Diana Mayo, the heroine, was 'a sister under the skin of [the Marquis De Sade's] Justine'.[2] What is particularly remarkable in contemporary commentary on *The Sheik* is that, regardless of the critics' platform and the readers they addressed, it is the best-selling *book*, not the best-selling *writer*, they focus on. The same may be said about the bulk of the reviews of love-in-the-desert' novels. And this obliteration of the persona of the writer (significantly, no photograph of E. M. Hull survives) at a period when best-selling writers made headlines is striking. For contemporaries, the novels of E. M. Hull and the many imitations she inspired were not the works of individuals but novels written to a recognisable formula, known by the synonymous terms 'desert passion' story, 'desert romance' and 'Eastern romance'.

The genre flourished between two world wars. Its palmiest season was between the socially perturbed aftermath of the First World War and the economic atrophy of the Great Depression. The middle and late twenties were also the period of the rise of the male film star as a sex symbol. In the personas of such stars as Rudolph Valentino and Ramon Navarro mass audiences found the living embodiment of full-blooded romance. The first filmed version of *The Sheik* (1921) was seen by 125 million viewers, the majority of them – to judge from the contemporary press reports – women. Valentino became the object of a cult that, even before his mysterious death in 1926, verged on the psychic.[3] Many a youth imitated the mannerisms and gestures of the 'love god'. Arab garments, Arab cigarettes and Arab motifs in decoration became the craze. In New York the sales of brilliantine and of cosmetics and jewels for men boomed (in the film, Sheik Ahmed Ben-Hassan was extravagantly attired and bejewelled). Such was the sheik mania that newspapers in Britain and America pontificated that the emergence and spread of the stereotype of the Eastern lover was a threat to the ideals of Western manhood. The *Chicago Tribune* in a famous article entitled 'Pink Powder Puff', which almost cost Valentino his career, lamented the disappearing occidental male:

> It is time for a matriarchy if the male of the species allows such things to happen. Better rule by masculine women than effeminate men. . . . Are pink powder and parlor pinks in any way related? How does one reconcile masculine cosmetics, sheiks, floppy pants and slave bracelets with a disregard for law and aptitude for crime? . . . It is a strange social phenomenon and one that is running its course not only here in America but in Europe as well. Chicago may have its powder puffs. London has its dancing men and Paris its gigolos.[4]

The phenomenal success of the film stimulated enterprising writers and publishers to emulate E. M. Hull's pioneering formula of rape-*cum*-redemption in the Sahara. A myriad desert-passion novels, novelettes and feuilletons flooded the book and magazine markets. But Hull remained the queen of desert romance. *The Sheik* had, inevitably, a sequel, *The Sons of the Sheik*, published in 1925. In the interval she produced *The Shadow of the East* (1921) and *The Desert Healer* (1923). Of her many imitators two merit attention: Kathlyn Rhodes and Joan Conquest (both are probably the pseudonyms of women writers). Rhodes was the most prolific though the least original of the desert-love novelists. Her first Eastern yarn appeared in 1909, five years after the publication of Robert Hichens's best-seller *The Garden of Allah*, which acquainted the Edwardian reading public with the Sahara. *The Lure of the Desert* and *The Will of Allah* (a cunning tribute to Hichens's novel) appeared in 1916 and 1918. Rhodes responded with exuberance to the post-war appetite for escapist fiction, producing, in quick succession, *The City of Palms* (1919), *The Golden Apple* (1920), *Courage* (1920), *Under Desert Stars* (1921), *A Desert Cain* (1922), *Desert Justice* (1923), and so on. Joan Conquest, Werner Laurie's reply to Nash (Hull's British publisher), was, arguably, the most imaginative of all the contemporary desert-love novelists. And she was the only one whose expertise was acknowledged by the London literary magazines.[5]

Conquest specialised in knockabout burlesques which parodied the conventions of the genre. The titles of her works are brazenly emblematic: *Desert Love* (1920), *The Hawk of Egypt* (1922), *Zarah the Cruel* (1923), *A Light in the Harem Window* (1927), *Harem Love* (1930), and so forth.

In comparison with Arlen's and even Margaret Kennedy's novels, the typical desert-love romance is inoffensively euphemistic. Yet it incensed literary critics and self-appointed guardians of the public's morals and was regarded by them as prurient. And, significantly, the new genre came in the popular mind to epitomise the sex novels at their worst: literary works whose function was, solely, to excite and stimulate the reader. In the eyes of contemporaries the fantasy set in the desert was not merely 'an opiate' (Mrs Leavis's expression) but also a pernicious aphrodisiac. I have in mind, of course, D. H. Lawrence's indignant remark that 'the furtive, sneaking, cunning, rubbing of an inflamed spot in the imagination is the very quick of modern pornography and is a beastly and very dangerous thing'.[6] Yet it is evident that what most irritated Lawrence's contemporaries about *The Sheik* and similar novels was not their prurience or 'obscenity' as such, but the fact that they were obscene novels *for women*. Countless articles, burlesques and cartoons implied, or stated outright, that the desert romance was pornographic literature, manufactured by female writers for the consumption of a sex-starved mass female audience. And, paradoxically, the language of the censorious parodies is far more ribald and coarse than that of the texts they lampoon. A typical burlesque appeared in the *Daily Express* on 23 and 24 January 1924 and reads,

> Bronzed and brutal was Abdullah
> And his eyes were green and glowing
> With inscrutable suggestion
> With a concentrated menace
> And a sinister expression
> Full of oriental passion
> Full of dark and devious meaning . . .
> And the haughty Sheik Abdullah
> Spent his time in trapping women
> Sweet and youthful English maidens
> In the first flush of their girlhood. . . .
> He would snatch them from their mothers
> As they sipped their tea at Shephard's . . .
> Pressing scorching kisses on them
> Burning all their necks and elbows
> With a simply dreadful relish

Nor was the furore about oriental passion in novels and films confined to the satirical columns. Both the Rothermere and Beaverbrook presses published articles on the many dangers awaiting inexperienced female travellers wandering or camping in the Sahara – which, no doubt, helped spread the myth that English women went to the East in search of illicit love and adventure. Typical titles picked out at random from the *Express* include 'Sunrise in Sahara-Biskra [Moroccan garrison town, a favourite spot in Sahara novels]', 'From Biskra to Bloomsbury', 'Sheik Husband of English Girl, Film Hero and the Real Thing'.[7] One of the bawdiest burlesques can be found in the anonymous *Young Men out of Love* (1928), which relates, at great length, the abduction and rape of Ali Bim-Seid-Amarcujian by a sex-starved débutante, a comic reversal of the roles of abductor and abducted. The eponymous sheik ('Amarcujian' is a pun on 'America', the land of origin of the desert-love film, as well as on Michael Arlen's Armenian surname 'Kouyoumdjian') has the profile of Rudolph Valentino and the agility of Ramon Navarro but regrettably lacks their passion. Subtlety failing, the heroine resorts to brute force and ravishes the poor Ali:

> Was ever any man so possessed? Valentino humiliated his manhood.
> . . . Ali Bim Seid gave himself with rapture of being possessed. He was in the same prediction of those Sabine maidens helpless in the hands of their Roman conquerers, spoils of war.[8]

The parody is crude and its implication overt: feminine relish in masochism is universal. And, the more emancipated and modern a woman is, the greater her desire to be humiliated and violated. This assumption is quite explicit in the noisy publicity campaign for Valentino's films: 'Shriek or the Sheik will strike you' cried street placards in New York and all over America. The placards blatantly express what the parodies merely insinuate. The former invite the overwhelmingly female film audience to share, vicariously, a collective experience of rape. Yet, underneath the brazen salaciousness of the parodists and the indignant righteousness of moralists and critics, there may be detected a fear. It is the same anxiety as in the contemporary writings on Arlen's libidinous heroines: namely, that the modern, sexually emancipated woman can pursue pleasure without being punished for her presumption. For, unlike Clarissa, the English-woman who is ravished in the Sahara does not virtuously die but lives to enjoy a blissful state of concubinage in the imaginary desert.

Generically the desert romance is connected with an older literary form that had developed in relation to the historic contacts of Europeans with the Arab world: namely, travel and guide books on the Orient.[9] The geographical and cultural isolation of the war years was followed by a broadening of real and imaginary horizons, accurately described by Paul Fussell as 'the travel obsession of the age'.[10] Africa and India were no longer the main resorts of exotic romance. They were now being supplanted by areas hitherto barely known to the fiction- (as opposed to the travel-book-) reading public: Mesopotamia, parts of Arabia, and the French Sahara. This switch was provoked by the mystique of the Arab revolt, and the romantically supercharged legend of Lawrence of Arabia. Without doubt, the stereotype of the Englishman posing as a Bedouin was a dramatisation of Lawrence's life in the Hejaz. After the war there was a spate of travel books on Arabia catering for every taste. 1922 saw the publication of Harry St John Philby's *The Heart of Arabia* and *Arabia, a Record of Travel and Exploration*. 1926 was a distinctly prolific year. In January Duckworth issued *Wanderings in Arabia*, an abridged, cheap edition of Doughty's classic *Travels in Arabia Deserta*, and in April Jonathan Cape published a complete edition introduced by T. E. Lawrence. Lawrence's own *Seven Pillars of Wisdom* and the first volume of Gertrude Bell's memoirs appeared in June, and by the end of the year Elois Musil's *Arabia Deserta* and *The Manners and Costumes of the Arabs* were available in English translation. But more important in this context are the now neglected works of women travellers and explorers. Freya Stark, who embarked on her first Eastern journey in 1927, was preceded by Rosita Forbes, Lady Dorothy Mills and E. M. Hull herself. Hull, the critics discovered, was not only a depraved pornographer, a literary offspring of the Marquis de Sade, but a capable, 'straightforward' travel-writer. In 1925 or 1926, accompanied by an unidentified female friend, she made a 600-mile circular tour of Morocco, travelling from Touggourt to El-Coled and back to her starting-point. The experience was recorded in *Camping in the Sahara*. Hull is pre-eminently a case of life imitating fiction (for she had first fictionalised the landscapes of North Africa and only afterwards explored them).[11] The works of Rosita Forbes and Lady Dorothy Mills represent a reverse process. Both writers dramatised prior real-life experiences. Forbes stands out as one of the most intrepid travellers of the inter-war years. In 1920 she headed an expedition to Kufara in Libya, the first European to have gone there since 1879. In 1923 she ventured into the Atlas mountains with the purpose of writing the life of the Berber leader Raisuli. The biography appeared a year later under the title *The Sultan of the Mountains: The Life Story of Raisuli* and was followed by two travel books, *From Red Sea to Blue River* (1925) and *The Secret of Sahara Kufara* (1931). Dorothy Mills described her travels in West Africa in *The*

Road to Timboktu (1924), Episodes from the Road to Timboktu (1927) and
The Golden land: A Record of Travel in West Africa (1929). She was also the
author of a successful desert-passion novel, The Tent of Blue (1922).

Travel, Paul Fussell asserts, became in the twenties a metaphor for
freedom and flight. And the metaphor was not confined to the writings of
literary travellers but was diffused into romance and loomed very large in
the journalese of the period. To contemporaries the female traveller, or
explorer in particular, became the incarnation of the sense of release and
the urge to escape that followed the First World War. The pages of the
Rothermere and Beaverbrook papers overflow with articles about, and
photographs of, lady aviators, navigators and travellers. Explorers such as
Rosita Forbes, Dorothy Mills and, later in the decade, Freya Stark
personified the spirit of modern womanhood: independent and totally
free from restriction. Freedom of movement, like the much discussed
sexual freedom, symbolised the widening of the traditional feminine
sphere. In what follows I suggest that the popular travel book and the
oriental love fantasy are manifestations of one and the same motif: the
explorer's voyage to unknown places is, in more ways than one,
analogous to the discovery in the desert romance of the heroine's hitherto
suppressed sexuality.

The desert romance is one of the most consciously topographical and
ethnological genres in popular fiction. The geographical setting for this
romance is the Arabian peninsula, the eastern Mediterranean and North
Africa, from the Red Sea to the Atlantic. For the writers this area divides
into three similar territories: the Sahara, Egypt and Arabia. It is this
division that gives each of the three main types of story into which the
genre falls its own specific mannerisms. The romance set in the French
Sahara is the desert romance in its purest and least modified form. It
abounds with sexual violence and revolves around the theme of rape. Less
violent, but equally replete with erotic tension, is the story set in Arabia, a
newly discovered and enthusiastically explored literary landscape. The
romance located in the Egyptian urban centres of Cairo, Alexandria and
Ismailia depicts the Orient at its most Westernised and is, of all varieties
of the genre, the least sexually and physically violent. The biggest sellers
of oriental passion had each her own territory. Hull's was the French
Sahara. Kathlyn Rhodes wrote about Cairo, Alexandria, Damascus and
Constantinople – in her euphemistic novels the four cities are the
proverbial Babels. Joan Conquest favoured Arabia, and Dorothy Mills,
North-west Africa.

The pattern of the desert romance proper – that is, the exotic Sahara
love story – combines two intertwined strands: travel and sexual

violence. Typically, in this pattern, an aristocratic Englishwoman, economically and socially independent but sexually unawakened, embarks upon a voyage into the heart of the Sahara desert. She is abducted by an Arab potentate, is held in captivity and is violated and humiliated. From sexual degradation and servitude she emerges a 'real woman', a better human being and, paradoxically, one who is freer. Thus the heroine's journey in space may be interpreted as a journey in time. For invariably she changes from an androgynous juvenile into a mature female, capable of feeling. This transformation is effected both by the magic power of the arid landscapes of the desert and by the potency of the desert man, the oriental male incarnate. The inseparability of the twin themes of physical freedom and sexual bondage is laid out in the conventional structure of the romance. The narrative typically begins at an oriental coastal town, or at a garrison town, which symbolises the junction of East and West. It is here, where the two cultures meet, that the heroine cuts herself off from the 'civilised' Western world and its restricting conventions to explore the symbolic desert. Thus Robert Hichens's classic *The Garden of Allah* begins with a description of the Algerian port of Robertville. Hull's *The Desert Healer* opens with an account of the grim, depopulated township of Bildah. The narrative of *The Sheik* begins at the Hotel Biskra, a displaced European *Grand Hotel* in the midst of alien and exotic surroundings. Invariably the greater part of the narrative takes place in the desert and relates the heroine's journey and her captivity. The Sahara romance concludes in an oasis and the release from captivity also symbolises journey's end and the beginning, for the heroine, of a new life. Various modifications of the formula conform to the conventional tripartite structure of the travel book: the departure from home (home can be, of course, a metaphor of the familiar Western, or Westernised, world), the journey and the return.

The desert novelist seeks to validate her fantastic fabrications by an almost obsessive attention to scenic actuality. Accuracy in geographical and ethnographical details is the primary requirement of the genre. The wilder and the more fatuous the fantasy, the greater the pain that is taken to authenticate it. The novels of Hichens, Hull and Mills and the parodies by Joan Conquest all abound with overwritten passages whose function is, primarily, to make romance believable. Sometimes these passages fit into the narrative. But more often they are flamboyant and extraneous *tours de force* whose sole purpose is to impress the reader with the writer's knowledge of her subject matter and to establish her as the omnipresent traveller–narrator. The oriental coastal town, with which the Western reader was more likely to be familiar than with, say, the desert oasis or the inland townships, is painstakingly described. The bazaar and casbah are depicted with a realism that verges on the pedestrian. Not only local customs and manners, but also colloquialisms and dialects, are studiously reproduced. Arabic terms and, in the Sahara-romance, ordinary French and *patouète* (the dialect of the *pieds-noirs*, the European lower classes of the coastal towns of Algeria and Morocco) are extensively spread through the text. A typical descriptive passage is hard to distinguish from a comparable passage in a popular travel book. The following extracts depicting the oriental bazaar are taken at random from Hull's *Camping in the Sahara*; her fourth novel, *The Sons of the Sheik*; and Joan Conquest's *The Hawk of Egypt*. First Hull:

> Groups of Arabs of all classes, their flowing burnouses ranging from the spotless white of the well-to-do to the drab must colour of the beggar, drifted past in twos and threes by the open shops talking, eternally talking. A string of camels, in charge of wild-eyed desert-men and hung with heavy, pendulous sacks stuffed with henna from the South stalked disdainfully through the crowd with a soft pad-pad of cushioned feet on their way to the *fondouk*. Crouched in the sand and dust, ragged and filthy hawkers of sweetmeats . . . cursed shrilly. . . . Here and there the scarlet cloak of a Spahi, the striking black or brown of a chief's burnous, the tall black-bearded maharist in the tight frock-coat and the long, baggy trousers of the Saharan camel corps. . . .[12]

> Groups of better-class Arabs, in twos and threes, drifted through the press, talking intently and ignoring with grave aloofness the babel that surrounded them. Now and again a chief, superbly mounted . . . cantered slowly across the square, haughtily indifferent to all who might be in [his] way; while from time to time a French officer, his well-fitting uniform a distinctive note among the drab array of burnouses, walked smartly in the direction of the barracks . . . [a dervish], wild-eyed and foaming at the mouth, stark naked save for the ragged fragments of a faded crimson burnous, once the discarded property of some Spahi . . . strode swiftly past. . . .[13]

The stiffly adjectival scenes conjure up a kaleidoscopic but clichéd image of the oriental town and the urban Arabs. Typically the latter are described not as individuals but *en masse*, and are stereotyped as unclean, garrulous and, above all, lascivious. Joan Conquest's description of the Khan-El-Kalili is crammed still fuller of eyewitness details:

> Water-carriers, camels, sweetmeat-sellers, lowly women in black gowns and coffee-sellers, donkeys which continuously bray, and dogs

which bark; cracking of whips: shrill cries of *Dahrik ya sitt or musya* (Thy back, lady or sir); shouts of *U'a tt'a'*; clashing of bronze ware; snarls of anger; laughter; song; dust and colour, all the ingredients which go to the entrancement of the bazaar. . . .

Or elsewhere: 'curious eyes watched behind the shelter of *masharabeyeh*, the harem lattice of finely carved wood. . . . Yards of silk of every hue lay tumbled inside and outside the *dukkan* or shop'.

The fictional casbah, or Arab quarter, is a male-inhabited space. It is a place of depravity, a macrocosmic *maison tolerée* whose only female inhabitants are Arab prostitutes, procuresses, belly dancers and fortune-tellers. To European women the casbah (and in the 1920s not only the fictional one, but the real one as well) is a forbidden area. And, being forbidden, it has for the well-educated, high-born heroines all the allure of a *quartier reservé* with its fascinating aura of sensuality and vice. Robert Hichens introduced in 1904 the theme of the Englishwoman who ventures into the nub of the casbah, the *café maure* (literally an Arab restaurant, but in the desert novel, invariably, a mixture of cabaret and brothel). In *The Garden of Allah* Domini Elfinden visits, unchaperoned, a *café maure*, watches *Kabyle* belly dancers, inspects prostitutes and returns, intact and pleasantly intrigued, to the safety of the European quarter. E. M. Hull allows her French and Anglo-Catholic heroines into the forbidden quarter – the Protestant ones she keeps out of it. In the notoriously francophobe popular English novel the French have often been endowed with a propensity to sin and Catholics have always been regarded as more frivolous in their morals than their sober Protestant brothers and sisters. In *The Sons of the Sheik* Yasmin, the offspring of an ancient French house, who is mistaken for a Moroccan, performs belly dances to a leering male audience in the squalid *café maure*. The episode, which Conquest was effectively to parody in her *Desert Love*, is described through the eyes of an English gentleman, Caryll Glencaryll, one of the twins fathered by the famous Sheik on the lovely Diana Mayo:

A few steps farther on was the *Café Maure*, brilliantly lit and in full swing already, a deafening noise of tom-toms and brazen trumpets crashing through its open door. . . . [It was] a long narrow room with bare plastered walls stained and streaked with dirt, lit by cheap flaring lamps that flamed and smoked upwards to the grimy cobwebbed ceiling. At the farther end was a low dais on which lolled the tom-tom and trumpet players, and half a dozen heavily-built, sleepy eyed girls in tawdry velvet dresses that hung like strapless sacks about them. . . .

All around him were pleasure-seekers; better-class and scum of the
gutter, Soudanese soldiers and half-caste Frenchmen, nomads from the
desert, and here and there a doubtful looking European – Spanish for
the main part – rubbing shoulders indiscriminately. The expression on
the faces of all and each was identical. It was vice in its most blatant,
most repellent form, a crude viciousness that seemed to shout at him,
undisguised, from every corner of the room.[15]

Into that den of vice descends Caryll's twin-brother, kown as the 'Boy',
who proceeds to abduct Yasmin, storms with her to the outskirts of
Touggourt and there ravishes her at knife-point. Unlike her future
mother-in-law Diana (continuously raped in *The Sheik*) the Gallic Yasmin
shows no signs of resistance to the Boy's assault. The whole charade is
well within the desert romance's rules of propriety. Yasmin has
prostituted herself merely by *being* at the *café maure*. Moreover, she is
mistaken for a *Morrocan*. And, both in the romance and in the North
African *patois*, 'Morrocan [or Arab] women', *femmes maures*, is an epithet
which designates prostitutes.[16] The episode associates physical uncleanness with an inner depravity and lasciviousness. The former is taken as an
outward sign of the latter, especially in Arab males. The Arab *habitués* of
the café, not the European ones, are described as 'tawdry', 'dirty', 'scum of
the gutter'. It is because of this that Yasmin, who, it later transpires, is an
occidental woman, is singled out for her cleanness and purity: 'How had
she remained so clean, so virginal in such an environment? For clean and
virginal she was.'[17]

In contrast with the casbah – narrow, squalid and overcrowded – the
desert is vast, pure and unpopulated. Abduction and rape, which, when
they take place within the precinct of the oriental town, are lurid, become,
in the open space of the desert, redemptive acts. The landscapes of the
Sahara have a magical influence upon the traveller heroine. Their effect is
not gradual but instantaneous – a miraculous *fiat*, as it were. The moment
the heroine leaves behind her the town and civilisation, she is transformed
from the sophisticated and overcivilised person that she formerly was
into a free, unencumbered woman. Typically, in the desert romance, rapid
movement over a considerable distance is a metaphor for freedom. Riding
is a liberating and releasing activity laden with erotic symbolism. The
Arab stallion or mare becomes, like the Arab male, a sexual symbol that is
repeatedly evoked. Solitary riding; riding in company; chases on
horseback; the tending of horses and the taming of wild colts – all these
are highly conventionalised set pieces. They are intensely charged
physical and emotional experiences which prefigure, both thematically

and structurally, the climatic experience that the heroine is to undergo. The following described Diana Mayo's escape from the oasis where she has been held captive:

> Her mount galloped swiftly and the wind whistled past Diana's ears . . . she knew that she was mad to ride across the desert alone, but she could not mind. She was free. . . . She laughed and shouted like a mad thing and her madness communicated itself to the grey, who was going at racing speed. . . . The pace was less killing now. . . . Diana looked about her with glowing eyes. Everything seemed different. From the first she loved the desert. . . . She loved the endless, undulating expanse, stretching out before her . . . the ground rose and fell in monotonous succession, and then the desert grew level again, and quite suddenly she could see for miles.[18]

In another crucial and especially violent scene she watches, transfixed, the ruthless sheik taming a wild colt. The analogy with sexual violence is transparent, and, to Diana and to the reader, the breaking of the indomitable animal foreshadows her own complete physical and spiritual surrender to the brutality of the sheik:

> It was a punishment of which the tamed animal was never to lose remembrance. The savagery and determination of the man against the determination of the horse. It was a hideous exhibition of brute strength and merciless cruelty. Diana was almost sick with horror from the beginning; she longed to turn away, but her eyes clung fascinated to the battle that was going on. . . . The Sheik was standing on the ground beside the colt, who was swaying from side to side with heaving sides and held low to the earth, dripping blood and foam. And as she looked he tottered and collapsed exhausted. . . .[19]

These pieces and many interchangeable ones have certain resemblance to, at least, two passages by Lawrence. The second, taming-of-the-colt piece, superficially evokes the famous comparable scene in *Women in Love*, though no connection can be made between the two. And there is a more than spurious similarity between the first riding-scene and the woman's solitary ride across the Mexican Sierra in 'The Woman Who Rode Away' (1925). It is possible, even probable, that Lawrence, who knew Hull's best-seller and even paid oblique tribute to its self-consciousness in his 'Surgery for the Novel or a Bomb', had it vaguely in mind when he wrote 'The Woman Who Rode Away'.[20] For otherwise his remark that Lederman 'like any sheik . . . kept her guarded among the mountains of Chihuahua' is hardly comprehensible. Another curious mention of the oriental lover appears in 'In Love', written shortly after Valentino's death:' "What else does Rudolf [sic] Valentino do for you?" – "You like *him*." – "He's dead poor dear. But I loathed him really." '[21]

Of all the topoi that have been attached to the Arab male, the stereotype of the sheik retains only one: an extraordinary sensuality, a priapism that the euphemistic novels never quite mention explicitly but continuously celebrate. In all other respects the noble nomad is diametrically opposed to his urban brother. Where the latter is filthy and depraved, untrustworthy and a coward, the man of the desert is fastidiously clean, resplendently attired, a fearless warrior and a ruthless but just ruler to his subjects. Of course, the *Kabyle* (or, in the novels set in Arabia, the Bedouin chief) is a figment of the novelist's imagination. Yet it expressed a powerful wish fulfilment. For typically the noble Arab is a European fathered by an Anglo-Saxon on a non-English woman (though never an Arab one), or an eccentric Briton 'gone native'. The occidental man masquerading as an Arab acquires the latter's potency and unlimited powers over women. 'Civilised' Englishmen and European men tend to come off badly in the desert romance. They are pleasant but unexciting, and sexless, rather anaemic figures in comparison with the colourful, hot-blooded Arab or the European masquerading as an Arab. The English knight-errants are no match for the Amazonian heroine. To dominate the modern cold virago, brute force, not chivalry, is needed. And the idealised, primitive cave man, not the androgynous male, can and does tame her. Significantly, *The Sheik* opens with a description of a ball at the Hotel Biskra where the beautiful Diana, newly arrived from England, stirs the provincial and placid British colony. Men are attracted to her boyish lithe figure like moths to flame. But she, cold, ruthless, selfish and unwomanly, rebukes them all. To her virginal mind, the mere idea of copulation is repugnant:

> The idea of marriage – even in its highest form, based on mutual consideration and mutual forbearance – was repugnant to her. She thought of it with a shiver of absolute repulsion . . . to her cold, reserved temperament it was a thing of horror and disgust. That women could submit to the degrading intimacy and fettered existence of married life filled her with scornful wonder. To be bound irrevocably to the will and pleasure of a man who would have the right to demand obedience in all that constituted marriage, and the strength to enforce those claims, revolted her.[22]

Ironically, the beautiful Diana is to enter a bond that is not sacred, nor based upon 'mutual consideration'. On the eve of her voyage into the Sahara, sleep eludes her and, brooding on a terrace, she hears a voice singing in Arabic 'White Hands of the Shalimar' (a famous Edwardian music-hall song). The voice casts a spell on her and lulls her to sleep. Sleep and unconsciousness have in the Sahara romance a role which is similar to that in *Clarissa*. At the end of the second day of her voyage, Diana's caravan is raided, her escort disperses and she is abducted by a mysterious Arab who carries her away to his encampment and introduces himself as Sheik Ahmed Ben-Hassan (the singer with the magical voice, it transpires). He then ravishes her. Like Clarissa Harlowe, Diana is unconscious when she is raped. And on the face of it her sexual role, like that of Clarissa, is one of passive suffering. Both the eighteenth-century paragon of feminine delicacy and her distant twentieth-century relation are not permitted consciously to enjoy the physical and emotional experience they undergo and are, therefore, not responsible for it. Yet *The Sheik* departs from the traditional literary representation of abduction and rape in that for Diana sexuality does not entail death or destruction. During subsequent violent sexual experiences she is, symbolically, conscious and acquiescent and survives to flower under her suffering. As the story progresses it becomes more and more violent, and in a typical manner Diana becomes a willing victim. When the sheik – whose real identity has by now been revealed (he is the son and heir of a degenerate peer) – wants to release his captive and return her to the civilised world, she positively refuses and chooses the natural, primitive life of the desert man. Subsequent marriage is only vaguely implied.

At first glance *The Sheik* is a prudishly told tale of masculine dominance and complementary feminine masochism and passivity. The story falls well within two established literary traditions: the erotic novel set in the Orient, which can be traced from the end of the eighteenth century (one has in mind, of course, the anonymous *The Lustful Turk*);[23] and the theme of abduction and rape, deeply engrained in the Victorian novel. But the desert romance departs from these traditions in three significant ways. First, the story of a sado-masochistic relation that is transformed into a permanent state of blissful sensuality is told from a feminine, not a masculine, point of view (as in the oriental erotic novel). Second, *The Sheik* does not conclude in either of the ways which are characteristic of the traditional forms: retribution visited on one or both of the main characters, or marriage. Diana and Ahmed, we assume, do marry. But, as contemporaries observed, both the marriage and the discovery, by Diana, of Ahmed's 'real' identity are gratuitous. At no point in the whole story is matrimony presented as a necessary alternative to an unlawful but happy concubinage. Third, despite its being a 'feminine' novel, the typical desert romance has a male, not a female, as its central character. True, the romance juxtaposes a 'real', sensual and subdued femininity to modern independent womanhood. Yet what *The Sheik* and its many imitations ultimately celebrate is an ideal of masculinity: 'primitive' (as opposed to 'civilised'), virile and priapic. The importance of the male character is stressed in the titles of the novels. Most of these titles evoke the place of action, the imaginary desert. But many indicate the male protagonist as well: *The Sheik, The Sons of the Sheik, The Desert Healer, The Hawk of Egypt*, and so on. Typically, scenes of ravishment are prepared for by conventional passages in which the distressed victim scrutinises appreciatively the magnificent physique of the aggressor. Examples could be multiplied: 'He had flung aside the heavy cloak that enveloped him from head to foot and was standing before her, tall and broad-shouldered. . . . Diana's eyes passed over him slowly. . . .'[24] Or, in Joan Conquest's patiche:

A Man was he indeed, with a width of shoulder rarely seen in an Arab, standing well over six feet, in spotless white robes sweeping to his feet a cloak of the finest black cloth falling over all in swinging folds, failing, however, to hide that look of tremendous strength . . . in the long-limbed, lean, muscular inhabitants of the desert.[25]

And elsewhere: 'an Arabian youth, beautiful as a god, supple as a snake, quick upon the feet as any fighting stallion'.[26] The imagery speaks volumes.

The silent film with its emphasis upon expressive performance emulated and stylised the image of the oriental lover. In most of Rudolph Valentino's films the camera lingers on the faces and bodies of the male actors. Valentino himself appears, partly naked, in *Blood and Sand* (1922), where he played a bullfighter. In a rather prudish indoors scene he emerges half dressed from behind a screen. The first production of *The Sheik* cunningly exploited a variety of sexual symbols: the sheik's smouldering cigarette, among the disarrayed objects on Diana's dressing-table on the morning that follows the rape; close-ups of Valentino's ludicrously enlarged eyes and of his muscular arms; and so forth. *The Sons of the Sheik* was bolder. In the famous torture scene Valentino, naked to his waist and strung up by the arms to a board, is beaten by two sadistic Germans. Apparently the audience's hysteria knew no bounds.

The phenomenon of the best-selling desert romance casts some doubts on the orthodox theory of pornography. According to this view – shared by scholars representing different shades of opinion[27] – the pornographic novel is a generically masculine artefact, produced by men for men. The world depicted in this novel is *sui generis* – runs the argument – androcentric and phallic, a mirror of the concepts and ideals of a male-dominated, sexually aggressive culture. Yet the desert romance eludes this model. For, at a period marked by the political emancipation of women, as well as by significant changes in the patterns of sexual behaviour, there emerged a massive body of erotic literature written by women for a female audience. To regard the flowering of this literature merely as a backlash, the reaction of a patriarchal society to the new freedoms acquired by women, is to oversimplify matters grossly. There is no escaping the fact that the desert-passion industry catered for women. Nor can it be argued that the novels were not pornographic because they were linguistically pure. True, the best-sellers of Hull and Conquest were euphemistic in critical scenes. But there is no doubt that contemporaries regarded them a perniciously prurient, 'pretty pornography' (Lawrence's famous expression), books that aimed to stimulate a sexually excitable reading public. Furthermore, the desert-love novel and the films and gramophone records that thrived alongside it represent one of the earliest examples of mass, commercialised erotic literature. The bonanza in sexual escapist fantasies was made possible by the growth of a female audience with increasing spending-power and leisure. And this audience was particularly influenced by the changes that occurred in the patterns of sexual behaviour and in everyday life. How to grapple with the changing image of womanhood? How to come to terms with the new, much talked-about sexuality? The answers lay in transforming the familiar stereotype of the priapic male from a villain into a hero; in reviving and idealising what had seemed a stale pattern of romance; and in locating this romance in an exotic, remote and imaginary world.

Part Three
Realistic Fantasies: The World of the Story Papers

7

Class and Gender:
The 'Girls' Weeklies'

And yet the world of Oracle *and* Peg's Paper *is a pure fantasy world. It is the same fantasy all the time, pretending to be richer than you are. The chief impression that one carries away from almost every story in these papers is of frightful, overwhelming 'refinement'. Ostensibly the characters are working-class people, but their habits, the interiors of their houses, their clothes, their outlook and, above all, their speech are entirely middle-class.*

(George Orwell, 'Boys' Weeklies')

Every paper desiring a wide circulation must circulate, for the greater part among the working classes, for the single reason that they form nine tenths of the population.

('Frank Richards Replies to George Orwell')

The impression one carries away from old issues of story papers such as *Peg's Paper* is quite different from that recorded by Orwell in his famous essay. One does not have the sense of 'frightful, overwhelming refinement', of blissful domesticity, of an exclusion from real life and the real world. The papers do have a certain coarseness which is sincere. Their idiom is the idiom of a class, not the parroted jargon of an élite. In their form and subject matter they are examples of what Eliot would probably call the 'expressive art of the people'.[1] And of a sex.[2] The remainder of this book is about class and gender. The combination of large audiences and a massively capitalised press has usually been regarded as a primary cause for the rise of a mass rather than class press. In post-war Britain that particular combination brought about the emergence of a different kind of commodity: the down-market, consumer-oriented periodical which was, none the less, a class paper. It will be useful, then, to look at the story papers in the context of structural changes in both the market for periodicals and the periodical-reading public, before concentrating on the aesthetics of pulp fiction.

The 1840s or 1890s, not the 1920s, are usually thought of as the formative period in the history of the popular periodical.[3] Yet in the twenties the magazine bonanza seemed a phenomenon whose very scale marked the decade off from earlier periods. 'The highbrows', noted the *Bookman* in January 1920, 'are not having the journalistic field to themselves. We are being flooded by new monthly and weekly magazines and story papers.'[14] Four years later the writing and reading of stories reached what seemed like epidemic proportion. 'This is the magazine age', remarked *Punch*, 'and with it came a flood of literature in the form of books and correspondence courses designed to teach people how to write the stories that are required to fill the pages of the magazines. The thing is becoming a cult.'[5] The metaphor of a flood is characteristic and reflects an awareness of the break from familiar patterns of magazine-publishing and reading. Equally characteristic is the diagnosis offered by publishers and critics that the magazine boom, like the boom in the book industry, was a result of a universal hunger for escapism consequent on the First World War and life, in its aftermath, in the modern big city.

From a more practical angle, there were golden opportunities in the magazine market. In an era of recession and unemployment it offered much for little to the resourceful practitioner. The magazine business was an expanding field in which capital was useful, but not necessary. This simple commercial analysis is conspicuous in a myriad articles, advertisements and manuals, offering practical advice on 'professional writing'. Ranking high among the manuals are Michael Joseph's five guides for the aspiring writer and journalist (1922–5); *Short Story Writing for Profit, Journalism for Profit, The Commerical Side of Literature, How to Write Serial Fiction* and *The Magazine Story*. George G. Magnus's *How to Write Saleable Fiction* (1904) ran into 14 editions before 1925. The *Bookman* carried series on 'The Practical Side of Story-writing' and in 1922 announced the launching of 'a bureau of practical advice for writers, especially on the mechanical side of stories'.[6] That same year appeared *The Elinor Glyn System of Writing*, which revealed, in that author's familiar effusive manner, the secret of the art: 'Anyone, anywhere is welcome to the profession. For years the mistaken idea prevailed that you had to have a special knack in order to write . . . but happily this notion is now a thing of the past.'[7] The language and tone of the best-selling novelist curiously resemble those of the magazine-editor or the advertiser. The editor of *My Story Weekly*, significantly subtitled 'Love Romances Told by the Girls Themselves', promised readers ready cash for 'real life stories':

Big Money for Your Story. Everyone has a story to tell. You are sure to have an experience that would be a help to other girls. Will you tell it to me?

For what in my opinion is the best true story sent in each week, the sum of One Guinea will be paid, and the story published without revealing the name or address of the sender. All I want you to do is to write up any incident of your life which you think would be interesting.[8]

All the short stories and serials in *My Story Weekly* were allegedly by amateurs and all employed first-person narrative. The following titles and resumés, chosen at random, are revealing: 'How I Was Loved by a Sheik . . . adventure and romance, which make all the sheik stories ever written pale into insignificance' (October 1927); 'The Man Who Let Me Down' (November 1927); 'My London Life. The Confession of Ivy Trent, a Manchester Girl' (November 1927); 'Wooed by a Prince, by Yvonne Lester, a Sheffield Girl' (December 1927). It is hardly surprising that the *literati* regarded this influx of publications as a writing on the wall, a sign that the barbarians were at the gates of 'minority culture'. Because if – as it was popularly argued – 'anyone, anywhere' could write, then the boundaries between the writing and the reading public were disappearing. And the traditional distinction between artist and audience, the keeper of a shared cultural currency and its receivers, was now dangerously blurred. It became, to use Walter Benjamin's expression, a merely functional distinction. 'At any moment the reader is ready to turn into a writer.'[9]

One image in particular recurs in the handbooks. It is the image of the fiction industry as a free market, uninfluenced by big capital, in which individual interests compete with each other. In the context of the twenties the doctrine and idiom of *laissez-faire* and those of 'self-help' (the manuals remotely echo Samuel Smiles's homilies) were ludicrously anachronistic and distorting. Perversely, the diverse members of the industry – the publisher, the seller, the magazine-editor and, finally, the writer – are all described as small entrepreneurs. The main feature of the decade after the war was, as will later be shown, the ascendancy of big concerns and the disappearance, through merger or amalgamation, of the smaller firms. And, needless to say, in this imaginary market 'background' and education were superfluous. Writing was no vocation, but simply a trade like any other.

The connection between genre and gender was less obvious here than in the case of the sex novel, and contemporaries realised that the magazine story as such was *not* a generically feminine commodity. In the first place, hundreds of papers catered for juvenile male audiences and many others were aimed at a mixed public (there were few all-story papers for male adults). Secondly, all the publishers and the majority of advertisers, editors and writers of women's magazines were men.[10] Despite all this, the periodical press was popularly described as a feminine domain. Its post-war boom was related not to changes in the reading public as a whole, but to the emergence of a new female audience. This possessed three characteristics. It was heterogeneous, but predominantly working-class. Its members were economically independent or better off than they had ever been. Finally, the readership was more exposed to the external influences described earlier and, subsequently, more open-minded and of wider interests than its Victorian and Edwardian precursors. Naturally the new audience influenced not only the structure of the fiction market, but the scope and nature of periodical fiction itself. The territories of the 'masculine' and the 'feminine' story now began to overlap. Romance, the largest category of mass-circulation fiction, was, publishers thought, a feminine domain, as it had always been. And of all the popular genres it was the least susceptible to changes in fashion or fluctuations of the market. Between August and November 1924 *Punch* ran a 'Guide to Short Story Writing' in ten parts, of which no fewer than four were dedicated to the art of the love story. Their titles are revealing: 'The Simple Little Love-story'; 'The Business Love-story'; 'The Married Love-story' and 'The Neglected Wife Story'. Advice to the would-be writer of the 'simple little love-story' began in a practical, if somewhat terse, tone:

> If you are the fortunate sort of person who can exude this type of fiction you may begin at once enquiries as to the safest way of avoiding the payment of super-tax. The simple love-story must not be confused with the tense love-story, the analytical love-story, the married love-story, and all the love-stories which depend for their love interest upon nothing else than love pure and simple. Character and such obstruse matters as that have no place in the type of story we are now considering.[11]

In fact the new magazine reading public was no longer content with simple domestic stories. After the war both the topics and the geographical horizons of romance broadened. To the realistic 'bread-and-butter' yarn, set against a familiar, urban background, and the 'Ruritanian melodrama' were now added innovative types of story set in remote, exotic surroundings. Female audiences, especially adolescent readers, were interested in 'masculine' genres: adventure and detective stories, Westerns and 'sporting' yarns (a term covering 'turf' and 'ring' stories, and stories set in a football stadium or at Wimbledon; the last two were great favourites in women's periodicals). Male writers were repeatedly advised to adapt to the changes in the audience: 'The male writer . . . should study his female readership and its expectations. A male writer who cannot skilfully portray a woman's character will be severely handicapped.'[12] Underlying this and similar remarks there is a fear similar to that which underlies comments on the novel-reading public. It is the fear that fiction will become more and more effeminate.

Yet the women's press of the twenties may be graphically described as a parabola, reflecting the characteristics of the newspaper industry as such: a rapid expansion over a short span; a growth in the reading public; and, finally, a trend towards the concentration of ownership in the hands of a few firms. This description particularly applies to the story papers. *The Newspaper Press Directory and Advertiser's Guide* classifies 20 periodicals in 1914 as story papers for women. Its list for 1928 numbers 67 such publications. In a period when new newspapers rarely appeared and the issue of new novels declined, the number of story papers for female readers more than trebled. Of the 67 magazines, 29 were owned by the Amalgamated Press, five by the Family Herald Press, four by Hutchinson, three by Arthur Pearson, three by the Scottish firm of John Lang, three by George Newnes and two each by Odham and Allied Newspapers. The rest of the market was divided between small firms, most of which were eventually to be devoured by the big houses. The Harmsworths were succeeded by the Berry brothers as moguls of the industry. Lord Rothermere's hegemony came to an end in 1926, when he sold the Amalgamated Press empire, of which the women's papers constituted less than a third, to William (later Lord Camrose) and Gomer (later Lord Kemsley) Berry.

It would appear that the story papers are a classic example of the manipulation of the media by small interest groups. Indeed, the handful of publishing-firms which controlled the women's-magazine market also dominated the national daily and Sunday press. Rothermere's is, of course, the best-known case. The Berry consortium controlled 26 Sunday and daily newspapers against his 17. The Odham group, whose heyday was yet to come, owned the *People* and, from 1929, the *Daily Herald*. But the model of a controlled press manipulated by and serving big capital is rather too simple. In reality the women's and national presses of the twenties were two separate systems, even in those cases where they were financially related. The women's press was – had always been – *sui generis* outside the orbit of politics and therefore apolitical, though by no means without a coherent ideology. Consider in support of this contention the relation between the Harmsworths' dailies and the Amalgamated Press's story papers. The latter absorbed notions of modern femininity expounded by such organs as the *Mail* and the *Express*, depoliticised those notions and dramatised them. But so did the sex novels, and, unlike the newspapers, they were not editorially censored. Moreover, on the whole the general outlook of the Amalgamated Press's story papers was, as I hope to show, progressive, far more progressive than that of the dailies and Pearson's or Odham's publications. Some of the Amalgamated Press's papers were socially conscious, and in glaring contrast to the *Mail* their idiom and approach to life were idiosyncratically working-class.

The expansion of the industry coincided with and was influenced by changes in the structure of the readership. The First World War ended more than two centuries of unbroken middle-class domination of the female magazine-reading public.[13] 1918 saw a *coup-de-grâce*, concluding a progress that had begun in the 1870s and had culminated in the 1890s with the appearance of the first mass-market women's weeklies. *Home Notes*, a paper for lower-middle-class readers, was published in 1895. 1899 saw the emergence of the *Girls' Friend*, a weekly for working-class adolescents. Significantly, both these publications were launched by the enterprising Harmsworths. It was left, however, to their chief competitor, Arthur Pearson, to complete the process and transform the fiction magazine from a miscellany for middle-class consumers into a commodity aimed at the swelling working-class audience. In 1919 Pearson's editor-in-chief, F. J. Lamburn, and his wife Mollie Kennedy brought out a 40-page weekly in a small format that was more manageable than the folio publications of the Amalgamated Press. *Peg's Paper* survived the Great Depression and competed successfully with the colour glossies without changing its appearance. Its formula was emulated by a crop of weeklies and fortnightlies: *Polly's Paper* (1919–24), *Peg's Companion* (1924–32), *Bow Bells* (1919–25), *Ivy Stories* (1922–34), *Poppy's Paper* (1924–36), *Pam's Paper* (1923–7), *Eve's Own Stories* (1923–39), and so on. By the mid-twenties over half the fiction magazines for women catered for the adolescent and adult working-class market.

Ideologically and structurally these magazines showed a tendency contrary to that of the rest of the British press. The general trend was from a class to a mass industry, from regionalism to the dominance of the metropolis, from diversity to uniformity and standardisation. The inter-war years were justifiably described as the age of cultural *Gleichschaltung*. But the story papers were moving, although only for a while, in the opposite direction. Never before had they been less uniform and never before had they shown greater differentiation. In the early thirties they too became standardised commodities. The twenties were, thus, a peculiar period. And the phenomena described here were peculiar to the women's press. They had no equivalent in periodicals for male or mixed audiences. Consider, for example, the boys' weeklies of that period. They resembled the women's and girls' magazines in appearance, were published by the same companies and catered for the same class of readers as the women's weeklies. There was, however, one significant difference. The world of *Magnet* and *Chum* is the public-school world of the *Boy's Own Paper*: patriotic, gentlemanly and upright. It is, as Orwell remarked, the secure world of the educated classes at the turn of the century, reproduced for post-war, working-class adolescents.[14] In contrast to these papers and the evangelist *Girl's Own Paper*, *Peg's Paper* and its sister publications depict a way of life that is far from genteel, drawing working-class audiences, in an idiom that was distinctly theirs.

In appearance the story papers were a far cry from the 'society' glossy, or the middle-class 'service' magazine (C. L. White's term). They were printed, on the newsprint pulp paper from which they derived their somewhat derogatory epithet, in a two- or four-column layout. The typical story paper was a weekly (there were no monthlies for working-class female audiences and fortnightlies were scarce). Its potential readers were unmarried manual workers, shop assistants, domestic servants and office workers. Married women in their early and mid twenties formed a distinct group for which a host of periodicals more domestic in outlook than the publications for adolescents catered.

The main component of the pulp weekly was fiction. The relation between the role of magazine fiction and the social status of the magazine-reading public has been noticed.[15] The space given to fiction was in inverse proportion to the class of readers. The 'higher' this class, the smaller the story component. *Vogue*, started in Britain in 1915 and catering for élite audiences, did not publish stories. *Harper's Bazaar* (founded in 1929) printed short stories with an appeal to Bright Young People. *Vanity Fair* (1914–29) carried stories, but not regularly. *Eve, the Lady's Pictorial* (1919–28), a fortnightly which, more than any other women's periodical, typified the 'modern' spirit of the twenties, ran series of complete, self-contained vignettes. These, like much of the rest of the magazine's content, and that of similar magazines, such as *Harper's Bazaar*, were sophisticated anecdotes about the comings and goings of the smart set. At the other end of the prism fiction preponderated. A crude sample analysis of four representative weeklies, two of which led the market and two of which merged with other publications, clearly illustrates the trend. 64 per cent of the space of *Peg's Paper* was given to serials, 'complete novels' (stories averaging 6000 words) and short stories. The proportion in *Polly's Paper* was roughly the same and in *My Story Weekly* it increased from 64 per cent in 1927 to 86.5 per cent in 1929. In the older *Girl's Friend* fiction took up 80 per cent of the space.

Even more significant is the relation between the form of fiction and the class of readers. The serial story was peculiar to working-class periodicals. The weekly instalment or instalments (some of these periodicals carried two or more serials simultaneously) constituted their core and essence. And a particularly successful serial was a major sales-booster. Middle-class publications, on the other hand, had a distinct preference for shorter fiction. There were some exceptions. *The Girl's Own Paper* and *Woman's Magazine* ran, as late as 1928, serial stories, the monthly instalment being on average considerably shorter than the typical weekly instalment in a pulp paper. The Amalgamated Press introduced serials in several of its sevenpenny fortnightlies for middle- and lower-middle-class audiences (the *Violet Magazine*, *Yellow Magazine* and *Red Magazine*), but later returned to the safer short stories and to mini-series consisting of two or three parts or a sequence of anecdotal, self-contained tales. In the 'society' glossies the serial was virtually non-existent.

As Table 1 shows, the women's pulp press had no monopoly on the serial story. Older family miscellanies such as *Answers* and *Argosy*, as well as weeklies for adolescent male readers, carried serial fiction. Serials were the backbone of *Chum*, *Magnet* and *Union Jack* (the overall length of a serial story in *Union Jack* averaged 8000–12,000 words, far greater than the average for a serial in a typical girl's weekly). Moreover, unlike the novel the serial story had never been classified as 'feminine'. In fact it had arisen as a form of entertainment for the whole household, not for women only.

Is the serial *qua* serial, then, a class construct? Does it embody the inherent characteristics and attitudes of a class, or does it capitalise on the universal appeal of suspense and repetition? And what about the element of gender? Is fiction that is produced and consumed at intervals generically feminine? Finally, there is the economic aspect of serial-writing to be considered, the influence of the regular instalment on the sales of the product. The last problem is the easiest to grapple with. Publishers, printers and writers had capitalised on the popularity of serial-

TABLE 1 *Serials in Amalgamated Press's women's magazines and miscellanies with a domestic interest*

Title	Periodicity	Price	No. of serials per issue and average length of instalment	Publisher's specified requirements
Answers	Weekly	2d	1 (5000–6000 words)	'Of a type to appeal to a wide circle of readers'; 'strong dramatic plot and love interest'
Argosy	Monthly	7d	Not specified	'Classics' by well-known authors
Eve's Own Stories	Weekly	2d	Not specified	'Strong romantic fiction with plenty of movement', to appeal to middle-class girls from 16 upwards
Girls' Friend	Weekly	2d	4 (6000 words)	'Aimed at the average girl'
Home Chat	Weekly	2d	1 (3000–5000 words)	'Strongly romantic appeal'
Home Companion	Weekly	2d	3 (4000 words)	'Appeals strongly to working girls and women'
New Magazine	Monthly	1s	1 serial and 3 part stories	Humour, mystery and romance
Poppy's Paper	Weekly	2d	2 (about 4000 words)	'Strong love interest'; 'good curtains necessary'
Red Magazine	Fortnightly	7d	Not specified	'Good plot and sincerity'
Women and Home	Monthly	6d	1 (10,000–12,000 words)	'Strongly romantic and modern'

TABLE 1   *continued*

Title	Periodicity	Price	No. of serials per issue and average length of instalment	Publisher's specified requirements
Woman's Pictorial	Weekly	2d	1 (8 instalments of 6000 words)	Not specified
Women's Weekly	Weekly	2d	2 (about 4000 words)	Not specified
Woman's World	Weekly	2d	3 (average 4000 words)	'[Serials] of domestic and romantic character', modern setting of a type likely to appeal to the working-class woman'

This table is based on Michael Joseph's list of serial-buyers, made in 1930, and on my own close examination of a large sample of women's and girls' magazines. See Michael Joseph, 'How to Write Serial Fiction', *The Complete Writing for Profit* (Hutchinson, 1930) pp.855–72.

writing since the 1840s.[10] But the 1920s saw an unprecedented boom in serial fiction, consequent on the expansion of a working-class reading public as well as on the prospects which the American market and the film industry offered to British writers. The serial market was easier to penetrate and less competitive than the novel or short-story market. The public did not clamour for big names, and even an apprentice, as many a contemporary observed, could extract handsome profits. In 1930 the average fee for 1000 words was a little over one guinea. A first 80,000-word novel could fetch its author between 50 and 60 guineas. A first short story of about 5000 words could fetch between 10 and 15 guineas. A successful serial could bring in a small fortune (given that the average length of a first instalment in a magazine could reach 20,000 words and that the number of instalments could total 20 or more). Favourite stories were reproduced in book form in pocket-size, cheap editions comprising between two and four 'complete novels'. The 'novels' – or 'libraries', as they were called – appeared fortnightly or monthly, and their low price (4d) made them extremely popular. The Amalgamated Press alone had four women's libraries: the *Girls' Friend Library*, *Companion Library*, *Mizpah Novels* (incorporated in 1922 with *Forget-Me-Not*) and *Woman's World Library*, specialising in domestic melodramas for older age groups. D. C. Thompson ran the popular *Red Letter Library*, launched in 1902 and still in publication in the later thirties.

Yet an analysis of the market does not fully explain the explosion of serial-writing after the war. Why, for instance, did the serial preponderate in papers for *one* class and not in those for another? And why the sudden growth in the women's press? Was the serial, despite its origins and evolution before the First World War, a 'feminine' form? It has been observed that the serial is an interactive form of communication that involves a close, intimate relation between the artist and his public, that it 'gave back story-telling its original form of performance', where the narrator had performed in front of a collaborative audience. Far from being passively receptive, the serial-reading public is 'co-creative'.[17] And, it may be added, it has more control over the production of the form than the novel- or short-story-reading publics (the effects of the public's reaction on the composition of the great serials of the 1840s is a salient example). Such a form of communication was likely to attract working-class audiences, for whom a sense of solidarity and togetherness had special significance.

Furthermore, the serial, more than the individualistic novel or the short story, reflected an attitude to time peculiar to these audiences. This attitude, as both Peter Stearns and Richard Hoggart have shown, was characteristically fatalistic.[18] The notion of linear progress was absent from it. The concrete, the immediate, the moment counted. The basic unit in the calendar of the urban worker was the week, which had an economic as well as a cultural significance (both related to the wage). The weekly instalment in the pulp magazine, corresponding to that unit, regulated longer, incomprehensible durations such as the month or the year. Significantly, there were only a few all-story fortnightlies and monthlies for women and they all catered for middle-class audiences. Moreover, the weeklies did not carry historical series of the 'cloak and dagger' genre, nor 'scientific' stories set in a Utopian future, a type of story which was becoming increasingly popular with adolescent male readers. Time in the women's and girls' serials was always present time, and they therefore conveyed no sense of progress. The world they presented was a static and changeless one. Of course, the serials dramatised acute problems: the demographic crisis; the 'modern woman' phenomenon; the decline of the family; women's work; and so on. But external occurrences were referred to rarely and spuriously and they were never casually related to each other or to the characters. Even the First World War was a remote shadow, an isolated and abstract event, convenient as a point of reference but with no bearing upon the motionless world of the heroines. On the other hand, there is, in these serials, a distinct sense of place. Unlike the 'masculine' types of magazine story (the detective, mystery and adventure yarns) the 'feminine' genres were defined solely by their locus of action: the *domestic* love story, the *Ruritanian* romance (set in an imaginary Central European state), the *Lancashire* or *mill* love story, the *Empire* yarn and, of course, the *desert* romance. The major female stereotypes in periodical fiction were popularly perceived and presented not in terms of their development, or progress in time, but in their relation to a place or places (see Chapters 8 and 9).

Other characteristics of the serial stories were emulated and brought to their highest perfection in the women's weeklies. The personal relation between the addresser and the addressees, that sense of intimate partnership, spread from the fiction pages to the editorial columns. The editorial voice assumed a role that was similar to that of the narrator. Both these voices inspired confidence, a sense of warmth and friendliness. Since the 1890s periodicals for women, especially the down-market, low-price periodicals, had capitalised and thrived on the principle of the reader's identification. It was, however, after the war that patterns of editorial presence and manner of address and of the public's response to them – what I call the *addresser–addressee relation* – crystalised. From this perspective the publication of *Peg's Paper* was a watershed in the history of women's-fiction publication. Designed to appeal to working-class readers, Arthur Pearson's magazine formulated a tone and manner of address that were to be emulated in a number of successful mass-market weeklies. The new formula was articulated in *Peg's* first editorial 'talk':

Hello Girls! Here I am, and here is a copy of our paper. It is going to be your weekly pal, and it will greet you every Thursday.

My name is Peg, and my one aim in life is to give you a really cheery paper like nothing you've ever read before. So let's shake hands and settle down to a comfortable chat and I'll tell you all about things. Not so long ago I was a mill-girl, too, and my clogs clattered with yours down the cobbled street. Some day I'll tell you my story. Because I've been a worker like you, I know what girls like, and I am going to give you a paper you'll enjoy . . . remember that Peg is your pal. I want you to come to me with your joys and your sorrows, look on me as a real friend and helper, someone whose face you cannot see but whose hands will grip yours in ready sympathy, and who will advise you on any problem that may confront you in your daily life. So don't forget that in sunshine and rain your best pal is Peg.[19]

The tone and the carefully chosen vocabulary are innovative. The editor has an identity. The first-person narrative, the reference to Peg's past as a mill lass, and the name itself, all conjure up the image of a working-class girl, the same age as the readers. That this persona was an invention is irrelevant. The editorial voice and image constituted a break from the paternalistic pose of the majority of editors before the war (the editorial voice in the *Girls' Friend* being a notable exception). The key to the new formula is in the word 'pal', which denotes friendship, solidarity and a willingness to help. It is, significantly, a neutral term that can be applied to females and males alike and has, also, meaningful associations with working-class vocabulary. Indeed *Peg* and its sister papers, despite their celebration of romance, lack the blatant feminine, domestic ideology of the 'service' and 'society' magazines and, needless to say, there is a gap between their language and that of the later publications. A wrong dose of one of *Peg's* identifiable ingredients could kill a paper. *Polly's Paper* (1919–24), probably the first imitation of *Peg*, was an attempt, which ended abortively, to capitalise on the mill-girl image. The paper had exactly the same proportion of fiction as *Peg*, about 60 per cent; a slightly higher proportion of advertisements; the same layout and type of print and even a similar pagination. But the editorial voice, seemingly *Peg's*, was, in fact, fatally different:

> I am not an ordinary woman, because I've had so many ups and downs. And those very experiences make me the more ready to understand your troubles, to sympathise with you, to help you. You know when you come to me for advice and help, you are writing to someone who had been through the mill . . . of course I shall be controlling the paper and I am anxious to be your friend . . . remember that I am a woman who has known what climbing the uphill path means – what it is to be lonely and disheartened – how gaunt and grim downright poverty can be, and because I've known all that, I am more able to sympathise with you than any other woman writer can be.[20]

The fact that the addresser has 'roughed it' in a mill fails to achieve the intended effect. For the nuances and very intonation of the editorial voice are those of a patronising, if well-intentioned, outsider. They both smack of middle-class complacency. The notion that poverty is 'grim' and degrading and that social mobility and an ambition to progress up the social ladder ('the uphill path') are desirable are equally alien to *Polly's* potential readers. But most fatal is the statement, 'of course I shall be controlling the paper'. Complicity and reciprocity is what adolescent working-class audiences sought, not control from above. Later the tendency to improve the reader became dangerously conspicuous. The paper's advice column was titled 'Polly's Straight Talk' and adopted an instructress tone.

The formula of collaboration, or co-editing, varied from one publishing-house to another. In Pearson's publications the editorial presence was obtrusive. *Peg*, for instance, ran two advice columns, a correspondence column ('Peg's Private Post') and a gossip page ('Whispers – Things I Heard about You'). The latter page comprises snippets of information such as 'Why did the Manchester girl refuse to attend the wedding of her best pal?' and 'Who is the matron in the Liverpool factory known as the "Black Cat"?'[21] The snippets are quite the reverse of the gossip columns in the glossier papers. Far from peeping into the glamorous world of 'society' and Bohemia, they are concerned with the reader's own world. The image they conjure up is that of an omnipresent, omniscient insider, familiar with the minutest details of her public's life. It is, basically, the same image as possessed by the ubiquitous narrator of the serials. In the Amalgamated Press magazines the editorial voice is hardly audible, and the sense of a regular, reciprocal rapport is relegated to the serials, which, through the decade, remained steadfastly working-class in their attitude and outlook.

Yet, despite different nuances, the girls' weeklies are all variations on one and the same idea. They are invitations to join a sorority of adolescents, a close-knit and privileged community of gender and age, but mainly one of class. Theirs is the world of working-class youth perceived and presented as the embodiment of the attitudes and values of that class. When Orwell described the girls' papers as organs of populist Toryism, the vehicles through which middle-class ideas are disseminated to a mass, he probably had in mind the thirties rather than the twenties. The decade before the Second World War saw the rise of the colour weekly, which imitated the up-market publications and gradually supplanted the pulp magazine. The post-war decade, however, still belonged to the class magazine. And nowhere were the class elements specified in this chapter so clearly articulated as in the story set in the heart of working-class Britain, the industrial 'Lancashire romance'.

8

'A Lass of Lancashire': The Mill Girl as Emblem of Working-Class Virtues

Why Lancashire should have become almost the official accent of music-hall humour is something of a mystery, for there are plenty of droll folk and music-halls elsewhere. But that rather flat but broad-vowelled speech . . . is admirable for comic effect, being able to suggest either shrewdness or simplicity, or, what is more likely than not, a humorous mixture of both.

(J. B. Priestley, *English Journey*, 1934)

Lancashire is the classic soil on which English manufacture has achieved its masterwork.

(Friedrich Engels, *The Condition of the Working-Class in Britain*, 1844)

The mill-girl story had emerged in the 1890s. Its heyday overlapped the decade between the end of the First World War and the Wall Street Crash; its decline and fall coincided with the Great Depression. The *Girls' Friend* (1899–1931), the first paper to have catered specially for women workers in the industrial centres, was emulated by a throng of weeklies whose titles exploited the appeal of the noun 'girl': the *Girls' Reader* (1908–15), *Girls' Home* (1910–15), *Girls' Weekly* (1912–22), *Girls' Mirror* (1915–33), and so on. Their reading public drew massively on the working-class and on a variety of occupations: the wool and cotton industries, domestic service, the clerical profession. And, to judge from the proportion of boarding-school yarns before the war, these publications could boast of large numbers of schoolgirls among their readers. Despite their heterogeneous audience, the weeklies published by the Amalgamated Press, D. C. Thompson and Pearson were popularly known as 'mill-girls' papers', a name that endured till the 1940s. Nor were the stories these papers printed confined to the world of the mill or to Lancashire. They covered the whole range of topical romance, from the

Ruritanian melodrama to the domestic romance. But the type of story that lent the papers their nickname, that embodied their style and epitomised the values they advocated was the romance set in a Lancashire mill.

The mill romance belonged to a regional tradition that had thrived in rural and urban Lancashire between the 1840s and the First World War. Lancashire dialect and Lancashire themes had been revived in the ballads and stories of local writers such as Edwin Waugh (1817–90), a Rochdale journeyman and printer, whose *Sketches of Lancashire Life and Localities*, first published in book form in 1855, earned him the title 'the Lancashire poet'. His contemporary Benjamin Brierley, poet and, from 1869 to 1891, publisher of *Ben Brierley's Journal*, was famous for his first collection of rhymes, *A Summer Day in Daisy Nook* (1859), still in demand in the 1910s. Apart from the local lore the 'mill' had a vogue on the 'illegitimate' London stage in the 1830s and 1840s, in the work of playwrights such as Douglas Jarrold and John Walker.[1] The Edwardian era saw the transformation of the local communal tradition into a national and commercial form of entertainment, aimed at large audiences. Lancashire music-hall artists and playwrights such as Harold Brighouse and Stanley Houghton modified dialect, stylised established themes and created a gallery of recognisable popular types: the ruthless 'maister' and the industrious, honest 'waver', the aristocratic toff, the incompetent 'fader' (Hobson instantly comes to mind) and, last but not least, the sensible, forthright Lancashire lass.

The story papers of the twenties represent the last and shortest phase in the history of mill-romance. After the war the Lancashire play and the vaudeville show on Lancashire themes were in danger of stagnation, consequent, no doubt, on the decline of the music hall and its replacement as working-class entertainment by the cinema. But the Lancashire tradition and Lancastrian characters were to have a short but significant flowering in what may seem unlikely quarters, the massively capitalised women's weeklies of the Harmsworth brothers (and, in the thirties, in Lancashire films; television series about Lancashire, which are distinctly less authentic than the older products of the tradition, are beyond the scope of this study). The war, which restructured the magazine market, hardly affected the mill-girls' papers. Most of the Edwardian weeklies had survived four years of acute paper shortage, and after 1919 they were joined by a spate of publications capitalising on the success of the *Peg's Paper* formula. In the output of the Amalgamated Press the Lancashire romance loomed very large. Taken together, the mill-girl yarns occupied more space than any other type of romance. And, significantly, their proportion was larger than before the war.

A handful of writers spun out thousands of mill yarns for the Press's weeklies. The most prolific of them was Henry St John Cooper, who wrote for girls' and women's magazines under the pseudonym Mabel St John. Cooper is best remembered now for his madcap school character Pollie Green, who was created in 1908 for the *Girls' Friend* and whose adventures were subsequently issued in book form.[2] What is less well known about him is that he was the author of numerous Lancashire stories featuring full-blooded working-class characters and drawing a realistic picture of working life. The extraordinarily fertile Cooper also contributed regularly to the *Boy's Realm, Pluck* and the *Union Jack*. Hundreds of his stories were reissued in pocket editions in the Amalgamated Press's 'libraries'. The British Library catalogue lists about 112 reissues between 1919 and 1928. Their titles are immensely revealing: 'Daughter of the Loom, or Go Marry Your Mill Girl' (*WWL*, 1922), 'He Married a Mill Lass' (*WWL*, 1924), 'I Shall Not Marry a Mill Lass' (*Companion Library*, 1921), 'The Mill Girl's Bargain' (*GFL*, 1924), 'Mill Lass o' Mine' (*GFL*, 1920), 'My Man of the Mill' (*WWL*, 1924), and so on.

The mill-romance writer *par excellence* was 'William E. Groves' (probably a woman, Mrs Wellesley-Smith). Groves specialised in 'clogs and shawl' series, skilfully reproducing Lancashire dialect and colloquialisms that even today bring to life the idiom of the Northern weavers and spinners. The emblematic titles of his/her series are exchangeable with those of St John Cooper or of any of the other writers for the Rothermere weeklies: 'Snubbed by the Mill, a Thrilling Industrial Romance' (*MN*, 1919), 'A Mill Girl's Soul' (*GF*, 1920), 'A Work-girl's Temptation' (*GFL*, probably 1922), 'Cinderella of the Loom' (*WWL*, probably 1921), 'Bess o' Bolton. This is What Happened to Sweet Bess o' Bolton the Belle of the Mill' (*WWL*, 1923). The stories stand out for their genuine concern with social conflicts and their militant class consciousness, conspicuous even in a genre distinguished by its realism.

Three other names recur in the pages of the weeklies and deserve to be mentioned: Effie Scott, Madge Crichton and Lewis Essex. Scott had a knack for complicated mystery stories set against the background of popular seaside resorts (Blackpool was a favourite) and wrote for the Press's weeklies and later for D. C. Thompson's *Red Letter Library*. 'Lewis Essex' was, probably, one of the pseudonyms of Ursula Harvey Bloom, who contributed regularly to the Press's weeklies and to middle-class fortnightlies such as the *Violet Magazine, Red Magazine* and *Yellow Magazine*.

The newer story papers modified the classic, Lancashire romance. *Peg's Paper* was initially aimed at workers in the cotton and wool industries (legend has it that Mollie Kennedy, its architect and first editor, lived in Wigan to get first-hand knowledge of local manners and local idiom). It was, without doubt, a working-class periodical, possessed of that strong sense of identity which Richard Hoggart described as the 'Them-and-Us' dichotomy. *Peg* advocated friendliness, solidarity and a tribal loyalty to one's clan, class and neighbourhood. Yet these values were distinctly less manifest than in the older Edwardian weeklies and they were slowly being eroded. The heroine in a typical *Peg's Paper* serial is invariably 'of the people', but rarely a mill lass; the locus of action is not Lancashire but London, the French Riviera and non-existent Ruritanian principalities; dialect is hardly ever used and, on those rare occasions that it is, there is a clear preference for Cockney. Compiling a check list of serials published between May 1919 and December 1928, I discovered seven that can be classified as Lancashire stories proper – that is, stories set in a Lancashire mill. Of these, three appeared in 1919, two in 1920 and two in 1921. The fiction pages of the middle and late twenties abound with wildly escapist yarns and domestic melodramas which have nothing of the realism of the industrial romance.

The mill-romance proper departed from its Victorian and Edwardian antecedents in one significant way: the female persona became the *exclusive* emblem of the working man's virtues. Lancastrian womanhood, not Lancashire or Northern 'folk', came to epitomise a set of 'authentic' values of the British working class: a simplicity that is not simplemindedness, an unbending spirit, fierce independence and a defiant local chauvinism – curiously coupled with class allegiance. Significantly, the nearest equivalent to this image can be found neither in the boys' weeklies, nor in fiction for adult males or mixed audiences, but in the performance of a variety artist such as Gracie Fields. To her audience, the Rochdale-born performer (who had once been a 'tenter') was working-class femininity incarnate. She was not strictly a singer, nor merely a comedian, but an 'expressive' actress and a true successor of Marie Lloyd. J. B. Priestley's famous description of Gracie in his *English Journey* may also be applied to the figure of the mill girl:

Gracie Fields . . . is not only the most popular and most dominating personality of the English variety stage but is also a sort of essence of Lancastrian femininity. Listen to her for a quarter of an hour and you will learn more about Lancashire women and Lancashire than you would from a dozen books on these subjects. All the qualities are there: shrewdness, homely simplicity, irony, fierce independence, an impish delight in mocking whatever is thought to be affected and pretentious. That is Lancashire.[3]

But why was it Lancastrian femininity, and not, for instance, Yorkshire or Cockney womanhood, that became the popular symbol of working-class characteristics and values? And, more important, why did this happen in the twenties? Why did this particular symbol emerge at the very time when Lancashire and the Lancashire cotton industry were at a low ebb? Lancashire, to repeat Engels's trivialised remark, had been 'the classic soil on which English manufacture has achieved its masterwork'. After the 1840s the area, and the 'shock city' of Manchester in particular, had come to symbolise the achievements of the Industrial Revolution as well as the economic and social injustice it had wrought. Lancashire had also been the classic area of female labour, concentrated in the predominantly female weaving-industry. As late as 1920 the proportion of women to men in the cotton industry as a whole was 17 to 10, and over a third of the female labour force consisted of married women – the highest proportion of Britain.[4] It was precisely this combination of historical factors that made the figure of the female loom-operative a national symbol. To explain the incongruence between myth and reality – between the rise, after the war, of a working-class *anima*, and material conditions in Lancashire at that time – the specificities of the romance have to be examined in the context of a number of demographic and economic changes.

In the mill romance proper the world divides into two unequal halves, geographically, socially and culturally apart – the North and the South. The North encompasses the spinning and weaving towns and townships of Lancashire. The rest of the world is referred to as 'the South', a term full of opprobrium that may apply to the Midlands as well as to remoter regions. Significantly, 'to be sent to Coventry', which in the idiom of the stories means 'to be given the cold shoulder', to be ostracised, is the worst possible insult:

it happens that tha'rt aboot t'only friend she's got left here. . . . We've sent her to Coventry – all of us.[5]

We've sent you to Coventry. . . . You've betrayed your own workmates, and we are going to see to it that you don't do it again![6]

We're sending Winnie Dawson to Coventry. And if tha go on chattering to her, we shall tak' it that tha'rt siding wi' her against us.[7]

The North–South dichotomy may be traced back to the social novels of the 1840s and it evokes an image of Lancashire that is ambivalent and somewhat equivocal, juxtaposing dynamic vigour and coarse materialism (notably in Mrs Gaskell's *North and South* and Disraeli's *Coningsby* and *Sybil*). What is so peculiar to the popular mill stories is that they present Lancashire as the nub of a curiously centripetal world. And this imaginary Lancashire is shown to the reader not from the point of view of a detached (if sympathetic) observer, but from that of an insider, the raconteur who identifies with his or her working-class characters. The 'other world', outside Lancashire, is alien and alienating. It is undefined and incomprehensible and, therefore, threatening.

By contrast, the urban landscape of the North is familiar and hospitable and the characters are in harmony with it. The details in that landscape are minutely depicted. And the feel of life in it is invoked by the systematic use of dialect, by descriptions of everyday life in the workplace and by the crude but stiffly stylised illustrations. Boldly drawn in black and white, these present a glaring contrast to the fanciful Art Deco drawings of the up-market product. Rarely is the urban environment made beautiful. Back-to-back terrace houses, cobbled alleys, dirty canals and ugly High Streets – all are realistically described. Yet the grim realism of the descriptive parts of the narrative is softened by a personal, affectionate tone that makes these descriptions cheerful and optimistic. 'Branchester,' begins a typical serial by Earl Danesford, 'for all its dirt and grime, for all its stark, squat houses and teeming cluttered streets, could show you some of the most wondrous lilies. . . . And Branchester knew it and was proud of it.'[18] The direct address ('Branchester . . . could show you') is characteristic and re-establishes that intimate relation between the narrator–guide and an audience which expected such familiarity and appreciated it. A passage from another favourite by W. E. Groves reads,

It was dark now, but the lights were springing up everywhere – along the canal, and from the High-Street. The huge chimneys from the mill just loomed out, too. A grim, grimy sort of town this, but prosperous, paying its way even in these bad times and with a magnificent future as soon as the tide was turned.[9]

'Mill Lass o' Mine', by Henry St John Cooper, opens with a stiffly adjectival passage, interchangeable with numerous others:

The Headbury Mills were a huge, ugly, forbidding-looking block of yellow brick buildings rising many floors high, covering an immense space of ground. . . . Headbury had been nothing five-and-twenty years ago – a mere waste, with a few derelict cottages here and there –

when Roger Burton [the self-made mill-owner who eventually wins the heart of the madcap heroine] had come here and built that small shed that was to prove the beginning of an immense business.[10]

North and South do meet. The classic collision between the antipodal two Englands is conventionally reflected in the clichéd encounter between the mill operative and the oily and idle flirt from the South, an easily identifiable and remorselessly lampooned type. Typically, the Southerner (a Londoner, or even a foreigner) who ventures to penetrate the closed world of the Northern town is fiercely resisted. In 'A Lass of Lancashire', Ivan Strenoff, a millionaire spy from Moscow (a rather dubious combination), descends on a small community near Manchester and kidnaps, by mistake, the plucky Poppy Merridew. Of course, the indomitable weaver scares off the villainous Russian and his gang and rescues single-handed her imperilled bosom pal, Natalie Nef, whom Strenoff is really after (Natalie is, in fact, an Anglo-Russian aristocrat compelled to 'rough it' in the mill and to learn the hard way what life is about). The following passage is typical:

> 'You're going to be sensible,' he said. 'That's just as well. We don't want to use force.'
> 'Not more than you have used already, for instance', Poppy said sarcastically.
> She was not going to show the white feather, 'Lancashire and proud of it.' Such has been her motto all through life. It was possible that she was in considerable danger just now, but she would keep her spirit up all the time. . . .
> 'I've never met any one quite like this Poppy Merridew before' (quoth Strenoff) which was true enough. It was the first time that Strenoff had come into contact with a Lancashire lass.[11]

Elsewhere Sidney Flint, the proverbial West End toff, is rebuked by an Oldham mill girl:

> Kate laughed when he complimented her on her dancing. 'Ay but I'm more used to clog-dancing. . . . During Wakes-Week they 'a' special bands on the piers at Blackpool. Hast ever been to Blackpool during a Wakes Week?'
> He murmured that he had not had that pleasure.
> 'Ah, well, tha've missed a treat, that's all I can say. I reckon that good

owd Blackpool is t'best place in all t'world, special at Wakes Week!
There is every thing! There's t'ball-rooms in t'Tower and Winter
Gardens and then t'special dances on the piers, Fiene!'[12]

The encounter between North and South may conclude – though it
seldom does – in the marriage, both literal and metaphorical, of these
separate worlds. The toff – mill-girl encounter had a popular equivalent in
the romance between a male mill-hand and a Southern lady, a curious
reversal of the customary sex roles in the Cinderella formula. But the
resemblance to the formula is superficial, because significantly, in the mill
romance the bridegroom does not benefit materially from the union. The
Southerner has to prove herself worthy of her mate and the community of
operatives by doing manual work and climbing up the labour hierarchy.
Most stories of this type have a Perdita theme as sub-plot, though here
again the old formula is inverted: instead of a shepherd's daughter who
turns out to be a princess, we invariably have an aristocrat who proves to
be 'a daughter of the people'.[13]

Underneath the bravura of the words 'Lancashire and proud of it' there
is a sensible attitude towards life and love. Society is static and mobility
by marriage improbable (though not altogether impossible) and undesira-
ble. Most importantly, marriage as a means of improving the woman's
social or economic status is categorically condemned. To forsake one's
'own people' – which may denote a clan, a community or a class – is to
violate the code of friendship and solidarity. This is perhaps why there are
so few Cinderella, Pamela and Perdita stories in the weeklies of the older
type. On the other hand, these do include some stories of romantic rivalry
between a mill-hand and a toff, fighting for the heart and hand of a mill
girl. Usually it is the honest, industrious Lancastrian who wins. On the
whole, the concept of marriage as a bond that benefits economically or
socially one or both of the parties is alien to the spirit of the Lancashire
romance. Matrimony is not an economic partnership, or a sanctioned
sexual relationship, but a lifelong friendship between two adolescents, an
extension of the 'matiness' of the mill.

The new weeklies represent an altogether different attitude. There are
social tensions, but they are soluble. Hypergamy – that is, marriage above
one's (usually the bride's) station – is the rule rather than the exception.
Characteristically, the symbolic encounter between the two Englands
takes place not in a provincial Northern town but in the metropolis. The
North–South dichotomy has a parallel in the familiar division of London,
the locus of most of the serials in *Peg's Paper* and *Polly's Paper*, into two
neighbouring but socially and culturally distinct parts: the East and West

Ends. These symbolic territories reflect the separate worlds of poor and rich, 'us' and 'them'. But society here is not as immutable as in the mill romance. Love smooths the tensions between the classes. And mobility is invariably upwards: it is the working-class heroine who leaves her home environment (the industrial Northern town, a small village or the East End) and moves up West. The symbolic movement is a change of place, as well as of social status. Compare a typical encounter between a West End toff and a Cockney with the passages quoted earlier. The following is from 'Blinkeyes', a serialisation of a film starring Betty Balfour and Tom Douglas, which appeared in *Peg's Paper* between March and September 1927. Millionaire Kenneth Clay becomes infatuated with little Blinkeyes, whom he watches dancing at street corners in her native Whitechapel. In the eighth instalment the bold Cockney still addresses him in her native dialect:

> 'I 'ate all aristocrats'. . . .
>
> 'But, my dear child, I'm not an aristocrat', Clay informed her. 'My father was merely a millionaire who made a fortune out of pickles. Certainly, I have a sister who is the wife of an Earl, but beyond that, I have no connection with the aristocracy. I'm merely a middle-class man!' . . .
>
> 'Don't tell me! You're one of the nobs right enough, and you can't 'ide it up! You've got Park Lane and Leicester Square written all over you. Think I want to marry a bloomin' duke and live in a swell 'ouse full of 'ot-'ouse flowers! Give me the East-End and some smells! It's what I'm used to – fish and chips and Chinese joss-sticks and river mud, all mixed up. If you take me away, I'd die.'[14]

Fifteen instalments on she surrenders. The final episode takes place in a South American jungle and the removal of the protagonists from the scene of social conflict to exotic surroundings is revealing. The final words are reserved for the loquacious Blinkeyes: 'It's Heaven', she murmurs. She has learnt not to drop her aitches. This is not the sort of ending typical of the Lancashire romance.

In the Lancashire romance life oscillates between home and the mill, representing the antipodal poles of domesticity and work. Authority, whether the authority of parents and elders or that of employers, is constantly questioned and often defied. The parental home is relegated to the background, and parents and siblings, on those occasions when they make an appearance, are merely decorative or grossly caricatured. Significantly, foster families, guardians and custodians outnumber natural parents. In the tradition of popular juvenile literature, the female character is a free agent, homeless and rootless – an orphan or a foundling, an outsider, poor and unprotected, but unencumbered by family, lineage or a past. Unlike in the post-war boys' magazines, the role of school and education in the girls' weeklies is peripheral. The boarding-school series, which had enjoyed a certain vogue before the war, lost its appeal to working-class female audiences in the early twenties. In the newer periodicals the school story is not conspicuous. And school, like the state, the Church, the propertied classes and the patriarchal home, is an abstract entity associated with 'them'. The imaginary, Utopian community of female workers is thus self-sufficient and autonomous, completely cut off from the outer world. Life centres on the mythical mill, which is more than a work place. It is the sole source of livelihood; the hub of social life; the stage on which personal and social dramas unfold; a substitute for home and family; the locus of romance; and, in a broader, symbolic sense, a metaphor for society and the universe.

The heroine's primary allegiance is to the community of her fellow workers. Filial obligations or romantic relations come second. The key words in the vocabulary of the mill are 'pal', 'mate' and 'popular' – neutral words that can be applied to males and females:

She is the most popular girl at Carbury gaffer – ay, one of t'best workers too.[15]

We've only known thee for eighteen months but tha've made thyself popular.[16]

. . . he was a popular hero at the mills. A young fellow of twenty-three, he had been captain of the football team for the past four seasons . . . up in the North they swear by *football* – many of the girls as well as the men.[17]

Defection to the 'other' camp, or a romantic entanglement with an 'enemy', is a serious violation of the code of behaviour; 'she was one of us all along – a working-class lass, who married a working-class man. And she's gone to the enemy';[18] or, 'Tha gives thyself airs – airs that seems silly enough to me.'[19] Against such breaches the community has its own punitive measures, of which the most humiliating is a 'sending to Coventry' (see above, p. 125). The distinctive local idiom reflects notions of friendship and solidarity of class as well as gender. For the idealised world of the weaving-shed is that of a compact and exclusive sorority. The only males who are admitted to it are the overlooker or 'tackler' and the owner or 'gaffer' – both, significantly, of working-class origins.

This intimate yet somewhat claustrophobic world is faithfully constructed in long, richly descriptive passages. The daily routine in the sheds, the machinery, relationships in the mill – all these and many other details are painstakingly recorded, as the following extracts show. The first introduces a 'tenter' – a part-time pupil – apprentice in her early teens, who is paid by a skilled weaver in charge of four or more looms – on her first day in the mill. The initiation of the tenter into the community of workers has a symbolic parallel in the introduction of the reader to imaginary Lancashire.

They passed through the outer office, across a yard, and past some sheds, from each one of which came the sound of whirring machinery. . . . As they entered a man approached them. This was the overlooker of that particular shed – the 'tackler', as he is commonly known to the mill girls. The gaffer spoke a few words to him, and they then went over to the looms, to where a girl named Meg Burnley was working. 'I want you to take over this girl', the gaffer said. 'She'll be your tenter for the time being, until she picks things up'. . . .

'I can't afford it, gaffer', said Meg briefly.

'Can't afford it?'

'Not wi' work slack as it is now, I can't afford to pay my tenter out o' my wages.'

The mill owner smiled.

'I'm not asking you to do that miss. . . . I want her to learn the job, that's all.' . . . When work comes in with a rush, an operator controlling four looms may employ a 'tenter' – generally a young girl straight from school – who acts as an assistant – pieces together broken threads, and so forth. In that way she may save the operator a deal of time, and is paid by her separately. . . .[20]

There was a clatter of clogs on the cobbled yard. Shawls in Lancashire have been discarded to a great extent, but the clogs are still worn by the majority of mill girls for their work, leaving the daintier footwear, the high-heeled shoes, for wear in leisure time.[21]

There is in these and numerous similar descriptions an admission that the world they set out to recapture no longer exists. The photographic attention to the most trivial details and the laborious manner of the narrative are aimed at that part of the audience to whom a cotton mill was *terra incognita*. Readers are taken by the confident, knowledgeable narrator on tour of instruction through the unfamiliar territories of the weaving towns. It is, despite the characteristic realism of the genre, a nostalgic journey through time to an idealised and rapidly vanishing world. The result is an odd mixture of undisguised sentimentality and shrewd observation, a mixture which manifests the central dilemma of the genre and the paradox behind it. The explosion of romantic fiction on Lancashire coincided with the worst crisis ever in the cotton industry. Of course, Lancashire had suffered periodic depressions before, but the war brought about one from which it seemed impossible to recover. Egypt and India ceased to be Britain's major markets for cheap cloth. Export production of cotton fell prodigiously and the industry was fatally affected by the speculation craze of 1919 and early 1920, when Lancashire mills worth £10,815,000 in total were bought for £71,815,000.[22] The inevitable result of the over-capitalisation of an ailing industry was the liquidation of mills and chronic unemployment and underemployment through the decade. During the relatively stable years 1923–6 unemployment in the cotton industry reached 12.3 per cent, 1 per cent above the national figure. In 1930 unemployment reached a peak of 29.3 per cent, 20 per cent above the figure for London.[23] Furthermore, one of the main features of the post-war economy was the decline of the old 'staple industries' – cotton, the mining-industry, ship-building and engineering – and the rise of new ones, manufacturing consumer goods. This structural change was accompanied by migration from North to South. The social histories of the twenties and surveys of the early thirties record the reversal of the nineteenth-century relation between North and South. G. D. H. and M. J. Cole, Carr-Saunders and D. Caradog-Jones, and Allen Hutt describe a depopulated impoverished Lancashire and a prosperous South, and exactly the same picture emerges from the documented journey records of George Orwell and J. B. Priestley.

But the map of England drawn in the mill romance is different. Fictional Lancashire is a mirror image of the real one – not a 'problem area' but, as formerly, the thriving centre of an industrial nation. The model of the 1920s curiously resembles that of the 1840s and 1850s: a toiling, affluent North is juxtaposed to a decaying, corrupted South. Similarly the working class, personified in the figure of the female weaver, is perceived and presented as the backbone of industrial England. The idealisation of the cotton industry and of manual work during an age of spreading automatisation, when the demand for unskilled cheap labour soared, is equally significant. In the Lancashire yarn non-manual work is debilitating, unmanly and, of course, inferior to factory work. The middle-class clerk and the shop assistant belong to a gallery of easily recognisable caricatures.

The explosion of mill-girl fiction was a response to a three pronged transition: a socio-economic transition from the traditional staple industries to new ones; a change in the balance between the industrial North (notably Lancashire) and the Home Counties; and, most importantly, a transformation in the physical and cultural environment of most of Britain's working-class female population. As in any transitional age, so in the twenties, there could be two responses to such significant changes: a conscious adjustment, or even a deliberate assimilation, to the new way of life; or a withdrawal from the real world to the security of old, familiar traditions. *Peg's Paper* and its many imitations represent the former course, the mill girls' papers the latter. The mill-girl weeklies clung to a vanishing world. Their construction of Utopian urban community of female workers based upon solidarity of class and gender was a protection against 'modernity' and the emergence of mass culture. It is, perhaps, significant that the *Girls' Friend*, the first weekly for working-class women, ceased publication in 1931. The Great Depression, which finally ruined the Lancashire cotton industry, also gave the Lancashire romance its *coup-de-grâce*.

9

The Emigrant: Romance and the Empire

This wonderful, sun-drenched, multi-coloured paradise. . . . The sense of boundless space and freedom. The glorious, sparkling air of the mountains, the delicious coolness of the evenings after the hot and sweltering day – all, all were beckoning to her now, irresistibly, as they have beckoned to countless others, as they will beckon so long as Rhodesia the Golden exists.
(Earl Danesford, 'The Adorable Flirt', 1926)

The remedy is to find suitable mates for spinsters by a consular system. This would allow a constant flow of virgins to the colonies and dependencies.
(A. M. Ludovici, *Women: A Vindication*, 1921)

Alongside the tendencies towards insularity, entrenchment and regionalism there emerged another. Its brand-mark was nationalism. Its symbol was the Empire. Its main characteristic was the blurring of social differences and the effacement of class consciousness. The literary form in which this tendency manifested itself was the magazine romance set in the Commonwealth, or in a British colony of dependency. Where the world of Lancashire was narrow and claustrophobic, that of the Empire romance was broad and free. Where the former was intimate, close and familiar, the latter offered a new, adventurous way of life in remote, exotic places. The broadening of the horizons of magazine fiction was, of course, related to the impact of the First World War. Michael Joseph, quick to detect changes in attitudes among publishers and editors, noted the significant disappearance of the pre-war taboo on stories set in foreign countries.[1] The exotic romantic serial was gradually supplanting the traditional domestic or industrial melodrama. Some publishers still had a bias towards an English scene and English characters. F. J. Lamburn instructed new contributors to *Pearson's Weekly*,

Keep the scenes of a story mainly to England. The average reader of
Pearson's Weekly doesn't know enough about countries abroad and the
people who live there to want to read solely about them. Let the
characters go abroad and have experiences abroad, but let them come
back to England before the story ends, otherwise the story loses a lot of
its appeal for readers. All the characters should be English unless their
nationality has a definite dealing with the story, such as Dr Fu Manchu
has with stories. Introduce, if you like, a French Count or a Russian
Bolshevik, but keep the main characters British.[2]

The rule obviously did not apply to the new girls' and women's papers,
where traditionalist 'English' plots were far outnumbered by adventure
and travel stories and Ruritanian fantasies. In all three of these genres,
however, the setting has a limited role. 'Abroad' is a place to travel to, to
experience a resplendent and exciting life in, but only for a while. Home is
England. Even the most fanciful stories conclude and, occasionally begin
on English soil. The story papers of the Amalgamated Press were guided
by an altogether different policy. Their fiction pages abound with stories
in which remote lands are not merely resorts of pleasure and respite, but
actually places of residence. And the characters are neither travellers nor
adventurers, but immigrants and colonisers, in search of a permanent
home and a new, fulfilling way of life.

Examples abound. The sevenpenny *Violet Magazine* carried in January
1928 six 'complete tales' on the English emigrant who puts down roots in
one or another part of the Empire. Four tales appeared in February, five in
March and four in April. The titles are emblematic: 'Silly Little Woman: A
Romance of Wild Places and Wild Men', 'Something We Don't Know
What: Romance and Adventure in Wild Places', 'A Girl Alone: Australia
and Home', 'The Hopeless Case: A Romance of South Africa', and so on.
Two other all-story fortnightlies, identical to *Violet* in appearance, the
Harmsworth Red Magazine and the *Yellow Magazine*, specialised in
emigrant stories and Westerns with 'feminine' appeal. The *Red Magazine*
Christmas number of 1920 included the opening instalment of a 'Veldt
serial', 'Mashona Child: A story of South Africa and England'; the first in a
series of complete, self-contained Wild West stories; and a 5000-word
Western. The first issue of 1921 carried in addition to two series two
short 'Canada stories'. Even the most traditionalist mill-girl periodicals
were not proof against change. By the mid 1920s most them published
Empire love yarns regularly. The following titles, chosen at random from
the Press's weeklies and 'libraries', are, characteristically, more outspoken

than those of stories in middle-class magazines: 'A Bride for Australia: A Natural Love Story of the Feelings and Experiences of a Pretty Girl Emigrant' (*GF*), 'Bad Man – A Rare Pulsing Story of the West! A Romance that Goes Straight to the Heart of Every Reader' (*GF*), 'Man Apart – A Vigorous Romance of the Far North. A Thrilling Story of Canada' (*Eve's Own Stories*), 'The Girl Emigrants' (*GFL*), 'The Girl Bushranger: A Thrilling Romance of the Wilds' (*GFL*), and so on.

Several factors combined to prepare the ground for the explosion of romantic fiction set in the Empire. Thematically and ideologically the genre may be conceived in terms of both a continuation of and a break from Victorian and Edwardian imperialist fiction, whose golden age covered the years between the partition of Africa at the Berlin Conference (1878) and the Boer War. Of the twin concepts that had formed the basis of the ideology of the 'White Man's Burden', racism and altruism, the Empire romance embraced only the first.[3] The notion of the Anglo-Saxon as missionary, destined to civilise the coloured populations of the colonised territories, is virtually non-existent in fiction about the Empire for women. More important, the Victorian and Edwardian novel and story were 'masculine' products, written by men, about men, for a predominantly (though not exclusively) male audience. The world depicted in the stories of Henry Rider Haggard, G. A. Henty and Robert Louis Stevenson is a masculine world. The archetypal Empire-builder is the solitary, virile Anglo-Saxon who goes to the colonies, conquers them, rules them justly and ultimately civilises their native inhabitants. Romance is peripheral and, typically, the female characters are merely a foil to the male ones. It is at this point that the post-war romance broke with its nineteenth- and early-twentieth-century predecessors. It substituted female figures for male ones and romance for adventure and, needless to say, was directed at mass female audiences.

The transition from 'masculine' fiction on the Empire to the Empire romance was precipitated by the First World War, which brought about one of those periodic outbursts of interest in the Empire that punctuated British history between the 1870s and the Second World War. The broadening of the horizons of magazine fiction coincided with the revival, described earlier, of popular travel literature and the rise of the oriental love story and film. Large, heterogeneous audiences became acquainted with remote, exotic places, unfamiliar to the majority of nineteenth-century magazine-readers.

More important, however, is the connection between the emergence of the Empire romance and the debate on the surplus-of-women problem. The flowering of a genre that celebrated an imaginary society in which females were scarce and males plentiful may be seen as a response to the anxieties caused by the imbalance between the sexes. Significantly, it was in Rothermere's story papers that the romance advocating female emigration flourished. True, Rothermere's political interests alone do not account for the amount and the scope of Empire love stories in the Amalgamated Press's weeklies and fortnightlies. In the first place, neither was affected by the change of ownership in 1926. Secondly, it is impossible to find out if or to what extent the owner of the *Daily Mail* was personally involved in the editorial side of his magazines. It seems, however, that it was not merely fortuitous that the vogue for emigrant stories coincided with discussion of the 'superfluous' woman. And, even if it were, popular fiction on the Empire clearly dramatised the acute fears of a perturbed, demographically imbalanced society.

There are two patterns of romance. In the first, the emigrant story proper, an Englishwoman, newly arrived from the 'Old Country', finds a mate, a home and purposeful life in the unpopulated wilderness of a British dominion or colony. In the second pattern, the heroine, born of British parents in the 'New Country', is pursued and won by an Englishman. In both these patterns the main emphasis is upon the national and racial identity of the protagonists. The characters must be white and Anglo-Saxon. Their affiliation to race replaces other allegiances – to class, to the community, to occupation and even to gender. The Empire romance describes an imaginary classless and sexless society of free Britons, based on the racial purity of its members. The purity of blood is far more important than in the desert-love story, which condones marriage and extra-marital relations between white people of different nations (the salient example being the unfortunate union in *The Sheik* between the Sheik's Castilian mother and his English father) and may even tolerate interbreeding. Such lapses are categorically condemned in the Empire romance. Hence the otherwise incomprehensible obsession with the colour, physiognomy and physique of the male and female characters, particularly the latter. 'Some said that her mother was a lady born from England,' reads a typical example

> others that young Mrs Morgan had been a lady's maid in Sydney. And someone else had it that she had been on the stage. Anyhow, whatever was the truth, she had given to her girl, Sally, a beauty that was marvellous, dangerous, exquisite. Eyes of the darkest, clearest blue, a complexion to conjure with, hair of a deep, rich gold, in which shone, danced and sparkled a hundred reddish lights. . . .[4]

The evocation of the country of origin, the attention given to the smallest detail in the heroine's appearance, the fascination with her complexion ('of deep rich gold', yet not dark) and, finally, the use of an idiom that smacks of popular Darwinism – all these elements occur interchangeably in hundreds of descriptions. Henry St John Cooper was obsessed with the origin of his female characters. Several of his most successful plots revolve around the mysterious birth of his immigrant or settler: is she English, or a half-breed, the fruit of a forbidden love between an Englishman and a coloured woman? As with the imperialistic adventure story, so with the Empire romance, the hybrid is at the bottom of the social hierarchy, an outcast, the lowest of all human beings. Cooper constantly implies that the heroine is not Anglo-Saxon, only to reassure readers of the purity of her blood:

> Sally Verriner was young, not yet eighteen. She moved with the grace of a panther, or an Indian woman, whose body had never been hampered by the inventions of civilisation. Her hair – had the hot sun let it alone – might have been dark brown. As it was, it was bleached into a curious tawny shade of gold. Her eyes were grey and direct, honest, tender, yet sometimes they could be stern even menacing [a native's eyes are never 'honest'], their lashes were very dark, long and curled. If the sun had played tricks with Sally Verriner's hair, her complexion had defied its greatest effort, except that round and about the tiptilted, dainty, delicate little nose, there was a powder of gold-dust like freckles.[5]

Sally, it later transpires, is no other than Ermine Estella Verriner, heiress to a great fortune and in the best Cooperian tradition a former 'head girl'. In another favourite serial, 'Pearl of the West', published in the *Girls' Friend* and reprinted in the *Girls' Friend Library*, the heroine, who could be Sally's identical twin, is possessed of 'The most perfect and wonderful face. . . . The skin creamy white, yet tinged with a golden brown from the kiss of the wind and the sun. The lips just a trifle full, but scarlet as the poppies of far away England nestling among the stalks of the green wheat.'[6] The key words are, of course, 'creamy white skin'. The reference to the 'scarlet . . . poppies of far away England' is, however, equally revealing. For in 1926 the mention of this symbol of the battlefields of Flanders could still move a British audience.

The new environment of the immigrant is diametrically opposed to that depicted in the Lancashire romance. The ideal, imaginary mill and the urban landscape surrounding it are feminine territories, and the omnipresent sorority of mill-hands is suffocating and oppressive. By contrast, the world the immigrant encounters and ultimately comes to terms with is distinctly masculine. It is unconfined and untrammelled.

And, most important, it is a world in which women are outnumbered by men. The Australian sheep stations, the South African and Rhodesian mining-camps and cattle farms, the icy wastes of Alaska (a favourite setting, though not a British territory) and the Canadian forests are all male-inhabited spaces. Not surprisingly, the most typical sub-plot in the romance evolves from a clash between two males over a female. Characteristically it is the worthy hero (a cowboy in the Wild West stories; a rancher in stories set in Australia and New Zealand) who outmatches the intriguingly attractive outlaw. In the context of the Empire romance, the universal theme of the triangle acquires a specific meaning: the superfluous males compete for the scarce and elusive female. The competition and the stylised, ritual fight conventionally concluding it echo the vulgarised notions of the Darwinist concept of 'the survival of the fittest' and 'natural selection'. The villain conveniently withdraws from the stage, or perishes in a symbolically violent act. He may be captured by the representatives of law (an end typical of the Wild West story), or he may be killed by the hero, or a 'natural' calamity – flood, fire, snowstorm, drought – may be visited upon him.

For a 'feminine' genre the Empire romance is exceedingly violent. And, in contrast to the desert-love yarn, violence is not sexual, though it is a means to 'get a woman'. The realistic and often unsavoury fight scenes are the only ones in which the female figures assume the role of passive onlooker, helplessly watching the warring males. In 'Four Square', a representative *Violet Magazine* story, Conn Parrat, a renegade station-manager, and the worthy Phil Eshelby almost perish in a raging 'swaggie' fire before the latter can win the heart of the lovely station-owner, Mona Flowerdew. In 'The Idolator', also published in *Violet*, there are only three characters – Helen and Rex Bronner and Simon Halket. Husband and wife, both notorious bushrangers, plan to rob Halket and kill him. But Helen falls in love with the upstanding Briton, elopes with him and is shot by her vengeful husband. Before the story concludes, the miraculously recovering heroine and her saviour watch, from a safe distance, the villain disappearing into the desert, where he will probably die of thirst. 'The Way of a Woman' is another variation on the theme of the male hunter and the hunted woman. Dick Trail and Ben Dorne are rival hunters, competing with each other for the lovely Delia Show. After Dick has tricked his prey into a marriage of misery and humiliation, Ben resorts to brute force: 'It would only be justice, the justice of all wild things, all primitive things, to fight for the woman they love, to fight to the death.'[7] Dick, however, is to be trapped in one of his own bear traps. The imagery is transparent.

The immigrant's encounter with the new, wild environment reflects the familiar culture-*versus*-nature conflict and may conclude in two different ways. The young Englishwoman, a personification of the old, civilised way of life, may exert a mitigating influence upon her masculine surroundings. More characteristically, she yields to them. Rather than refine the male-inhabited environment and emasculate it, she herself becomes wild, hard and resilient. What makes her adjustment to the new world possible is a combination of physical prowess and a juvenile, masculine appearance. Domestic figures are very few. Women play some of the traditional feminine roles assigned to them in related genres such as the Western or the adventure story: ministering to the sick, reforming sinners and even keeping house.[8] But more typically they are presented outside the home. The ideal heroine is an Amazon who can face hardship like any man and who can shoot, hunt and ride. She is, or appears to be, an androgynous adolescent. Significantly, even adult women are depicted as boyish and are often mistaken for young men. It is precisely this effacement of gender marks and of distinct 'womanly' behaviour that enables the heroine to be accepted by the male characters as an equal. She is admitted to the intimate fraternity of cowboys, or rangers, not because of her feminine qualities, but because of her resemblance to men. They often regard her as a young 'pal', a fellow wanderer and adventurer, and address her as a kid brother. Cooper's ideal type is the indomitable colleen who looks and behaves like a young boy: 'She wore no womanly flounces and frills: hers was a workaday costume that scarcely differed at all from her father's';[9] or, 'she looked like a very slender, graceful and dainty boy in her quaint costume that was half womanly, half boyish'.[10] In Angus Leigh's 'On the Edge of the World: A Romance of the Australian Wilds', Bob Durrant finds in a deserted shanty a delirious boy afflicted by 'the fever' ('a common Australian disease'). He nurses the invalid, who, it later transpires, is a woman. Now it is Bob's turn to succumb to 'the fever', and the woman nurses him. Waking from delirium he again mistakes her for an attractive young boy, 'spruce and neat and lovely in leggings, in a rough, brown shirt'.[11] The curious mixture of innocent camaraderie and implicit homosexuality seems out of place in an editorially censored girls' paper. Yet it *is* there, in the popular transvestite sub-plot as well as in the ambiguity lent by such conventional epithets as 'dainty' and 'quaint', or, in combination, 'spruce and neat'. The latter may even be applied to middle-aged characters who have seen and known the world.

The vocabulary of androgyny is revealing. For the yielding of the immigrant to her new environment does not involve the development of a feminine sexual identity. Unlike the violated captive in the desert romance, she is not transformed into a 'real woman'. True, the Empire yarn is full of sexual tensions, but they are implicit. Sexual experience and, needless to say, sexual violence are taboo. Technically and thematically the genre is and was seen as clean. Even marriage, the conclusion of each and every story, is a platonic bond between pals. Thus the character of the immigrant never develops or changes. Hers is the blissful state of eternal, never-ending pubescence. Even the world around her is timeless. Apart from insignificant, passing references to women's hair-style or clothes there is no sense of time in the stories. The genre has no monopoly on the idealisation of adolescence. Magazine fiction has always glamorised youth and has tended to relegate sexuality, marriage and motherhood to an imaginary future, coveted, but unreal and unexplored. What is peculiar to the Empire romance is the centrality of the place of action: it is, more than any of the other geographically specific genres of the period, defined solely by its locus.

'Empire' yarns may be divided into roughly three geographical groups. The first group, sometimes known as 'Wild West' stories, are set in Alaska and the English-speaking provinces of Canada and around the US–Canadian border. The second group, the 'romances of the wilds', relate to Australia and New Zealand. The third group, which enjoyed a vogue in the late twenties, are the 'romances of the Veldt', set in South Africa and the regions of Matabeleland and Mashonaland in Southern Rhodesia, with the railway line from Cape Town to Bulawayo and Salisbury as both real and symbolic axis. The female characters, undeveloped as they are in their relation to time, are not only perceived but also presented in their relation to the open expanses of the new continents. Urban space, the matrix of the industrial and domestic melodrama, is depicted only rarely and has but one function: to provide a contrast to nature, unspoilt and unaffected by humans. Home is seldom described. Man-made dwellings, on those rare occasions when they are depicted, are simple, almost Spartan, poorly furnished and distinctly masculine. It is in the open, limitless spaces that the heroine is in her element. Characteristically, the development of her relation to the wild environment is articulated in the stylised, stiffly conventional riding-scene.

As in the desert romance, riding has various functions. It is not merely a sport but also a symbolic activity endowed with purifying and even redemptive powers; the ultimate test of the heroine's physical prowess and endurance, and, most important, a metaphor for her dynamic rapport with the surrounding landscape. Descriptions of riding in the wilderness constitute the best parts of the narrative. They are competently written, with an eye for detail, and they often help authenticate the fatuous plots. The following example is from 'The Woman Who Had Lots of Pluck', a typical romance of the wilds, set in New Zealand and Australia, serialised in *Violet Magazine* in August 1926 and later reprinted in several of the Amalgamated Press's 'libraries'. Hermione Otway, a disreputable actress, accompanies Jim Coreless, a down-at-heel sheep-station master, on a mysterious voyage whose destination she does not know. Their taciturn progress in the wilds is carefully chronicled. Special attention is given to the terrain, the flora and fauna:

> Larks sang overhead in the white blue sky and the road was bordered on either side by mile upon mile of white and pink flowering orchards; the hills around were almost bare of vegetation, but holding in their rocky hollows purple and mauve and indigo shadows; the swiftly swirling river upon which they had looked down last night, was green like clouded jade – it brought the snow-water down from the distant Southern Alps – and all along its banks were piled high the white mountains of silt cast out by the gold dredgers of a former day. After following the road for some miles they struck in along a bridle-track amongst the hills. Here it was necessary to ride in single file. Coreless rode first, the pack horse followed, and Hermione with the dogs brought up the rear. . . . The sun was dropping in the west when they entered the valley down which followed a rocky, tree-fern borded stream, and where a few forest trees – pines and black birch – grew amongst the Manuka and low undergrowth. It was possible to ride abreast here and Coreless, pointing to a slab hut on a plateau about half a mile distant, informed the actress that this was his place.[12]

Although the scenic route is described through the eyes of the riders (particularly through those of the heroine), they themselves are effaced to re-emerge only halfway through the passage. Their itinerary is the same on their way back to the civilised, populated world. But the landscape, which before had filled Hermione with high aspirations, now becomes desolate and threatening. Even the auspicious weather turns foul. It is these changes in the landscape and the proximity to urban civilisation and the refined way of life which she loathes that fill the heroine with despair: 'as they rode past the spot where she had sat down on the daisy starred grass in the sunshine only a week before, her heart contracted with a curious pang of loneliness and loss.'[33] The setting is thus not merely a background to the characters. They are themselves details in an integral part of the landscape. The completeness with which they merge into their surroundings is reflected in the deliberate use of pronouns, impersonal nouns and surnames ('he', 'the actress', 'Coreless') instead of, or interchangeably with, first names. The device, and the scene as a whole, seem to have been taken from a Western.[14] Indeed, the writer of this particular story, Lloyd Williams (the name appears in the British Library catalogue but is most probably a pseudonym), specialised in both genres, contributing Westerns to the Amalgamated Press's boys' weeklies and stories of the wilds to the girls' papers. Not only the characters are effaced, but so is the role of the narrator himself. Though no less knowledgeable than the raconteur in the mill romance, the narrator here is much less intrusive. And his tone lacks the directness and warmth of the garrulous narrator – guide in the typical Lancashire serial.

A confident and popular writer such as Cooper, with a large following, had no need to prove his credibility by burdening his readers with superfluous descriptive passages. Consequently his riding-scenes are not crammed with details of the scenery but are full of action. The following, taken from 'Pearl of the West', has all the classic components of the genre: the transvestite sub-plot; the symbolism of riding; and the dynamic interaction between the Amazonian heroine and her environment. It is significant that the scene is described from the point of view of a male spectator who watches the swift movement of the rider, while he himself remains static:

Ahead of him on the trail, the broken track, had appeared suddenly, as though the rocks themselves had disgorged it, the figure of a horse and rider. For a moment, in the hazy mist of the heat, he mistook the rider for a man. A moment later he discovered his mistake. It was a woman – a girl – yet her dress and the manner in which she bestrode the horse suggested a man rather than a woman. . . . She rode a black horse. Horse and rider were perhaps two hundred yards distant from him when he first saw them. There was a slight rise in the rocky ground and both stood against the skyline. . . . It happened in a moment. One instant the great black horse was standing motionless, as though carved in stone; the next it had shied and reared violently. A less skilled rider than she must have been flung down; but she kept her seat, and then, with head down . . . . the horse bolted. It bolted as Brown had never seen any horse in his life bolt. It shot like an arrow, its hoofs clanging on the rocks. He saw its staring, starting eye-balls; he saw in a flash the girl's face, calm, resolute, and unseared. The horse and rider were gone, whirling away in a moment.[15]

The implied eroticism of the ritualistic solitary ride recalls the coded language of the sex novel. The latter part of the scene is a curious reversal of the famous taming-of-the-colt episode in *The Sheik* – a reversal in that in Cooper's apparently 'clean' version it is an excited male who watches the heroine parading her horsemanship and quelling the wild animal. Curiously, tales set in Rhodesia are substantially more intense than those stories set in other parts of the Empire. And, of all the idealised landscapes, the most exalted is that of the Rhodesian Veldt. The region is endowed with mythic powers and the scenes which take place in it are erotically charged. The terrain, characteristically, 'stretches enticingly'; the wind 'turns [one's] blood stirring' and 'scorchingly' kisses one's face; the rim of blue mountains 'invites' one to penetrate it.[16] Clearly the Empire, especially its unpopulous parts, promised not only a challenging life but also, it is hinted, genuine excitement – intriguing because so alien to the conservatism of the story papers.

The Lancashire romance and the love story set in the Empire are realistic fantasies. The apparent contradiction in terms can be explained. Both genres describe ideal imaginary societies. The sorority of mill-hands has, no doubt, some historical basis and the attitudes and values it idealises correspond to and even reflect notions typical to the working-class reader. But this sorority is completely cut off from the sexually and socially heterogeneous outside world. Society, as it is perceived and described in the Empire romance, is even more Utopian. Ostensibly the open landscapes and the towns and settlements depicted in the stories are topographically real. But the 'Golden Rhodesia' (or Canada, or Australia) is essentially Nowhere. Like the Lancastrian sorority, the classless community of Britons is changeless, a world that has reference only to itself. In other words, if the mill-girl melodrama is, essentially, a withdrawal to an idealised past, a movement in time, then the Empire love story is an escape to another place, a movement in space. The realistic element has two different aspects. First, there is the background realism of the Lancashire mill and the locations described in the Empire yarns. Secondly, and more importantly, each of the genres was a response to a specific socio-cultural problem. The nostalgia for the mill and for 'authentic' working-class values was, primarily, a reaction to the significant changes in the texture of life of most of the magazine-reading public. The Empire romance, seemingly a purely escapist form, had its roots in the important debate on the demographic imbalance at home and its wider economic and social implications. In summary, the two genres are realistic fantasies because they are dislocations. The solutions they offer to the acute problems of women are outside their context and time. The modern woman withdraws to a secure past, or she emigrates, never to return to the scene of discord.

Conclusion

'Flapper' did not suddenly vanish from the popular idiom. The equivocal, mysterious term and the host of images it conjured up subsided as they had once emerged, slowly and gradually. They can be found recurring in editorial pages, in novels and in recorded speech till the mid thirties. The furore in Rothermere's dailies had a curious sequel in sporadic outbursts of rhetoric in the spring and summer of 1928.[1] On 30 May 1928 *Punch* gleefully reported on 'the conspicuous absence of a peer who had violently attacked what he was pleased to call the flapper vote'.[2] Over a year later, John Blunt, MP, lamented the recruitment of yet another 'ten thousand flapper voters'[3] to the cohorts of female voters. In 1931 Elinor Glyn produced another of her records of the vagaries of cosmopolitan Bohemia, a collection of colloquial dialogues entitled *The Flirt and the Flapper*, describing an encounter between an eighteenth-century courtesan and a modern flapper. And as late as 1933 Osbert Sitwell referred to 'an old opponent to – as it had been called – the flapper vote'.[4]

The gradual disappearance of the key word of the vocabulary of sexuality reflected a slow but perceptible change in attitudes, which took place around the turn of the decade. It is difficult to draw a dividing-line, because obsession with the modern young woman petered out slowly. And feminine sexuality – indeed, sexuality as such – remained a popular interest through the thirties, especially during their first half. Yet the debate lost the intensity of the previous decade and its scope became significantly smaller. The discussion no longer had a specific *political* reference to make it authentic. After the spring of 1928 the issue of universal female suffrage had no importance. And it was precisely the figure of the disfranchised female and the rhetoric evolved in relation to it that acted as, as it were, the cement holding together the diverse autonomous discourses. The flapper as a popular myth died because it ceased to be politically relevant. And in a pluralistic society over time such relevance is all important, for it elevates the merely fictional or symbolic to popular myth and lends it the capacity actively to stir audiences. Once the specific context that had lent it relevance was gone, the flapper degenerated from myth to the earlier passive form (from 'myth' or fiction of the 'second degree' to mere fiction, to use Roland Barthes's terms).

But there were reasons other than political for the weakening of interest in the young woman, and these should be sought in the broader and complex social and cultural context of the inter-war era. It has now become a cliché to contrast the self-consciously disillusioned twenties to the socially and politically conscious 'devil's decade' that followed them.[5] The post-war decade came to be identified with a tendency towards escapism, assuming diverse cultural forms: indifference to politics and economics; nostalgia; promiscuity in marginal groups; and, in the masses, a collective withdrawal from 'real life' (the expression is the Leavises') to vicarious experiences provided by the new forms of popular entertainment. Conversely, the decade before the Second World War was 'realistic'. Popular interest shifted from forms and styles to economy and international politics. As Orwell was to put it in his penetrating comments on *Tropic of Cancer*, by the early thirties the *homme moyem sensuel* had fallen from grace. The *déclassé* and the libertine had ceased to be emblems of the age. 'The average sensual man is out of fashion. The passive, non-political attitude is out of fashion. Preoccupation with sex and truthfulness about the inner life are out of fashion. American Paris is out of fashion.'[6] The expatriate American is the ultimate metaphor of escapism, a tendency evident, particularly in the form of an obsession with sexuality, in most memoirs and personal histories of the twenties.[7] As I have attempted to show, it was not esoteric but clearly manifested itself in popular writings.

It is tempting to describe the twenties and their aftermath in dialectical terms: a period of release was followed by one of austerity.[8] The archetypes of wife and mother supplanted the image of the female as androgyne. The main danger in such an analysis is that it isolates the decade from its wider historical context. This book, admittedly, has all along emphasised the transitory and historically peculiar, almost to the exclusion of the long-term and universal. Yet, if the phenomenon of the twenties is to be perceived historically, it has to be approached in terms of both continuity and change. Even the most radically novel notions on women did not emerge from a cultural vacuum but were permeated with familiar myths. Indeed, the culturally most significant images − the 'flapper' and the 'superfluous woman' and the 'nymph' − had roots in the past as well as ties with the present, and this was the source of their power.

However, in a final, critical analysis the elements of change outweigh those of continuity. Of the former there are four: the scope of popular debate; the plurality of discourse; the 'new licence'; and, last but by no means least, the significant break with, on the one hand, the mainstream Victorian ideology on sexual and social matters and, on the other, its associated aesthetics. If, to repeat Foucault's trivialised phrase, the history of sex over the last three centuries has been one of continuous discourse on sexuality, then the twenties were a moment of explosion marked by a quickening of that discourse, which became extraordinarily intense and self-consuming. For what distinguishes the twenties from previous decades is not only the unprecedented volume of popular writings on the contemporary young female, but also the development of forms classified at the time as 'feminine' and the modulation of 'masculine' forms into 'feminine' ones. We may instance the 'sex novel', the oriental fantasy, the Empire romance, and traditionalist working-class fiction, which as revived received a new social significance. All these forms were to survive till the Second World War, but their heyday was, roughly speaking, the post-war decade.

Inseparable from the scope of the debate is the plurality of discourse, what I have called its 'polyphonic quality'. One of the assumptions underlying this book is that in a pluralistic society, especially in the socially mobile industrial society of the West, there cannot be *one* ideology of womanhood, a single feminine mystique, which dominates the attitudes and modes of thinking of society at large. Britain after the First World War is a noteworthy example of social and cultural pluralism, for it combined a demographic crisis with, on the one hand, profound social and economic changes, and, on the other, a transition from what had been pre-eminently a class culture to a mass consumer culture. The material changes outlined in Chapters 2 and 7 were ideal ground for the evolution of diverse and complex notions about women and sex. To describe the discourse as a 'conflict' between a dominant and an opposing ideology, or even as characterised by tension, would be fatally wrong. The post-war debate was not a dialogue between an 'official' doctrine of the roles of the sexes, articulating the ethos of a class, and a 'counter' or 'subversive' concept. What was so peculiar to the twenties was the exchange of a wide variety of popular notions and idioms, of more or less equal significance. Despite the indisputable importance of particular stereotypes (the 'flapper', or the 'superfluous woman'), they co-existed with, rather than dominated, other journalistic and literary images of the female androgyne.

In this plurality there are several structural features common to different genres and forms: a connection between class and language and between gender and class, plus certain unifying themes which occur in *all* the texts discussed. Working-class modes of feeling and thinking about women differed radically from those of the middle classes or élite audiences. The differences manifested themselves in both the *form* and the *language* of discourse. The 'sex novel' attracted socially heterogeneous audiences but remained, in essence, a form of communication between middle-class authors and a middle-class reading public. The serial, on the other hand, evolved into a genuine working-class artefact. In the best-selling 'sex novel' the break from the past was, pre-eminently, a thematic and ideological one, a rebellion against certain standards of sexual behaviour. That is to say, the 'new freedom' equalled *sexual freedom*. Significantly, even the 'masculine' documentary novel, which does not fall into the category of sex fiction proper, is, among other things, an assault on monogamous marriage and the family. By contrast, in periodical fiction for working-class women sex is peripheral and the topic of sexuality is muted. Romance triumphs. But love and sex are subsidiary to comradeship and the tribal solidarity of the group, the community, the class or even the race. The rebellion manifested itself in the appropriation of 'masculine' forms, such as the Western and the imperialistic action story, and their adjustment to the tastes and preferences of a female audience. Romance replaced adventure as the main line of dramatic action, and the new female stereotypes, notably those of the emigrant, were divested of distinct gender marks and endowed with the characteristics, both physical and mental, of the adolescent androgyne.

But the 'feminine' artefacts were not merely imitations of masculine models. Nor did they emulate the ideology of a class. It may be argued that the emerging community of open discourse constituted, in fact, an extended middle class, that the twenties saw not the liberation of discussion from bourgeois ideology but rather the diffusion of that ideology to the socially unconscious urban masses. This observation, paradoxically shared by critics of both the Right and the Left, suggests that there cannot be a reciprocal process of communication between writer and audience, only a one-sided transmission of indoctrinating ideologies. There appears to be more than a grain of truth in the familiar argument. The little that can be discovered about the few who controlled the women's press suggests that they all came from a middle-class background (with the exception of Lord Beaverbrook). The press moguls, the architects of the new concept of a working-class press, and the creators of working-class characters dealt with in this book – all came from the Edwardian middle-class milieu. But the Leavisite–Orwellian argument is irrelevant. The fact that working-class women did not write their literature – indeed, that it was, more often than not, written by middle-class men – does not mean that they did not have *a literature of their own*. The working-class fiction examined in this book did not mirror bourgeois ideologies, not did it imitate gender models. It projected working-class values in an idiosyncratically working-class language that was wholly different from that of its 'masculine' blueprints.

There is yet another difference between middle- and working-class fiction. The 'new licence' has been cited as a generic characteristic of the former. But 'outspokenness' and 'realism' are relative. The inoffensively euphemistic 'sex novels' employed various idioms which contemporaries could easily decipher. Hence the alarm at the prurience of best-sellers. The fashionable 'society' chronicle, exemplified in Arlen's works, employs the suggestive language of innuendo and *double entendre*. *The Constant Nymph*, which was universally regarded as 'clean' and 'straightforward', successfully combines forbidden themes and an erotically charged atmosphere with actual reticence. And the enormously popular oriental fantasy, technically the 'cleanest' of all sex novels (using the term broadly), aroused the greatest fears. In pulp fiction feminine sexuality was never *explicitly* acknowledged. Periodicals, especially those aimed at a female audience, were subject to severe editorial censorship. But, more significantly, their reticence manifested the trend towards what Peter Stearns termed traditionalism – that is, adherence to ideal historical sex-roles, characteristic of 'poverty' tradition – as a defence against change'.[9]

In its social and cultural connections, as well as in an overall historical perspective, the debate on freedom of expression in the novel was, pre-eminently, a discussion on the nature and trajectory of majority culture. And the controversy over the 'new licence' was the point at which the discourse on sexuality and that on the popular artefact and its audience met. The central question was: would the reading public be a minority public, educated, middle-class in composition and sexually balanced? Or would it develop (as it was feared it would) into a mass public, semi-literate, socially heterogeneous and predominantly female or effeminate? The forebodings felt about the novel and the novel- (and magazine-) reading public – that they were undergoing a process of emasculation – are exactly comparable to those felt about the composition of the new electorate. And, baseless as they may have been, these forebodings were real enough. More significantly, as I have all along attempted to show, the discourse on popular culture was instrumental in the evolution of a discourse on feminine sexuality, and *vice versa*.

The unity of theme manifests itself against the diversity of idiom and tone. The motif of the young female as androgyne is universal and transcends the differences of discourse, class and gender and even the idiosyncrasies of genre and the individual work. It looms large in the myth of the 'flapper' and the image of the 'superfluous woman'. It appears in the figure of the libidinous adult and, concealed and almost muted, behind the classical archetype of the precocious adolescent. And it is conspicuous in the images of traveller and emigrant. The rise of the androgyne motif can be fully comprehended only in relation to, or against the break from, the ideology and aesthetics of 'separate spheres'. The most culturally significant phenomenon in discourse on women, after the First World War, was the disappearance of the 'home' as *the* locus of the female's interests and the feminine experience of reality. To be sure, the ideology of domesticity survived and even prospered – in the national press, in the numerous 'service magazines', studied by Cynthia L. White, and in influential texts such as Leonora Eyles's *The Woman in the Little House* (1922) and Elinor Rathbone's *The Disinherited Family* (1924). Nevertheless, the central, most salient feature of the twenties was the redefinition and remodelling of the woman's place, in both the metaphorical and ideological senses of the term. Accepted classifications of literature according to gender were reviewed. And, significantly, both these classifications and the emerging 'feminine' genres were described mainly in geographical terms. The 'geographic' genres – the desert romance, the Empire or emigrant story, and the working-class Lancashire melodrama – display, like the 'sex novel' and the 'misogynist' social novel, a marked trend away from the home. In all these genres the domestic figure is non-existent or merely a caricature, and in most of them travel, migration or merely a change of place becomes the central metaphor for a move towards economic, social and sexual freedom. What is more, an analogue may be found in the domestic English form: in the 'masculine' novel of the early twenties the central contrast is between 'home' – signifying in this context civilian life – and the 'front', as the distinct territories of the sexes.

Yet the break from the notion of a defined feminine sphere and the aesthetic conventions of domestic fiction was incomplete, because largely confined to fantasy. Social and sexual freedoms were displaced into imaginary or Utopian societies, and the 'new freedom' or 'new licence' dissociated from the mundane and familiar. The flapper was relegated to Bohemia or Utopia, or she was sent abroad, not to imperil the perturbed, unbalanced post-war society. But clearly fantasy was not opposed to 'real life', but reflected it. The trend towards escapism was a response to the changes in attitudes consequent on material and cultural changes. Furthermore, despite universal, unchangeable elements, popular discourse and the popular new notions about the young female could develop only in the context of an acutely felt demographic crisis and political reform, combined with the emergence of modern mass-market fiction and journalism. This is precisely why the myth of the flapper has such a short history. It could not survive its place and historical moment, those specific material conditions and collective experiences to which it owed its rise.

Appendixes

(A) BEST-SELLING AUTHORS: BIOGRAPHICAL NOTES

MICHAEL ARLEN (DIKRAN KOUYOUMDJIAN, 1895–1956), novelist and essayist. Born in Bulgaria to a family of Armenian textile merchants; brought to England in 1901; educated at Malvern College and Edinburgh University, which he shortly left to embark on a journalistic and literary career. Before he became a successful writer Arlen wrote regularly for *Ararat: A Search-light on Armenia* and the *New Age*. His biggest seller was *The Green Hat* (1924). Other important works are *These Charming People* (1924), *May Fair* (1925) and *Lily Christine* (1929).

WARWICK DEEPING (1877–1950), doctor and novelist. Educated at Cambridge, served in the First World War with the Royal Army Medical Corps. His principal works are *Sorrell and Son* (1925) and *Old Pybus* (1928).

ETHEL M. DELL (ETHEL MAY SAVAGE, 1881–1939), novelist. Her first and most successful work was *The Way of an Eagle* (1912).

GILBERT FRANKAU (1884–1952), prosperous wholesale cigar merchant and then successful writer and polemicist. His best-known works are *The Love Story of Aliette Bronton* (1922), *Men, Maids and Mustard* (1924) and *Life and Erica* (1925).

PHILIP HAMILTON GIBBS (1887–1962), journalist, distinguished war correspondent and novelist; brother of the writer Cosmo Hamilton. Gibbs wrote for the *Daily Mail*, *Tribune*, the *Daily Graphic* and the *Daily Chronicle* and became famous for his coverage of the Second Balkan War and the famine in the USSR in 1921. During the First World War he was one of the five accredited correspondents with the Allied forces. Among his non-fictional works are *The Street of Adventure* (1900) and *Battles of the Somme* (1016). His best-known novel is *The Middle of the Road* (1923).

RICHARD LE GALLIENNE (1866–1947), poet and essayist, literary critic of the *Star*. Known mainly for *The Quest of the Golden Girl*.

ELINOR GLYN (1864–1943), journalist, romantic novelist and script-writer. Remembered for her biggest seller, *Three Weeks* (1907). Among her other works are *The Visits of Elizabeth* (1900), her first novel; *His House* (1910); *The Career of Katherine Bush* (1917); and *It* (1927).

ROBERT SMYTHE HICHENS (1864–1950), music critic, satirist, romantic novelist and traveller. Educated at Clifton College and the Royal College of Music; art critic for the *World*. His principal works are the anonymously published *The Green Carnation* (1984), a satire on Wilde's circle; a classic horror tale, 'How Love Came to Professor Guilda' (1900); and *The Garden of Allah* (1904).

E. M. HULL (EDITH MAUD WINSTANLEY, dates uncertain), novelist and traveller. Author of *The Sheik* (1919), *The Desert Healer* (1923) and *The Sons of the Sheik* (1925).

ARTHUR STUART MENTETH HUTCHINSON (1880–1971), journalist, editor and novelist; son of General H. D. Hutchinson of the Indian Army. Hutchinson cut his medical studies to embark on a journalistic career. Between 1912 and 1916 he was editor of the *Daily Graphic*. His greatest success was *If Winter Comes* (1921).

ROBERT KEABLE (1887–1927), clergyman and novelist. Educated at Magdalen College, Oxford; between 1911 and 1917, missionary in Basutoland; during the war, chaplain to the South African Corps in France; resigned from the ministry in 1918 and embarked on a literary career. His best-remembered novels are *Simon Called Peter* (1921) and its sequel *Recompense* (1925).

MARGARET KENNEDY (1896–1967), novelist and essayist. Educated at Cheltenham Girls' School and Somerville College, Oxford. Her best-seller was *The Constant Nymph* (1924). Her other main works are *Come with Me*, a play (1928); *Together and Apart* (1936); *Lucy Carmichael* (1951); and *Troy Chimneys* (1952).

FRANK RICHARDS (Charles Hamilton, dates uncertain), serial-writer, the creator of several blueprints of school-story characters, notably Billy Bunter.

HENRY DE VERE STACKPOOLE (1863–1951), doctor, biographer and novelist. Educated at Malvern College and St George's and St Mary's Hospitals, London; close to the *Yellow Book* circle. He is best remembered for *The Blue Lagoon* (1908).

PERCIVAL CHRISTOPHER WREN (1885–1941), sailor, navvy, schoolmaster, trooper and mercenary soldier. His life in the Foreign Legion was the model for his celebrated Geste novels: *Beau Gest*, (1924), *Beau Sabreur* (1926), *Beau Ideal* (1928) and *The Good Gestes* (1929).

(B) MARGARET KENNEDY ON *THE CONSTANT NYMPH*

The undated 40-page paper, extracts from which are quoted here, was written in the early thirties and not intended for publication. It is a self-conscious post-mortem and, so far, the most penetrating comment on a best-seller, whose contemporary English and foreign critics had overlooked some of its main weaknesses. Of special interest are the paragraphs on Lewis, Florence and the novel's end.

Lewis

I began to ponder upon the theme of an entirely single mind, and of the havoc which such a mind creates in the field of personal relationships. . . . He was more maturely conceived and free from a kind of juvenility which clung to Vera (Tessa*) and her family, who were, after all, a legacy from my childhood. And when eventually, I attempted to describe him, he turned to be too much for me. He needed a writer with more intellectual force, more mental stature, than I had got. I still think that a great artist might have made a great piece of work of him. He reminded me of Bazorov in *Fathers and Children* . . . only in a very few passages of *The Constant Nymph* did I regain anything of my first conception. . . .

Florence

. . . Florence and Lewis in *The Constant Nymph* , are examples of two different kinds of faults in a novelist. Lewis was fine in conception but he came to grief in the 'cellarage'. Florence was brought out of limbo too soon, and set down on paper before she had been properly cooked. She is reported, the only character in the book who was 'drawn from somebody I know'. I did not realise it at the time, but I see it now. Arnold Bennett complained that she was *conventional*. By this he said that that meant she was a novelist's character. She might have strayed in from somebody else's book. . . . She was to be cultured and he [Lewis] was to be an artist. I had just about then, discovered that culture and art are not at all the same thing. . . . They were to live in an exquisite house, overflowing with pictures. . . . She was to wrap him round with appreciation and understanding, treating his Arts as something utterly sacred. . . . He had no wish to be useful to society. The pleasure or edification of his audience did not concern him. He was to maintain that culture springs from an attempt to harness this passion of the artist, to make use of the labours of the artist for ends of which he knows nothing; it asks him to become the minister of a finer, a more civilised pattern of living. All this was to be shown in the clash between Florence and Lewis. . . . But Lewis could not have fallen in love with her in her customary surroundings. These would have frightened him away. They must have met in a place where she was unsure of herself. . . . He must not see her as a cultured young woman, she must have some motive for temporarily suppressing her culture. . . .

The order of events was, roughly, this. I got the Sangers quite complete, in their house in the Tyrol. All the four sisters and the little boy Sebastian . . . were in

---

*Tessa was a composite portrait of 'Vera', a memory from Kennedy's childhood, and 'Esther', a fellow student at Cheltenham Ladies College and the literary *alter ego* of Kennedy the adolescent. Esther's family was, probably, the model for the 'Sanger Circus' and the John ménage provided additional details.

their places. Papa Sanger was to die as soon as the family had been introduced. The relations of the children's mothers were to arrive and to take them to England. The main subject of the book was to be the tragi-comedy of Vera–Esther, transformed from Bohemia to Kensington, and the attitudes towards the new set of values which would be thrust upon her. The family was first to be seen through the eyes of two people arriving to stay. . . . I was a little put out when I discovered that one of them was to be Lewis. I accompanied Lewis and Trigonin through their first meeting and the various stages of their journey until they met two of the Sanger children, Pauline, who was the child Vera, and Tessa, who was Vera–Esther. And I got them all into a little cart, driving across a valley. Here a new surprise awaited me. There was some kind of bond between Lewis and Tessa. Their stories were going to be linked. I had not originally paired them. . . . In the Art V. Culture passages I was badly hampered by the weakness of Florence as an imagined character. . . . Florence was not an effective advocate for culture, and I could not feel that both sides of the question were being adequately put before Tessa. . . . The great and final difficulty was to decide which choice Tessa would make. When Lewis walked out, should she walk with him? In the first version she did not. But it did not sound right. . . . I sketched out another ending in which she did. She ran away with him to Brussels. Florence, unforgiving, yet determined to do her duty, pursued and found them. She brought Tessa back to England. Lewis was hustled off to America. Tessa died nine months later, in a neat spare bedroom, surrounded by every possible attention. But I could not carry this thing out. . . . I did not know how to manage anything so grim without resorting to crude violence. The unconscious callousness of Lewis would not take him to the point of deserting Tessa. So I let her die before even Florence got to Brussels.

(C) WOMEN'S STORY PAPERS, 1919–30: A CHECK LIST OF FICTION MAGAZINES WITH 'FEMININE' INTEREST

Title	Category	Price	Periodicity	Publisher/years	Location in UK Libraries
Betty's Paper	Story paper for girls of all ages	2d	W	Allied Newspapers	BL PP6004 sat
Blue Bird	Girls' magazine	1½d (after 1924, 2d)	W	AP (1922–4)	BL PP5993 wbb
Blue Magazine	Complete stories	1s	M	Walbrook & Co. (1919)	BL PP6018 tal
Bow Bells	Home stories	1½d (after 1924, 2d)	W	AP (1919–25)	BL PP6004 sam
Butterfly (new series)		1½d (after 1924, 2d)	W	AP (1900–40?)	BL PP6004 gmz
Choice Story Magazine	Fiction in handy pocket form	2d	W	Family Herald Press (1923–6)	BL PP6004 taa
Companion Library	Stories	4d	B	AP (1919–32)	BL 12645 bl
Complete Novel Weekly	Fiction and articles	1s	W	AP (1925–40)	BL PP6004 seo

Title	Description	Price	W/M	Publisher (dates)	Location
Complete Story Magazine	Fiction	7d	W	Family Herald Press	
Complete Story-teller	Love stories	2d	W	Newnes (1927–8)	BL PP6004 scc
Eve's Own Stories	Stories	2d	W	AP (1923–39)	BL PP6004 sau
Forget-Me-Not Novels	Complete story paper for women	2d	W	AP (1919–26)	BL 12644 c1
Girls' Favourite	Romantic fiction for girls	2d	W	AP (1922–7; then incorporated into *Eve's Own*)	Colindale
Girls' Friend	Powerful melodramatic love stories	2d	W	AP (1889–31)	Colindale
Girls' Friend Library	Complete novels		W	AP (1899–31)	BL 12606a
Girls' Mirror	Up-to-date fiction	2d	W	(1915–33)	Colindale
Grand Magazine	Fiction	1s	M	Newnes (1905–40)	BL PP6004 gmo
Handy Stories	Long complete tales	2d	M	AP	Not seen

Title	Category	Price	Periodicity	Publisher/years	Location in UK Libraries
Happy Hour Stories	Complete stories	2d	W	Family Herald Press	Not seen
Happy Magazine	Complete stories and humorous pictures	7d	M	Newnes (1922–40)	BL PP6018 tas
Home Chat	Ladies' paper	2d	M	AP (1895–1956)	Colindale
Home Companion	Long complete story and serial	2d	W	AP (1897–1941; continued until 1956 as *Home Companion and Family Friend*)	
Home Mirror Novels	Fiction and interesting articles for women	2d	W	AP (1919–26)	BL PP6004 san
Home Stories	Complete story and serials	2d	W	AP (started 1900)	BL PP6004 sab
Hutchinson's Story Magazine	Serials and short stories	1s	M	Hutchinson (1919)	BL PP6018 tak
Ivy Stories	Complete stories for young women	4d	F	John Leng (1922–32)	BL 12819 al

Joy	Love stories	2d	W	AP (1925–8)	BL PP6004 say
Lily Library	Complete stories	2d	W	Pickering and Inglis (started 1921)	BL WP1001
Marry Magazine	Fiction	6d	M	Macdonald and Martin (1924–30)	BL PP6004 goz
Mizpah Novels	Fiction	4d	M	AP (1919–22; afterwards incorporated into *Forget-Me-Not Novels*)	BL 12644 aaa1
Monthly Magazine of Fiction	Complete novels and short stories	6d	M	Family Herald Press (1885–1927, continued as the *Magazine Series* 1927–8 and then as the *Magazine of Fiction and Complete Story-teller*)	BL PP6004 s
My Pocket Novels	Long complete novel	1½d (after 1924, 2d)	W		Not seen
My Story Weekly	Love stories	2d	W	AP (1927–8)	BL PP6004 scb
My Weekly	Complete tales and serial	2d	W	John Leng (1910–60)	Colindale

Title	Category	Price	Periodicity	Publisher/years	Location in UK Libraries
New Magazine	Illustrated fiction	1s		AP (1909–30)	BL PP6004 god
Newnes Pocket Novels	Love stories	4d	B	Newnes	Not seen
Own Story Magazine	All-fiction	3d	W	Family Herald Press	Not seen
Pam's Paper	Story paper	2d	W	Allied Newspapers (1923–7)	BL PP6004 saw
Peg's Companion	Fiction	2d	W	Arthur Pearson (1919–32)	BL PP6004 sar
Peg's Paper	Fiction	2d	W	Arthur Pearson (1919–40)	BL PP6004 sal
Polly's Paper	Stories	2d	W	(1919–24)	BL PP6004 sao
Poppy's Paper	Stories	2d	W	AP (1924–34; continued to 1936 as *Fortune*)	BL PP6004 sax
The Popular	Complete stories	2d	W	AP (1920–31?)	Not seen
Red Letter and Home Weekly	For home circle, containing fiction	2d	W	D. C. Thompson	Colindale

Red Letter Novels	Complete novels	4d	M	D. C. Thompson (1920–33)	BL 012604 1.1.
Red Magazine (Harmsworth Red Magazine)	Stories of love, adventure and mystery	7d	F	AP (1908)	BL PP6018 tad
Romance, Every Woman's Story Magazine	Women's magazine	9d	M	Odham (1923–7)	BL PP6018 tax
School Friend	School stories for girls	2d	W	AP (1919–29)	BL PP5993 ndm
Schoolgirls' Own	Stories	2d	W		BL PP5993 wc
Schoolgirls' Own Library	Stories	4d	B	AP (1922–)	BL PP12607 c1
Schoolgirls' Weekly	Stories	2d	W	AP (1922–39)	BL PP5993 wba
Smart Fiction	Complete story	2d	W	(1913–24; then incorporated into the *Duchess Novelette*)	BL PP6004 cat
Smart Novels	Complete tales and serial	2d	W		Not seen

Title	Category	Price	Periodicity	Publisher/years	Location in UK Libraries
Smart Set (not to be confused with an American periodical of the same name)	Fiction	1s	not certain	Hutchinson (1924)	Not seen
Sunday Stories	Complete stories	2d	W	AP (1896–1940)	BL PP268 el
True Story Magazine (British edn)	Stories from real life	1s	M	Hutchinson (1922–?)	Bodleian Per25612d 24
Violet Magazine	Women's magazine	7d	F	AP (1922–40)	BL PP6018 tat
Weekend Novels	Serials and short stories	2d	W	Allied Newspapers (1919–35)	BL PP6004 sap
Woman's Friend	Home magazine and fiction	3d	W	Newnes (1924–50; then continued as *Glamour*)	Colindale
Woman's Pictorial	Fiction and articles fully illustrated	3d	W	AP (1920–56)	Colindale
Woman's Weekly	Women's magazine	2d	W	AP (1911–61; then continued as *Woman's Weekly and Woman's Companion*)	Colindale

Woman's World	Complete stories and serial	2d	W	AP (1903–58)	Colindale
Woman's World Library	Fiction	4d	M	AP (started 1913)	BL PP12646 c1
W. T. Novels	Complete story	6d		W. T. Leng	
Yellow Magazine	Fiction	7d	F	AP (1921–?)	BL PP6018 tao

Abbreviations: AP – Amalgamated Press; B – bi-monthly; BL – British Library; F – fortnightly; M – monthly; W – weekly.

Notes

INTRODUCTION: 1918−28, CONTEXTS AND TEXTS

1. See *Parliamentary Debates, House of Commons*, 5th ser., vol. 215, pp.1359ff. For additional information see David E. Butler, *The Electoral System in Britain, 1918−51* (Oxford University Press, 1953) pp.15−38; Neal Blewett, 'The Franchise in the United Kingdom 1885−1918', *Past and Present*, vol. XXXII (Dec 1965) pp.27−57; Martin Pugh, 'Politicians and the Women's Vote 1914−18', *History*, vol. LIV (Oct 1974) pp.358−74; and Pugh's *The Making of Modern British Politics 1867−1939* (Blackwell, 1982) pp.174−5; 188−9, and *Electoral Reform in War and Peace 1906−18* (Routledge and Kegan Paul, 1978) pp.136−55.

2. *Statistical Abstract for the United Kingdom*, no. 72 [1913−27] p.398.

3. Usefully surveyed in Jeffrey Weeks, *Sex, Politics and Society: The Regulation of Sexuality since 1880* (Longman, 1981) pp.19−28.

4. See especially Steven Marcus, *The Other Victorians: A Study of Sexuality and Pornography in Mid Nineteenth-Century England* (Weidenfeld and Nicolson, 1967); Brian Harrison, 'Underneath the Victorians', *VS*, vol. X, no. 3 (1967) pp.239−63; Peter T. Cominos, 'Late Victorian Social Respectability and the Social System', *International Review of Social History*, vol. VIII, no. 8 (1963) pp.8−48, 216−50; and Peter Gay's recent *The Bourgeois Experience*, vol. I: *Victoria to Freud* (Oxford University Press, 1984).

5. Imported advice was equally successful. Of the plethora of American and continental books on conjugal love, Judge B. Lindsey and Wainwright Evans's famous tract *The Companionate Family*, first published in Britain in 1928, deserves special mention. For the impact of Marie Stopes's writings see Ruth Hall (ed.), *Dear Doctor Stopes: Sex in the 1920s* (Andre Deutsch, 1978).

6. Simone de Beauvoir, *The Second Sex*, tr. H. M. Parshley (Bantam Books, 1961). It is, characteristically, the anthropologist's interpretation. See, for instance Claude Lévi-Strauss, *Mythologiques*, vol. III *L'Origine de manières de table* (Plon, 1968); Shirley Ardener (ed), *Perceiving Women* (Dent and Halsted, 1957); *Defining Females: The Nature of Women in Society* (Croom Helm, 1978). For the psychological aspects of the notion of the female as 'other', see Helen Deutsch's influential *The Psychology of Women*, 2 vols (Crane and Stratton, 1949).

7. Ian Watt, *The Rise of the Novel: Studies in Defoe, Richardson and Fielding* (Penguin, 1981) pp.175−6; Antonia Fraser, *The Weaker Vessel: Women's Lot in Seventeenth-Century England* (Methuen, 1984).

8.   On the literary aspects of the notion of 'separate spheres', see particularly Walter H. Houghton, *The Victorian Frame of Mind 1830–70* (Yale University Press, 1975) pp.341–72; and Alexander Welsh, *The City of Dickens* (Clarendon Press, 1971) pp.149–61. On the political aspect see Brian Harrison, *Separate Spheres: The Opposition to Women's Suffrage in Britain* (Croom Helm, 1972) pp.56–61. For a discussion of 'woman's sphere' in America see Nancy F. Cott, *The Bonds of Womanhood: 'Woman's Sphere' in New England, 1780–1835* (Yale University Press, 1977).

9.   A. M. Carr-Saunders and D. Caradog-Jones, *A Survey of the Social Structure of England and Wales* (Oxford University Press, 1927) p.4.

10.   Ibid, pp.3–4.

11.   *Statistical Abstract for the United Kingdom*, no. 74 [1916–29] p.29.

12.   See Weeks, *Sex, Politics and Society*, p.187.

13.   Arthur J. B. Marwick, *Women at War, 1914–18* (Croom Helm, 1977) p.166, table 3.

14.   G. D. H. and M. J. Cole, *The Condition of Britain* (Victor Gollancz, 1937) p.247, which also provides a comparison with the average income of male workers.

15.   Michel Foucault, *The History of Sexuality*, vol. I: *An Introduction*, tr. Robert Huxley (Penguin, 1981) esp. pp.1–49. See also Jeffery Weeks's important 'Foucault for Historians', *History Workshop*, no. 14 (1982) pp.107–19.

16.   Nichola Beauman's *A Very Great Profession: The Woman's Novel 1914–39* (Virago, 1983), is an exception.

17.   Martha Vicinus, *Independent Women, Work and Community for Single Women, 1850–1920* (Virago, 1985). For theory and authority in the study of women's history see Sally Alexander, 'Women, Class and Sexual Differences in the 1830s and 1840s: Some reflections on the Writing of a Feminist History', *History Workshop*, no. 17 (Sep 1984) pp.225–50. See also Richard J. Evans's 'The History of European Women: A Critical Survey of Recent Research', *Journal of Modern History*, vol. LII (Dec 1980) pp.656–75. Arthur Marwick's *Women at War* and his *The Deluge: British Society and the First World War* (Macmillan, 1979) ch. 3 are notable exceptions.

18.   Raymond Williams, *The Long Revolution* (Penguin, 1980) p.233.

19.   Ibid., p. 191; Michael Joseph, 'The Commerical Side of Literature', *The Complete Writing for Profit* (Hutchinson, 1930) pp.404–7.

20.   See especially Leo Lowenthal, *Literature, Popular Culture and Society* (Prentice-Hall, 1961), and the following important collections: C. W. E. Bigsby (ed.), *Approaches to Popular Culture* (Edward Arnold, 1976); Bernard Rosenberg and W. P. Manning (eds), *Mass Culture: The Popular Arts in America* (Free Press, 1964). For the media see particularly James Curran, Michael Gurevitch and Janet Wolacott (eds), *Mass Communication and Society* (Edward Arnold, 1977).

CHAPTER 1   THE SUPERFLUOUS WOMAN, THE FLAPPER, THE DISFRANCHISED FEMALE AND THE ROTHERMERE PRESS

1. Q. D. Leavis, *Fiction and the Reading Public* (Penguin, 1979) p.203.
2. Ibid., pp.146–52; F. R. Leavis, *Mass Civilisation and Minority Culture* (Minority Press, 1930) pp.6–7; F. R. Leavis and Denys Thompson, *Culture and Environment* (Chatto and Windus, 1933) pp.8–10; R. C. K. Ensor, *England 1870–1914* (Clarendon Press, 1966) pp.311–15. For a more recent and somewhat different interpretation, see James Curran, 'Capitalism and the Control of the Press, 1800–1975', in Curran, Gurevitch and Wollacott, *Mass Communication and Society*, pp.195–231.
3. In addition to the Leavises see Theodor Adorno and Max Horkheimer, *Dialects of Enlightenment* (Allen Lane, 1973); and Graham Murdock and Peter Golding, 'Capitalism, Communication and Class Relations', in Curran, Gurevitch and Wollacott, *Mass Communication and Society*, pp.12–44. The notion of communication is, of course, taken from Raymond Williams, *Communications* (Penguin, 1979) p.11.
4. Murdock and Golding, in Curran, Gurevitch and Wollacott, *Mass Communication and Society*, pp.134–5; Piers Brandon, *The Life and Death of the Press Barons* (Secker and Warburg, 1983) p.124.
5. According to his biographer he seldom wrote editorials before the early thirties. See A. J. P. Taylor, *Beaverbrook* (Hamish Hamilton, 1972) p.228.
6. Marwick, *Women at War*, p.154; Pugh, *Electoral Reform in War and Peace*, pp.145–6.
7. For the Victorian debate on 'redundant Women' see Martha Vicinus, *Independent Women*, especially the Introduction and Chapter 1, pp.1–46.
8. *Daily Mail*, 18 Jan 1921 and 21 Dec 1921.
9. 'When the young woman has the vote she will see to it that we have a better distribution of the population of this country in the waste spaces of the dominions'; and elsewhere: 'One of the results of giving the franchise to women will be that we shall get much more responsible schemes of emigration and some provisions for large numbers of women to go out to these remote parts of the Empire where young men are plentiful' – *Parliamentary Debates, House of Commons*, 5th ser., vol. 215, pp.243, 246. For nineteenth-century schemes see Una Monk, *New Horizons: A Hundred Years of Women's Migration* (HMSO, 1963); James A. Hammerton, 'Feminism and Female Emigration, 1861–86', in Martha Vicinus (ed.), *A Widening Sphere: Changing Roles of Victorian Women* (Methuen, 1980).
10. Quoted in Charles L. Mowat, *Britain between the Wars, 1918–39* (Methuen, 1978) p.226.
11. *Punch*, vol. 174 (27 July 1928) p.724.
12. *Daily Mail*, 9 Nov and 9 Dec 1920 and 12 Oct 1921.
13. The correspondence column of 18 April is headed 'Paying Women not to

Work. Honest Toil Shirked. Idling on the Dole'. The introductory note states,

> Complaints from readers about the demoralising effect of the dole upon women continue to pour into the offices of the *Daily Mail*. . . . From the evidence of the letters there is no doubt that many girls prefer a life of idleness eked out of the dole, to life of honest work as domestic servants.

Readers' letters on the matter continued to appear until June.

14. Jonathan Swift, *Gulliver's Travels*, in *The Works*, Scott's edn (Bickers, 1883), vol. XI, p.193.

By chance I came across an unknown and elsewhere unrecorded early example. A fortnightly bearing the title *The Flapper* had appeared in Dublin between 2 February 1796 and 10 September 1797. *The Flapper* disguised anti-British propaganda in lofty Swiftian belle-lettrism with great success.

> With all due deference to the prerogative of the Executive government and to the functions of the college of arms I have assumed the office together with the name and title of flapper to the people of Ireland. It is my task to call their attention to propriety and decorum in their social communications and to warn them of such dangers as may beset their ways. As it is impossible for me to attend personally on each individual, I am driven to avail myself of that multiplied prescence which the press offered me.

Quoted from *The Flapper: A Periodical Work*, vol. I, no. 1 (2 Feb 1796) p.2.

15. Joseph Wright (ed.), *The English Dialect Dictionary* (Henry Frowde, 1900) vol. II, pp.383–91; John S. Farmer and William E. Henley, *Slang and its Analogues Past and Present* (Kraus, 1965) vol. III, pp.5–6. See also J. A. H. Murray, *A New English Dictionary on Historical Principles* (Clarendon Press, 1901) vol. IV, p.287.

16. 'She was in the last stage of what slangy men call "flapperdom" and her hair was gathered on the nape of her neck with a big black bow' (1907); 'That was during her childish beauty, before she passed into her red-faced flapperhood' – *Oxford English Dictionary: Supplement*, vol. I, p.1097. For earlier examples see Farmer and Henley, *Slang and its Analogues*; and Albert Barrere and Charles G. Leland, *A Dictionary of Slang, Jargon and Cant* (Gale Research, 1967) vol. I, p.237.

17. Wright, *The English Dialect Dictionary*; and Eric Partridge, *A Dictionary of Slang and Unconventional English* (Routledge and Kegan Paul, 1961) vol. I, p.282.

18. This usage is idiosyncratically British. For the contemporary American

usages see Sukimo Higashi, *Virgins, Vamps and Flappers: The American Silent Movie Heroine* (Eden Press Women's Publications, 1978); and G. E. Mowry (ed.), *The Twenties: Fords, Flappers and Fanatics* (Prentice-Hall, 1963).

19. *Punch*, vol. 175 (30 Nov 1927) p.591.
20. *Daily Mail*, 1 Sep 1919.
21. *Daily Mail*, 31 Mar 1927.
22. William Empson, *Seven Types of Ambiguity* (Chatto and Windus, 1930) p.299.
23. *The Times*, 30 Mar and 1 Apr 1928.
24. One anonymous pamphlet is worth quoting:

> It is evident that of the women admitted to the Register between 21 and 25 years of age
> 415,000 would be over 21 and under 22
> 405,000 would be over 22 and under 23
> 390,000 would be over 23 and under 24
> 380,000 would be over 24 and under 25. . . .

See *Not the Flapper Vote* (19 June 1928), Fawcett Library fiche 51.
25. *Daily Mail*, 28 Oct, 3 Nov and 9 Nov 1922.
26. The press as a whole made much of the fact than an unusually large number of MPs were absent from the division on the second reading of the Equal Franchise Bill (29 Mar 1928). The *Mail* referred to 'party dissension' (31 Mar), 'Loyal Conservatives who are in a quandary' (3 Apr) and to 'passive resisters' to the Bill (4 Apr). According to the *Mail*, 146 Conservative members were absent from the division. According to *The Times* (31 Mar) there were only 135 Conservative absentees, as well as 53 Labour and 12 Liberal absentees.
27. *Parliamentary Debates, House of Lords*, 5th ser., vol. 71, pp.213–56. The third reading was on 18 June and the bill received the Royal Assent on 2 July (ibid., pp.407–50, 502, 808).

CHAPTER 2 'SEX NOVELS': A NEW KIND OF BEST-SELLER

1. For the early American usages see John A. Sutherland, *Bestsellers: Popular Fiction of the 1970s* (Routledge and Kegan Paul, 1980) pp.12–13; Frank L. Mott, *Golden Multitudes: The Story of Best-sellers in the United States* (Macmillan, 1947; Bowker, 1966); Alice P. Hackett and James H. Burke, *80 Years of Best-sellers 1895–1971* (Bowker, 1977).
2. J. A. H. Murray, *New English Dictionary*, p.74.
3. Joseph, 'The Commercial Side of Literature', *The Complete Writing for Profit*, pp.407–8.
4. Elizabeth A. Drew, *The Modern Novel: Some Aspects of Contemporary Fiction* (Jonathan Cape, 1926) p.61.

5.   *Daily Mail*, 8 Nov 1927.

6.   For the eighteenth century see Watt, *The Rise of the Novel*, pp.102–83. For nineteenth-century classifications see Elaine Showalter, *A Literature of their Own: British Women Novelists from Brontë to Lessing* (Virago, 1978) pp.1–73.

7.   'The Londoner', *Bookman*, vol. 55, no. 5 (July 1922) p.503.

8.   Joseph, 'How to Write Serial Fiction', *The Complete Writing for Profit*, p.849.

9.   Williams, *The Long Revolution*, pp.191–2.

10. The term 'edition' is used here simply to indicate a number of copies issued at one time, i.e. including new impressions (unaltered reprints from standing type or plate) as well as editions proper (the original printing and newly set or altered reprints).

11. Per Gedin, *Literature in the Market Place* (Faber and Faber, 1977) p.67.

12. On the growth of suburbia see Cole and Cole, *The Condition of Britain*, pp.36–8; Carr-Saunders and Caradog-Jones, *The Social Structure of England and Wales*; M. C. Carr, 'The Development and Character of a Metropolitan Suburb: Bexley, Kent', in F. M. L. Thompson (ed.), *The Rise of Suburbia* (Leicester University Press and St Martin's Press, 1982) pp.211–69.

13. Drew, *The Modern Novel*, p.61.

14. *Bookman*, vol. 55, no. 4 (Apr 1922) p.503. See also Joseph Collins, 'Sex in Literature', *Bookman*, vol. 49, no. 2 (Apr 1924) pp.92–133.

15. Marwick, *The Deluge*, pp.302–5; Mowat, *Britain between the Wars*, pp.27–8.

16. T. S. Eliot, 'Marie Lloyd', *Selected Essays* (Faber and Faber, 1951) pp.459–60.

17. Rachel Low, *History of the British Film, vol. IV: 1918–28* (George Allen and Unwin, 1971) p.47.

18. Walter Benjamin, 'The Work of Art in the Age of Mechanical Reproduction', *Illuminations*, tr. Harry Zohn (Jonathan Cape, 1970) p.233.

CHAPTER 3   1921: *IF WINTER COMES*—A 'MASCULINE' NOVEL

1.   *The Times*, 26 Apr 1922.

2.   'Spring after the Winter of War', *NYTBR*, 14 Aug 1921, p.14.

3.   *Bookseller*, Sep 1922, quoted in John A. Attenborough, *Living Memory: Hodder and Stoughton Publishers, 1868–1975* (Hodder and Stoughton, 1975) p.94.

4.   *The Times*, 28 Apr 1922.

5.   'Mr Hutchinson Writes on Woman's Place', *NYTBR*, 3 Sep 1922; *The Times*, 28 Apr 1922.

6.   *The Times*, 24 Apr 1922.

7.   The programme of the Council of People's Delegates effectively gave all German women over the age of 21 the vote (12 Nov 1918). French women were enfranchised only in 1945.

8.   One exception that should be mentioned is Elinor Glyn's *Six Days* (1924), a repeat of her notorious *Three Weeks* set in post-war Normandy.

9.   *The Times*, 2 May 1922.

10.   Q. D. Leavis, *Fiction and the Reading Public*, p.69.

11.   *TLS*, 16 Nov 1922, p.746.

12.   A. S. M. Hutchinson, *If Winter Comes* (Hodder and Stoughton, 1922) p.145.

13.   Ibid., pp.146–7.

14.   *NYTBR*, 3 Sep 1922; *The Times*, 22 Apr 1922; *TLS*, 27 July 1922, p.491. The first and last reviews are on *This Freedom*.

15.   Hutchinson, *If Winter Comes*, pp.33–5.

16.   Ibid., pp.18–19.

17.   *TLS*, 15 Sep 1921, p.594.

18.   *TLS*, 27 July 1922, p.491.

19.   A. S. M. Hutchinson, 'Author's Preface to the Popular Edition', *This Freedom*, 5th edn (Hodder and Stoughton, 1924).

CHAPTER 4   1924: *THE GREEN HAT*

1.   'The Green Hat', New Statesman, 5 July 1924, p.382.

2.   Drew, 'Sex Simplexes and Complexes', *The Modern Novel* pp.53–61.

3.   Claude C. Washburn, 'Sophistication', *Opinions* (Constable, 1926) p.53.

4.   Alec Waugh reviewed it as 'Is this George Moore?' – Michael J. Arlen, *Exiles* (André Deutsch, 1971) p.65.

5.   On the relationship with Orage see Martin Wallace, *The New Age under Orage* (Manchester University Press, 1967); Philip Mairet, *A. R. Orage: A Memoir* (Dent, 1969); Harry Keyishian, *Michael Arlen* (Twayne, 1975) p.21.
         Arlen saw Lawrence in 1915 and 1916 and in Florence in 1927 (Lawrence was then revising *Lady Chatterley*, into which he wrote Arlen as Michaelis). Lawrence mentions him in seven letters, and one, to Lady Ottoline Morrell, is especially perceptive: 'Kouyoumdjian seems a bit blatant and pushing . . . but it is because he is very foreign even though he does not know it himself. In English life he is a strange alien medium' – *The Collected Letters*, ed. Harry T. Moore (Heinemann, 1962) I, 396.

6.   For the American stage production see Katherine Cornell, *I Wanted to be an Actress* (Random House, 1938). For the London production consult James Agate, *The Contemporary Theatre, 1925* (Chapman and Hall, 1926); and Noël Coward, *Present Indicative: An Autobiography* (W. Heinemann, 1937).

7. Evelyn Waugh, *Brideshead Revisited* (Penguin, 1982) p.117.

8. Keyishian, *Michael Arlen*, p.129, n.19.

9. Michael Arlen, *The Green Hat: A Romance for a Few People* (Collins, 1924) p.6.

10. Roger Abingdon, *The Green Mat: A Romance for Askew People* (Collins, 1925) p.15.

11. Ford Corey, 'Three Rousing Cheers!!! The Parody Adventures of our Youthful Heroes. The Rollo Boys with Sherlock in Mayfair or, Keep it under your Green Hat', *Bookman*, vol. 62, no. 5 (Jan 1926) p.584.

12. *TLS*, 19 June 1924, p.386.

13. *NYTBR*, 21 Sep 1929, p.9.

14. *New Republic*, vol. 49 (30 Sep 1924) p.153; *New Statesman*, 5 July 1924, p.382; *Saturday Review of Literature*, vol. 1, no. 10 (4 Oct 1924) p.159.

15. Arlen, *The Green Hat*, pp.10–11.

16. Corey, in the *Bookman*, vol. 62, no. 5, p.586.

17. Arlen, *The Green Hat*, p.33.

18. Ibid., p.47.

19. Ibid., p.45.

20. Ibid., p.41.

21. See, for instance, *TLS*, 19 June 1924, p.386.

22. Ibid.

23. Drew, *The Modern Novel*, p.60.

24. Arlen, *The Green Hat*, pp.22–4.

25. See Grant Overton, *Cargoes for Crusoes* (Appleton and George J. Doran, 1924) pp.272, 275.

26. The best study of Nancy Cunard's life is Anne Chisholm's well documented *Nancy Cunard* (Penguin, 1981). For additional information see Daphne Fielding, *Emerald and Nancy: Lady Cunard and her Daughter* (Athenaum, 1968); and Hugh Ford (ed.), *Nancy Cunard: Brave Poet, Indomitable Rebel, 1896–1965* (Chilton Books, 1968).

27. Chisholm, *Nancy Cunard*, pp.100–1.

28. Ibid., p.103.

29. *NYTBR*, 22 Mar 1925, p.2.

CHAPTER 5   1924, *ANNUS MIRABILIS: THE CONSTANT NYMPH*

1. *TLS*, 13 Dec 1923, p.880.

2. 'I've fallen in love with your Tessa. I wished somebody like her existed' – William Gerhardie to Margaret Kennedy, unpublished letter, 22 June 1925, JBA.

3. Arnold Bennett to Margaret Kennedy, unpublished letter, 5 Oct 1924, JBA.

4. Letter of 14 Sep 1927, in Antonio Gramsci, *Letters from Prison*, tr. L. Lawner (Jonathan Cape, 1975) p.104, n.1.

5. Q. D. Leavis, *Fiction and the Reading Public*, pp.43–5.

6. Margaret Kennedy on *The Constant Nymph*, in Appendix B, p.153.

7. Ibid., pp.154–5.

8. Ibid., p.154.

9. Ibid., p.155.

10. W. Heinemann to Margaret Kennedy, 30 Sep 1925, JBA.

11. Michael Holroyd, *Augustus John: A Biography* (W. Heinemann, 1974) vol. II, p.225, n.53.

12. *TLS*, 30 Oct 1924, p.684.

13. *NYTBR*, 22 Feb 1925, p.5; *Punch*, vol. 167 (17 Dec 1924) p.698.

14. Charles Churchill, who is a classical scholar, wishes to teach the child Tessa the ancient languages. Mythological themes and images recur in *Red Sky at Morning* (1927) and *Troy Chimneys* (1952).

15. Margaret Kennedy, *The Ladies of Lyndon* (W. Heinemann, 1923) p.122.

16. Ibid.

17. Margaret Kennedy, *The Constant Nymph* (W. Heinemann, 1924) pp.72–3.

18. Ibid., pp.78–9.

19. Margaret Kennedy on *The Constant Nymph*, in Appendix B, p.153.

20. *NYTBR*, 15 Mar 1924, p.14. Margaret Kennedy was also a founder member of the Charlotte Yonge Society.

21. Kennedy, *The Ladies of Lyndon*, p.164.

22. Kennedy, *The Constant Nymph*, p.189.

23. Ibid., pp.205–6.

24. *Punch*, vol. 167 (17 Dec 1924) p.698.

CHAPTER 6   1919–28: 'THE SHEIK OF ARABY' – FREEDOM IN CAPTIVITY IN THE DESERT ROMANCE

1. Q. D. Leavis, *Fiction and the Reading Public*, p.116.

2. Quoted in Stanley J. Kunitz, *Twentieth Century Authors* (1942) p.686.

3. The most perceptive assessment of the film's impact is in John Dos Passos's 'The Adagio Dancer' (1930). See John Dos Passos, *USA* (Penguin, 1960) pp.883–6. For more details consult Natacha Rambova, *Rudy: An Intimate Portrait of Rudolph Valentino* (Hutchinson, 1927); Alexander Walker, *Rudolph Valentino* (Penguin, 1972).

    The first (Famous Players Lasky) production of *The Sheik* was released on 30 October 1921. Other screen idols, such as John Gilbert and Edmund Carew, appeared in a succession of less blooded, albeit popular imitations: *The Arab* (1924), *Arabian Love* (1922), *The Song of Love* (1923) and *Desert Night* (1929).

4. Quoted in Brad Steiger and Chaw Mank, *Valentino* (Corgi, 1976) p.12.

5.   See *TLS*, 20 Apr 1922, p.262, and 15 Feb 1923, p.110.

6.   D. H. Lawrence, *Pornography and Obscenity* (Alicat Bookshop, 1948) p.17.

7.   *Daily Express*, 26 Jan, 28 Jan and 1 Feb 1924 and 10 June 1927.

8.   *Young Women out of Love, Being a Commentary on the Genius Peculiar to Michael Arlen* (Stanley Paul, 1923) p.114.

9.   See Edward E. Said, *Orientalism* (Routledge and Kegan Paul, 1978) pp.170–97; Mohamad Ali Hachicho, 'English Travel Books about the Arab Near East in the 18th Century', *Die Welt des Islams*, vol. IV, nos 1–4 (Leiden, 1964) pp.1–207. On the nineteenth-century travelogue on the Middle East see Rashad Rashdy, *The Lure of Egypt for English Writers and Travellers during the 19th Century* (Cairo, 1950).

10. Paul Fussell, *Abroad: British Literary Travelling between the Wars* (Oxford University Press, 1982) p.11.

11. *NYTBR*, 8 May 1927, p.14; 'Liberia and the Sahara', *TLS*, 4 Nov 1926, p.760.

12. E. M. Hull, *Camping in the Sahara* (Evelyn Nash and Grayson, 1926) pp.9–10.

13. E. M. Hull, *The Sons of the Sheik* (Evelyn Nash and Grayson, 1926) pp.95–6.

14. Joan Conquest, *The Hawk of Egypt* (Werner Laurie, 1922).

15. Hull, *The Sons of the Sheik*, pp.103–4. Cf. Joan Conquest, *Desert Love* (Werner Laurie, 1920) pp.158–60.

16. Emanuel Sivan, 'Colonialism and Popular Culture in Algeria', *Journal of Contemporary History*, vol. XIV (1979) pp.21–53, esp. pp.34–5.

17. Hull, *The Sons of the Sheik*, pp.101–2.

18. E. M. Hull, *The Sheik* (Evelyn Nash, 1919) pp.119, 120, 121.

19. Ibid., pp.103–4.

20. On the self-consciousness of the desert-love novels and their effect upon large audiences see D. H. Lawrence, 'Surgery for the Novel or a Bomb', *Selected Literary Criticism* (Heinemann, 1955) p.116.

21. D. H. Lawrence, 'The Woman Who Rode Away' and 'In Love', *The Woman Who Rode Away and Other Stories* (Penguin, 1978) pp.48, 116.

22. Hull, *The Sheik*, p.38.

23. On the oriental love tale and oriental motifs, see Maria Pike Conant, 'The Oriental Tale in England in the 18th Century', *Studies in Comparative Literature* (Columbia University Press, 1908); and Marie de Meester, 'Oriental Influences in the English Literature of the Early 19th Century', *Anglistische Forschungen*, no. 46 (1915). On the erotic tale see particularly Marcus, *The Other Victorians*, pp.197–217.

24. Hull, *The Sheik*, p.58.

25. Conquest, *Desert Love*, p.24.

26. Conquest, *The Hawk of Egypt*, p.85.

27. For instance Marcus, *The Other Victorians*, pp.212–16; Susan Griffin, *Pornography and Silence: Culture's Revenge over Nature* (Women's Press,

1981); J. A. Sutherland, *Offensive Literature: Decensorship in Britain, 1960–80* (Junction Books, 1982). Marcus's well-known model of 'pornotopia', which may be taken as an exemplar of the Freudian motif of sexuality *versus* social order, is manifest, though naturally with different emphases, in feminist writings on the topic of sexual violence.

CHAPTER 7   CLASS AND GENDER: THE 'GIRLS' WEEKLIES'

1. Eliot, 'Marie Lloyd', *Selected Essays*, p.457.
2. A classic on the connection between gender and class is Richard Hoggart's study of *Peg's Paper* in *The Uses of Literacy: Aspects of Working-class Culture with Special Reference to Publications and Entertainment* (Penguin, 1981) pp.120–31. See also Cynthia L. White, *Women's Magazines 1693–1968: A Sociological Enquiry* (Michael Joseph, 1970); and Mary Cadogan and Patricia Craig, *You're a Brick Angela! A New Look at Girl's Fiction from 1839 to 1975* (Victor Gollancz, 1976).
3. Kathleen, M. Tillotson, *Novels of the 1840s* (Oxford University Press, 1954) pp.24–33; Margaret Dalziel, *Popular Fiction 100 Years Ago: An Unexplored Tract of Literary History* (Cohen and West, 1975).
4. 'The Hutchinson's Magazine', *Bookman*, vol. 50, no. 5 (Jan 1920) p.348.
5. 'A Guide to Short Story Writing', *Punch*, vol. 167 (July 1924) p.122.
6. *Bookman*, vol. 55, no. 1 (Mar 1922) pp.41–9; no. 2 (Apr 1922) pp.126–33; no. 3 (May 1922) pp.252–8; no. 4 (June 1922) pp.368–75; no. 5 (Aug 1922) pp.485–91.
7. Elinor Glyn, *The Elinor Glyn System of Writing* (Writer's Press, 1922), p.17.
8. *My Story Weekly*, no. 1 (15 Oct 1927) p.24.
9. Benjamin, in *Illuminations*, p.234.
10. Two notable exceptions are Flora Klickman, who dominated the *Girl's Own Paper and Woman's Magazine* from 1908 until her retirement in 1931, and Mollie (Nel) Kennedy, architect and first editor of Pearson's *Peg's Paper*.
11. 'A Guide to Short Story Writing. Lesson II: The Simple Little Love-story', *Punch*, vol. 167 (13 Aug 1924) pp.180–1.
12. Joseph, 'How to Write Serial Fiction', *The Complete Writing for Profit*, p.845.
13. According to Cynthia L. White, the First World War strengthened rather than weakened the middle-class orientation of the women's press. But her study concentrates on 'service magazines' and excludes the story papers. See *Women's Magazines*, pp.93–123, esp. pp.95–7.
14. George Orwell, 'Boys' Weeklies', *The Collected Essays, Journalism and Letters*, vol. I: *An Age Like This 1920–40*, ed. Sonia Orwell and Ian Angus (Penguin, 1982) pp.516, 518.
15. White, *Women's Magazines*, p.87; Williams, *Communications*, p.57.

16. Tillotson, *Novels of the 1840s*, pp.30 – 31. See also Graham Pollard, 'Serial Fiction', in John W. Carter (ed.), *New Paths in Book Collecting* (Constable, 1931).

17. Robin G. Collingwood, *The Principles of Art* (Clarendon Press, 1938) pp.323 – 4; Tillotson, *Novels of the 1840s*, pp.33 – 7; Dalziel, *Popular Fiction 100 Years Ago*, pp.36 – 42.

18. Hoggart, *The Uses of Literacy*, pp.132 – 6; Peter N. Stearns, 'The Effort at Continuity in Working-class Culture', *Journal of Modern History*, vol. LIV, no. 4 (Dec 1980) p.268. See p.177, n.9.

19. 'Let's Be Pals', *Peg's Paper*, no. 1 (15 May 1919) p.1.

20. 'Who is Polly? My Own Life Story', *Polly's Paper*, no. 1 (17 Nov 1919) p.40, and no. 6 (22 Dec 1919) p.40.

21. *Peg's Paper*, no. 1 (15 May 1919) p.19.

CHAPTER 8 'A LASS OF LANCASHIRE': THE MILL GIRL AS EMBLEM OF WORKING-CLASS VIRTUES

1. Sally Vernon, 'Trouble Up at t'Mill: The Rise and Decline of the Factory Play in the 1830s and 1840s', *Victorian Studies*, vol. XX (Autumn 1976) pp.117 – 41.

2. For additional information see Cadogan and Craig, *You're a Brick Angela!*, pp.132 – 5.

3. J. B. Priestley, *English Journey, Being a Rambling but Truthful Account of What One Man Saw and Heard and Felt and Thought During a Journey through England during the Autumn of the Year 1933* (W. Heinemann and Victor Gollancz, 1934) p.259.

4. Hutt, *The Condition of the Working Class in Britain*, p.58.

5. W. E. Groves, 'Snubbed by the Mill', *MN*, no. 1 (probably 1919) p.27.

6. W. E. Groves, 'A Work-girl's Temptation', *GFL*, old ser., no. 336 (probably 1922) p.46.

7. W. E. Groves, 'The Bride Who Would Not Say I Will', *GFL*, old ser., no. 526 (7 Mar 1924) p.9.

8. Earl Danesford, 'The Adorable Flirt', *GF*, no. 1391 (10 July 1926) p.1.

9. W. E. Groves, 'The Story of Kate Wayward', *GF*, no. 1151 (26 Nov 1921) p.2.

10. Mabel St John, 'Mill Lass o'Mine', *GF*, no. 1074 (5 June 1920) p.217.

11. W. E. Groves, 'A Lass of Lancashire', *GF*, no. 1373 (27 Feb 1926) p.12, and no. 1374 (6 Mar 1926) p.13.

12. Groves, 'The Story of Kate Wayward', *GF*, no. 1155, p.2.

13. One typical example is Effie Scott, 'Her Ladyship Mill Girl': 'A strange adventure in very truth, the Lady of title and a working man . . .' – *GFL*, new ser., no. 42 (5 Mar 1926) p.2.

14. Oliver Sandys, 'Blinkeyes. A Story of Laughter and Tears, Sunshine and Shadow', *Peg's Paper*, no. 417 (16 May 1927) p.25.
15. Groves, 'The Story of Kate Wayward', *GF*, no. 1151, p.2.
16. Groves, 'The Bride Who Would Not Say I Will', *GFL*, old ser., no. 526, p.1.
17. Groves, 'Snubbed by the Mill', *MN*, no. 1, p.5. See also 'a popular idol' (ibid., p.13).
18. Groves, 'A Work-girl's Temptation', *GFL*, old ser., no. 336, p.40.
19. Ethel Gardener, 'A Mill Lad's Bride', *MN*, no. 8 (probably 1919) p.26.
20. Scott, 'Her Ladyship Mill Girl', *GFL*, new ser., no. 42, pp.15−16.
21. W. E. Groves, 'The Woman in It', *GFL*, no. 106, new ser. (1 July 1927) pp.5−6.
22. According to the Labour Research Department; quoted in Charles L. Mowat, *Britain Between the Wars*, p.26.
23. Cole and Cole, *The Condition of Britain*, p.220; Hutt, *The Condition of the Working Class*, pp.54−7.

CHAPTER 9   THE EMIGRANT: ROMANCE AND THE EMPIRE

1. Joseph, 'How to Write Serial Fiction', *The Complete Writing for Profit*, pp.716−17.
2. Ibid., p.868.
3. On the notion of Empire in the Victorian and Edwardian popular adventure novel, see Elie Halévy, *History of the English People in the 19th Century*, vol. V: *Imperialism and the Rise of Labour*, tr. E. I. Watkin (Ernest Benn, 1951); Alan Sandison, *The Wheel of Empire: A Study of Imperial Idea in Some Late Victorian and Early Twentieth-Century Fiction* (Macmillan, 1967); and Christine Bolt, *Victorian Attitudes to Race* (Routledge and Kegan Paul, 1971). On the idea of Empire in periodical fiction for boys, see Patrick R. Dunae, 'Boys' Literature and the Idea of Empire', *VS*, vol. 24, no. 1 (1980) pp.105−23.
4. Madge Crichton, 'The Girl Bushranger: A Romance of the Wilds', *GF*, no. 1410 (20 Nov 1926) p.2.
5. Mabel St John, 'Girl of the Prairie', *GFL*, probably 1922, p.2.
6. Mabel St John, 'Pearl of the West', *GFL*, new ser., no. 56 (4 June 1926) p.3.
7. Ursula Bloom, 'The Way of a Woman', *Violet Magazine*, no. 115 (4 Feb 1927) pp.20−1.
8. For the roles of women in the Western, see John G. Cawelti, *Adventure, Mystery and Romance: Formula Stories as Art and Popular Culture* (University of Chicago Press, 1976). Cawelti deals briefly with the 'transvestite theme', common to the Western and the Empire romance.
9. St John, 'Pearl of the West', *GFL*, new ser., no. 56, p.2.
10. Ibid., p.8.
11. Angus Leigh, 'On the Edge of the World', *Violet Magazine*, no. 97 (14 May 1926) p.65.

12. Lloyd Williams, 'The Woman Who Had Lots of Pluck', *Violet Magazine*, no. 102 (6 Aug 1926) pp.6–7.

13. Sequel in *Violet Magazine*, no. 103 (20 Aug 1926) p.108.

14. For the role of landscape in the Western, see Cawelti, *Adventure, Mystery and Romance*.

15. St John, 'Pearl of the West', *GFL*, new ser., no. 56, p.2.

16. The examples are from Danesford, 'The Adorable Flirt', *GF*, no. 1393, p.6.

CONCLUSION

1. Following the discussion of the Equal Franchise Bill in a House of Commons committee, the second reading of the Bill in the House of Lords, and the division of the Lords committee. See the *Daily Mail*, 18 Apr, 19 Apr, 22 May, 23 May and 13 June 1928; and *Daily Express*, 22 May 1928.

2. *Punch*, vol. 174 (30 May 1928) p.605.

3. J. A. H. Murray, *A New English Dictionary, Supplement* (Clarendon Press, 1933) p.375.

4. *OED Supplement*, vol. 1, pp.1096–7.

5. See, for instance, Robert Graves and Alan Hodge, *The Long Weekend: A Social History of Great Britain 1918–39* (Faber and Faber, 1940) pp.248, 298–9; Mowat, *Britain between the Wars*, pp.201, 480; William M. Medlicott, *Contemporary England 1914–64* (Longmans, 1967).

6. George Orwell, 'Inside the Whale', *Collected Essays*, vol. I, p.540.

7. See, for instance, Bertrand Russell, *The Autobiography*, vol. II: *1914–44* (1968); Dora Russell, *The Tamarisk Tree: My Quest for Liberty and Love* (1975); Anthony Powell, *To Keep the Ball Rolling*, vol. I: *Infants of the Spring*. On a somewhat different level, but conveying a similar sense of escapism through sex and sexuality, are Tallulah Bankhead, *Tallulah: My Autobiography* (1952); Barbara Cartland, *The Isthmus Years* (1941) and *We Danced All Night* (1972); Coward, *Present Indicative*; and Nerine Shutte, *We Mixed Our Drinks: The Story of a Generation, an Autobiography* (1945).

8. For instance, Kate Millett, *Sexual Politics* (Equinox Books, 1964) pp.62–3. See also Weeks, *Sex, Politics and Society*.

9. Peter N. Stearns, 'Working-Class Women in Britain, 1890–1914', in Martha Vicinus (ed.), *Suffer and Be Still: Women in the Victorian Age* (Methuen, 1980) pp.100–21. But Stearns argues the textile-workers were less prone to adopt a conservative 'poverty-tradition'.

Select Bibliography

1 PRIMARY MATERIAL

(a) Government records and official publications

Parliamentary Debates, House of Commons, 5th ser., vols 215–20.
Parliamentary Debates, House of Lords, 5th ser., vol. 71.
League of Nations International Statistical Year Book, 1926–8.
The Register General's Statistical Review of England and Wales, new annual ser.,
 nos. 1–9 (1921–9).
Statistical Abstract for the United Kingdom, nos 72 [1913–27], 73 [1915–28], 74
 [1916–29] and 75 [1917–30].

(b) Newspapers, periodicals and pamphlets

The Bookman: A Handbook of British and Foreign Literature
Boy's Own Paper
Daily Express
Daily Mail
Eve (from March 1921, Eve, the Lady's Pictorial)
Eve's Own Stories
The Flapper: A Periodical Work
Flapdoodles about Flappers
Fortnightly Review
Girls' Friend
Girls' Friend Library
Girl's Own Paper and Woman's Magazine
Harmsworth Red Magazine
Mizpah Novels
My Story Weekly
New Republic
New Statesman
New York Times Book Review
Not a 'Flapper' Vote
Peg's Paper
Polly's Paper
Punch, or the London Charivari
Revue de Paris
Saturday Review of Literature

Sunday Dispatch
The Times
The Times Literary Supplement
True Story Magazine (British edn)
Vanity Fair
Violet Magazine
Vogue (British edn)
Woman's World
Woman's World Library
Yellow Magazine

(c)   Fiction

Arlen, Michael, *The Green Hat: A Romance for a Few People* (Collins, 1924).
——, *May Fair* (Collins, 1925).
——, *Men Dislike Women: A Romance* (Heinemann, 1931).
——, *These Charming People* (Collins, 1923).
——, *Young Men in Love* (Hutchinson, 1927).
Conquest, Joan, *Desert Love* (Werner Laurie, 1920).
——, *The Light of the Harem Window* (Werner Laurie, 1927).
——, *Zarah the Cruel* (Cassell, 1923).
Deeping, Warwick, *Sorrell and Son* (Cassell, 1925).
Dell, Ethel M., *The Way of an Eagle* (Fisher Unwin, 1912).
Ford, Ford Madox, *Some Do Not* (Duckworth, 1924).
Frankau, Gilbert, *Life and Erica: A Romance* (Hutchinson, 1925).
Gibbs, Philip, *The Middle of the Road* (Hutchinson, 1922).
Glyn, Elinor, *The Flirt and the Flapper: Dialogues* (Duckworth, 1930).
——, *It and Other Stories* (Duckworth, 1927).
——, *Six Days* (Duckworth, 1924).
——, *Three Weeks* (Duckworth, 1907).
Hichens, Robert, *The Garden of Allah* (Methuen, 1904).
Hull, E. M., *The Sheik* (Evelyn Nash, 1919).
——, *The Sons of the Sheik* (Evelyn Nash and Grayson, 1925).
Hutchinson, A. S. M., *If Winter Comes* (Hodder and Stoughton, 1921).
——, *This Freedom* (Hodder and Stoughton, 1922).
Keable, Robert, *Recompense: A Sequel to Simon Called Peter* (Constable, 1924).
——, *Simon Called Peter* (Constable, 1921).
Kennedy, Margaret, *The Constant Nymph* (W. Heinemann, 1924).
——, *The Fool of the Family* (W. Heinemann, 1930).
——, *The Ladies of Lyndon* (W. Heinemann, 1923).
——, *Red Sky at Morning* (W. Heinemann, 1927).
Mills, Dorothy A. M., *The Tent of Blue* (Duckworth, 1922).
Remarque, Erich Maria, *All Quiet on the Western Front*, tr. A .W. Wheen (G. P. Putman, 1929).

Rhodes, Kathlyn, *The Will of Allah* (Hutchinson, 1908).

Stackpoole, H. De Vere, *The Blue Lagoon* (Fisher and Unwin, 1908).

Wassermann, Carl Jacob, *Faber; or the Lost Year*, tr. Harry Hansen (George Allen and Unwin, 1930).

Wren, C. P., *Beau Geste* (John Murray, 1924).

(d)   *Other literary material*

NOVELS AND SHORT STORIES

Austen, Jane, *Mansfield Park* (1814; Penguin, 1981).

Drieu La Rochelle, Pierre, E., *Gilles* (Gallimard, 1939).

Giraudoux, Jean, *Siegfried et le Limousin* (Bernard Grasset, 1922).

Hemingway, Ernest, *The Sun also Rises* (Scribner, 1926).

Huxley, Aldous, *Antic Hay* (Chatto and Windus, 1923).

——, *Point Counter Point* (Chatto and Windus, 1928).

Lawrence, D. H., 'In Love' (1927), in *The Woman Who Rode Away and Other Stories* (Penguin, 1978).

——, *Lady Chatterley's Lover* (1928; Penguin, 1983).

——, *Women in Love* (1920; Penguin, 1982).

——, 'The Woman Who Rode Away' (1925), in *The Woman Who Rode Away and Other Stories* (Penguin, 1978).

Swift, Jonathan, *Gulliver's Travels* (1726), in *The Works*, Scott's edn (Bickers, 1883) vol. XI.

Waugh, Evelyn, *Brideshead Revisited* (1945; Penguin, 1982).

PARODIES AND PLAYS

Abingdon, Roger, *The Green Mat: A Romance for Askew People* (Collins, 1925).

Arlen, Michael, *The Acting Version of The Green Hat: A Romance* (George H. Doran, 1925).

Brighouse, Harold, *Hobson's Choice: A Three Act Comedy* (Constable, 1910).

——, *Three Lancashire Plays: The Game, The Northerners, Zack* (Samuel French, 1920).

Ford, Corey, 'Three Rousing Cheers!!! – The Parody Adventures of Our Youthful Heroes. The Rollo Boys with Sherlock in Mayfair or, Keep it Under Your Green Hat', *Bookman*, vol. 62, no. 5 (Jan 1926).

Frank, Leonard, *Carl and Anna*, tr. Cyrus Brooks (Peter Davies, 1929).

Houghton, W. Stanley, *Hindle Wakes: A Play in Three Acts* (Sidgwick and Jackson, 1912).

Hutchinson, A. S. M., and Hastings, B. M., *If Winter Comes: A Play in Four Acts* (Hodder and Stoughton, 1928).

Kennedy, Margaret, 'Tessa, la nymph au coeur fidèle, pièce en trois actes et six tableaux . . . , adaptée pour la scene française par Jean Giraudoux', *Revue de Paris*, nos. 23 (1 Dec 1934) and 24 (15 Dec 1934).

Kennedy, Margaret, and Dean, Basil, *The Constant Nymph, from the Novel of Margaret Kennedy* (W. Heinemann, 1926).

Menzel, Gerhard, *Tobboggan, Drama* (Gustav Kiepenauer, 1928).

Plain, Barry E. O., *If Summer Don't: A Parody of If Winter Comes by A. S. M. Hutchinson* (Werner Laurie, 1922).

——, *This Charming Green Hat Fair: A Parody of The Green Hat by Michael Arlen* (Werner Laurie, 1925).

Toller, Ernst, 'Hinkemann. A Tragedy in Three Acts', *Vision and Aftermath: Four Expressionist War Plays*, tr. J. M. Ritchie and J. D. Stowell (Calder and Boyars, 1969).

Young Women out of Love. Being a Commentary on the Genius Peculiar to Michael Arlen ((Stanley Paul, 1928).

(e)   Films

Numbers in square brackets are those of British productions as listed in the British Film Catalogue.

Beau Geste (Paramount, 1926).

Blood and Sand (MGM, 1922).

Cobra (Paramount, 1925).

The Constant Nymph (Gainsborough, 1928) [08314].

The Flapper and the Curates (Fitz Films, 1916) [03648].

The Flapper and the Fan (Crusade, 1914) [05277].

The Flapper goes to School (1916) [06113].

The Flapper's Elopement (Fitz Films, 1912) [03491].

The Flappers and the Nuts (Urban Trading Company, 1913) [04342].

Flesh and the Devil (MGM, 1927)

The Irresistible Flapper (Broadwest, 1919) [06671].

It (Paramount, 1927).

Outcast Lady (MGM, 1934).

The Sheik (Famous Players Lasky, Paramount, 1921).

The Sons of the Sheik (United Artists, 1926).

A Woman of Affairs (MGM, 1928).

(f)   Criticism and writings on popular culture

Arnold, Matthew, *Culture and Anarchy: An Essay in Political and Social Criticism* (Smith and Elder, 1869).

Drew, Elizabeth A., *The Modern Novel: Some Aspects of Contemporary Fiction* (Jonathan Cape, 1926).

Eliot, T. S., 'Marie Lloyd', *Selected Essays* (Faber and Faber, 1951).

Empson, William, *Seven Types of Ambiguity* (Chatto and Windus, 1930).

Kennedy, Margaret, *Jane Austen* (Arthur Barker, 1950).

——, *The Outlaws on Parnassus: On the Art of the Novel* (Cresset Press, 1958).

——, 'The Novelist and his Public', *Royal Society of Literature, Essays by Divers Hands*, vol. XXXII (1963).

Lawrence, D. H., *Pornography and Obscenity* (1929; Alicat Bookshop, 1948).

——, 'Surgery for the Novel – or a Bomb', in *Selected Literary Criticism*, ed. Anthony Beal (W. Heinemann, 1955).

Leavis, F. R., *Mass Civilisation and Minority Culture* (Minority Press, 1930).

—— and Thompson, Denys, *Culture and Environment* (Chatto and Windus, 1933).

Leavis, Q. D., *Fiction and the Reading Public* (1932; Penguin, 1979).

Orwell, George, 'Boys' Weeklies' and 'Inside the Whale', in *The Collected Essays, Journalism and Letters*, vol. I: *An Age Like This 1920–40*, ed. Sonia Orwell and Ian Angus (Penguin, 1982).

Richards, Frank, 'Frank Richards Replies to George Orwell', in George Orwell, *The Collected Essays*, vol. I (see preceding entry).

Washburn, Claude C., 'Sophistication', *Opinions* (Constable, 1926).

Woolf, Leonard, *Hunting the Highbrow* (Hogarth Press, 1927).

Woolf, Virginia, 'Women and Fiction', in *Collected Essays*, vol. II, ed. Leonard Woolf (Hogarth Press, 1966).

(g)   *Other material*

Agate, James, *The Contemporary Theatre, 1925* (Chapman and Hall, 1926).

Brittain, Vera, *Testament of Youth: An Autobiographical Study of the Years 1900–25* (Victor Gollancz, 1938).

——, *Testament of Experience: An Autobiographical Study of the Years 1925–50* (Victor Gollancz, 1957).

Carr-Saunders, A. M., and Caradog-Jones, C., *A Survey of the Structure of England and Wales* (Oxford University Press, 1937).

Cole, G. D. H. and M. J., *The Condition of Britain* (Victor Gollancz, 1937).

Coward, Noël, *Present Indicative: An Autobiography* (W. Heinemann, 1937).

Dilnot, George, *The Romance of the Amalgamated Press* (Amalgamated Press, 1925).

Engels, Friedrich, *The Conditions of the Working Class in England* (1845; Granada, 1982).

——, *The Origin of the Family, Private Property and the State* (1884: Lawrence and Wishart, 1941).

Eyles, Margaret Leonora, *Commonsense about Sex* (Victor Gollancz, 1933).

——, *The Woman in the Little House* (Grant Richards, 1922).

Forbes, J. Rosita, *From Red Sea to Blue River: Abyssinian Adventures* (Cassell, 1925).

——, *El Raisuli, the Sultan of the Mountains: His Life Story* (Thronton Butterworth, 1924).

Glyn, Elinor, *The Elinor Glyn System of Writing*, 2 vols (Writer's Press, 1922).

Gramsci, Antonio, *Letters from Prison*, tr. Lynne Lawner (Jonathan Cape, 1975).

Hull, E. M., *Camping in the Sahara* (Evelyn Nash and Grayson, 1926).

Hutt, Allen, *The Condition of the Working Class in Britain* (Martin Lawrence, 1933).

Joseph, Michael, *The Complete Writing for Profit* (Hutchinson, 1930).

Lawrence, D. H., *The Collected Letters*, ed. Harry T. Moore, 2 vols (W. Heinemann, 1962).

Magnus, George G., *How to Write Saleable Fiction* (Cambridge Literary Agency, 1925).

Masterman, C. F. G., *England after War: A Study* (Hodder and Stoughton, 1922).

Mills, Dorothy R. M., *The Golden Land: A Record of Travel in West Africa* (Duckworth, 1929).

———, *The Road to Timboktu* (Duckworth, 1924).

The Newspaper Press Directory and Advertiser's Guide, 1914.

Priestley, J. B., *English Journey, Being a Rambling but Truthful Account of What One Man Saw and Heard and Felt and Thought During a Journey through England during the Autumn of the Year 1933* (W. Heinemann and Victor Gollancz, 1934).

Rathbone, Elinor, *The Disinherited Family* (Edward Arnold, 1924).

Russell, Bertrand, *Marriage and Morals* (George Allen and Unwin, 1929).

Stopes, Marie, *Married Love: A New Contribution to the Solution of Sex Difficulties* (A. C. Field, 1918)

———, *Wise Parenthood* (A. C. Field, 1918).

2   SECONDARY MATERIAL

Abrams, Mark, *The Condition of the British People 1911–45* (Victor Gollancz, 1946).

———, *The Population of Great Britain, Current Trends and Future Problems* (George Allen and Unwin, 1945).

Arlen, Michael J., *Exiles* (André Deutsch, 1971).

Adorno, Theodor W., *Prisms*, tr. Samuel and Shirley Weber (Neville Spearman, 1967).

Adorno, Theodor W., and Horkheimer, Max, *Dialectics of Enlightenment*, tr. John Cumming (Allen Lane, 1973).

Alexander, Sally, 'Women, Class and Sexual Differences in the 1830s and 1840s: Some Reflections on the Writing of a Feminist History', *History Workshop*, no. 17 (Sep 1984).

Altick, Richard D., *The English Common Reader: A Social History of the Mass Reading Public, 1800–1900* (University of Chicago Press, 1957).

Ardener, Shirley (ed.), *Perceiving Women* (Dent and Halsted, 1975).

———, *Defining Females: The Nature of Women in Society* (Croom Helm, 1978).

———, *Women and Space: Ground Rules and Social Maps* (Croom Helm, 1981).

Baker, Laura H., 'The Flapper in American Fiction 1919–33' (MA dissertation for the University of Louisville, Kentucky, 1974).

Banks, George A. and Olive, *Feminism and Family Planning in Victorian England* (Liverpool University Press, 1964).

Barrow, Margaret, *Women 1870–1928: A Select Guide to Printed Archive Sources in the United Kingdom* (Mansell, 1981).

Barthes, Roland, *Mythologies*, tr. Annette Lavers (Granada, 1979).

Beauman, Nichola, *A Very Great Profession: The Woman's Novel 1914–39* (Virago, 1983).

Beauvoir, Simone de, *The Second Sex*, tr. H. M. Parshley (Bantam Books, 1961).

Benjamin, Walter, 'The Work of Art in the Age of Mechanical Reproduction', *Illuminations*, tr. Harry Zohn (Jonathan Cape, 1970).

Bigsby, C. W. E. (ed.), *Approaches to Popular Culture* (Edward Arnold, 1976).

Blewett, Neal, 'The Franchise in the United Kingdom 1885–1918', *Past and Present*, vol. XXXII (Dec 1965).

Brandon, Piers, *The Life and Death of the Press Barons* (Secker and Warburg, 1982).

Butler, David E., *The Electoral System in Britain since 1918* (Clarendon Press, 1963).

Cadogan, Mary, and Craig, Patricia, *You're a Brick Angela! A New Look at Girls' Fiction from 1839–1975* (Victor Gollancz, 1976).

Cawelti, John G., *Adventure, Mystery and Romance: Formula Stories as Art and Popular Culture* (University of Chicago Press, 1976).

——, 'The Concept of Formula in the Study of Popular Literature', *Journal of Popular Culture*, vol. III, no. 3 (Winter 1969).

Chaney, David, *Fiction and Ceremonies: Representation of Popular Experience* (Edward Arnold, 1979).

Chisholm, Anne, *Nancy Cunard* (Penguin, 1981).

Clarke, John, with Critcher, Chas and Johnson, Richard (eds), *Working-Class Culture: Studies in History and Theory* (Hutchinson, 1980).

Cockburn, Francis C., *Bestseller: The Books that Everybody Read, 1900–39* (Sidgwick and Jackson, 1972).

Collingwood, Robin G., *The Principles of Art* (Clarendon Press, 1938).

Cunningham, A. R., 'The "New Woman Fiction" of the 1890s', *VS*, vol. XVII, no. 2 (1973).

Curran, James, with Gurevitch, Michael, and Woolacott, Janet (eds), *Mass Communication and Society* (Edward Arnold, 1977).

Curran, James, with Boyce, George, and Wintage, Pauline (eds), *Newspaper History from the 17th Century to the Present Day* (Constable, 1978).

Dalziel, Margaret, *Popular Fiction 100 Years Ago: An Unexplored Tract of Literacy History* (Cohen and West, 1957).

Davison, Caroline, *A Woman's Work is Never Done: A History of Housework in the British Isles, 1650–1950* (Chatto and Windus, 1982).

Deutsch, Helen, *The Psychology of Women*, 2 vols (Crane and Stratton, 1949).

Escarpit, Robert Charles, *The Book Revolution* (George Harrap, 1966).

Evans, Richard G., *The Feminists: Women's Emancipation Movements in Europe, America and Australasia* (Croom Helm, 1977).

——, 'The History of European Women: A Critical Survey of Recent Research', *Journal of Modern History*, vol. LII (Dec 1980).

Foucault, Michel, *History of Sexuality*, vol. I: *An Introduction*, tr. Robert Huxley (Penguin, 1981).

Freud, Sigmund, 'Femininity', in *The Complete Psychological Works*, vol. XXV: *New Introductory Lectures on Psycho-analysis*, vol. xxv, tr. James Strachey (Hogarth Press, 1964).

——, 'Three Essays on Sexuality', in *The Complete Psychological Works*, vol. VII: *A Case Hysteria, Three Essays on Sexuality and Other Works*, tr. James Strachey (Hogarth Press, 1964).

Fryer, Peter, *The Birth Controllers* (Secker and Warburg, 1965).

Fussell, Paul, *Abroad: British Literary Travelling between the Wars* (Oxford University Press, 1980).

Gay, Peter, *The Bourgeois Experience*, vol. I: *Victoria to Freud* (Oxford University Press, 1984).

Gedin, Per, *Literature in the Market Place* (Faber and Faber, 1977).

Graves, Robert, and Hodge, Alan, *The Long Weekend: A Social History of Great Britain 1918–39* (Macmillan, 1941).

Hackett, Alice P., and Burke, James H., *80 Years of Best-sellers, 1895–1975* (Bowker, 1977).

Halévy, Elie, *A History of the English People in the 19th Century*, vol. V: *Imperialism and the Rise of Labour*, tr. E. I. Watkin (Ernest Benn, 1951).

Harrison, Brian, *Separate Spheres: The Opposition to Women's suffrage in Britain* (Croom Helm, 1972).

——, 'Underneath the Victorians', *VS*, vol. X, no. 3 (1967).

Higashi, Sukimo, *Virgins, Vamps and Flappers: The American Silent Movie Heroine* (Eden Press Women's Publications, 1978).

Hoggart, Richard, *The Uses of Literacy: Aspects of Working-Class Culture with Special Reference to Publications and Entertainment* (Penguin, 1981).

Holroyd, Michael, *Augustus John: A Biography*, 2 vols (W. Heinemann, 1974).

Houghton, Walter H., *The Victorian Frame of Mind 1830–70* (Yale University Press, 1975).

Keyishian, Harry, *Michael Arlen* (Twayne, 1975).

Lane, Michael, and Booth, Jeremy, *Books and Publishers: Commerce against Culture in Postwar Britain* (Lexington Books, 1980).

Lévi-Strauss, Claude, *Mythologiques*, vol. I: *Le Crue et le cuit* (Plon, 1964); vol. II: *Du miel aux cendres* (Plon, 1966); vol. III: *L'Origine de manières du table* (Plon, 1968).

——, La Pensée sauvage (Plan, 1962).

Lewis, Jane, 'The Ideology and Politics of Birth-control in Inter-war England', *Women's Studies International Quarterly*, vol. II, no. 1 (1979).

——, *Women in England, 1870–1950: Sexual Divisions and Social Change* (Wheatsheaf Books, 1984).

Low, Rachel, *History of the British Film*, vol. IV: *1918–28* (George Allen and Unwin, 1971).

Lowenthal, Leo, *Literature, Popular Culture and Society* (Prentice-Hall, 1961).

Macluhan, H. Marshall, *The Mechanical Bride: Folklore of Industrial Man* (Routledge and Kegan Paul, 1967).

Marcus, Steven, *The Other Victorians: A Study of Sexuality and Pornography in Mid Nineteenth-Century England* (Weidenfeld and Nicolson, 1966).

Marcuse, Herbert, *One Dimensional Man: Studies in the Ideology of Advanced Industrial Society* (Beacon Press, 1964).

Marwick, Arthur J. B., *The Deluge: British Society and the First World War* (Macmillan, 1979).

——, *Women at War* (Croom Helm, 1977).

Mead, Margaret, *Male and Female* (William Morris, 1949).

Medlicott, William N., *Contemporary England 1914–64* (Longmans, 1967).

Millett, Kate, *Sexual Politics* (Equinox Books, 1964).

Mott, Frank L., *Golden Multitudes: The Story of Best-sellers in the United States* (Macmillan, 1947; Bowker, 1966).

Mowat, Charles L., *Britain between the Wars, 1918–40* (Methuen, 1978).

Mowry, George E. (ed.), *The Twenties: Fords, Flappers and Fanatics* (Prentice-Hall, 1963).

Peel, J., 'The Manufacture and Retailing of Contraceptives in England', *Population Studies*, vol. XVII (1963).

Pollard, Graham, 'Serial Fiction', in John W. Carter (ed.), *New Paths in Book Collecting* (Constable, 1931).

Pound, Reginald, and Harmsworth, Arthur G., *Northcliffe* (Cassell, 1959).

Powell, Violet, *The Constant Novelist* (W. Heinemann, 1983).

Pugh, Martin, *Electoral Reform in War and Peace 1906–18* (Routledge and Kegan Paul, 1978).

——, *The Making of Modern British Politics 1867–1939* (Blackwell, 1982).

——, 'Politicians and the Women's Vote 1914–18', *History*, vol. LIX (Oct 1974).

——, *Women's Suffrage in Britain 1867–1928* (Historical Association, 1980).

Rosenberg, Bernard, and Manning, W. P. (eds), *Mass Culture: The Popular Arts in America* (Free Press, 1964).

Rougemont, Denis de, *L'Amour et L'Occident* (Plon, 1939).

Sandison, Alan, *The Wheel of Empire: A Study of Imperial Idea in Some Late Nineteenth- and Early Twentieth-Century Fiction* (Macmillan, 1967).

Said, Edward, *Orientalism* (Routledge and Kegan Paul, 1978).

Showalter, Elaine, *A Literature of their Own: British Women Novelists from Brontë to Lessing* (Virago, 1978).

Sivan, Emanual, 'Colonialism and Popular Culture in Algeria', *Journal of Contemporary History*, vol. XIV, no. 1 (Jan 1979).

Stearns, Peter, 'The Effort at Continuity in Working-Class Culture', *Journal of Modern History*, vol. LIV, no. 4 (Dec 1980).

Stevenson, John, *The Pelican Social History of Britain, British Society, 1914–45* (Penguin, 1984).

Sutherland, John A., *Bestsellers: Popular Fiction of the 1970s* (Routledge and Kegan Paul, 1981).

——, *Offensive Literature: Decensorship in Britain 1960–82* (Junction Books, 1982).

Taylor, A. J. P., *Beaverbrook* (Hamish Hamilton, 1972).

——, *English History, 1919–45* (Pelican, repr. 1979).

Thompson, F. M. L. (ed.), *The Rise of Suburbia* (Leicester University Press and St Martin's Press, 1982).

Thomson, David, *England in the Twentieth Century (1914–79)* (Penguin, 1981).

Tillotson, Kathleen M., *Novels of the 1840s* (Oxford University Press, 1954).

Turner, Ernest Sackville, *Boys Will Be Boys: The Story of Sweeney Todd, Deadwood Dick, Sexton Blake, Billy Bunter, Dick Barton et al.* (Michael Joseph, 1948).

Vicinus, Martha, *Independent Women: Work and Community for Single Women, 1850–1920* (Virago, 1985).

—— (ed.), *A Widening Sphere: Changing Roles of Victorian Women* (Methuen, repr. 1980).

—— (ed.), *Suffer and Be Still: Women in the Victorian Age* (Methuen, repr. 1980).

Watt, Ian, *The Rise of the Novel: Studies in Defoe, Richardson and Fielding* (Penguin, 1981).

Waites, Bernard, with Bennett, Tony and Martin, Graham (eds), *Popular Culture Past and Present* (Croom Helm, 1977).

Weeks, Jeffrey, *Sex, Politics and Society: The Regulation of Sexuality since 1800* (Longman, 1981).

Welsh, Alexander, *The City of Dickens* (Clarendon Press, 1971).

White, Cynthia L., *Women's Magazines 1693–1968: A Sociological Enquiry* (Michael Joseph, 1970).

Williams, Raymond, *Communications* (Penguin, 1976).

——, *Culture and Society, 1870–1950* (Penguin, 1979).

——, *The Long Revolution* (Penguin, 1980).

Index